A WALK
A DAY

A WALK A DAY

365 SHORT WALKS IN NEW ZEALAND

PETER JANSSEN

CONTENTS

INTRODUCTION	6
NORTH ISLAND	**11**
26 short walks in **Northland**	12
22 short walks in **Auckland**	30
8 short walks in **Hauraki Gulf**	46
16 short walks in **Coromandel**	54
27 short walks in **Waikato and King Country**	64
13 short walks in **Bay of Plenty**	84
17 short walks in **Rotorua and Central North Island**	94
21 short walks in **East Cape, Gisborne and Hawke's Bay**	106
13 short walks in **Taranaki**	120
14 short walks in **Whanganui, Rangitikei, Manawatu, Horowhenua and Kapiti**	130
24 short walks in **Wairarapa and Wellington**	142
SOUTH ISLAND	**160**
12 short walks in **Marlborough and Kaikoura**	162
18 short walks in **Nelson and Golden Bay**	172
19 short walks on **the West Coast**	184
14 short walks in **Buller and Lewis Pass**	196
10 short walks in **Canterbury and Arthur's Pass**	206
18 short walks in **Christchurch and Banks Peninsula**	212
19 short walks in **South Canterbury, Mackenzie Country and North Otago**	226
16 short walks in **Central Otago**	242
19 short walks in **Dunedin, South Otago and the Catlins**	254
20 short walks in **Southland, Stewart Island and Fiordland**	266

INTRODUCTION

Over the years in the course of researching several books, I've clocked up over 700 walks throughout this country and still haven't covered every track. While the experiences have been variable, I never failed to be impressed by the beauty of the natural and human landscape of New Zealand. From our intriguing flora and fauna and magnificent vistas, through to our rich Maori and European history, this is my pick of the best walks from previous books, along with some new discoveries.

I'm a firm believer that walks should be enjoyable and relaxing and needn't involve heavy boots, even heavier packs and tasteless food. All walks in this book are under three hours, the vast majority under two and many take less than 30 minutes. Even those of modest fitness can undertake most of them, and nearly all are suitable for family groups. None require complicated maps or special gear, certainly no heavy backpacks or awkward tramping boots. Very rough, overgrown or hard-to-follow tracks have been excluded and most are accessible from a main road.

As the walks are short and straightforward, some descriptions are correspondingly simple and basic.

Grade

The walks are graded *Easy, Medium* and *Hard*.

Easy are suitable for all ages and family groups. Mostly flat, well-maintained and easy to follow.

Medium walks require a little more effort with a bit of uphill, but well within the range of average fitness. May not suit very young children and occasionally the track might be uneven and muddy.

Hard means this track is uphill, though the grades and conditions vary considerably from very good to a bit rough. Not suitable for very young children and good footwear is recommended.

Time

The times given in this book are for a very leisurely pace. Anyone with good fitness can take 25 percent off the time.

How to get there

Simple maps and instructions are provided on the assumption that the traveller has GPS, a smart phone complete with maps or reasonable paper road and street maps. The excellent network of information centres and Department of Conservation offices will be able to help out if you don't have a local map or are really unsure of directions.

Gear

While no special gear is required, New Zealand weather is notoriously fickle and track conditions vary considerably, so be prepared. The weather in the South Island can turn cold quickly, even in summer, and the West Coast of the South Island is famous for high rainfall. In winter thermal underclothing is a good option, very light to carry and wear. In summer the northern areas of the country are exposed to the tail end of tropical cyclones, which can bring high winds and heavy rain, though usually short-lived.

Shoes: Tramping boots aren't necessary. You'll be much more comfortable with a good pair of trainers you don't mind getting dirty, but make sure they have a good tread as tracks are often muddy or have slippery sections over rocks and wooden steps.

For summer there are very good, sturdy walking sandals available, with excellent tread.

Jacket: Invest in a genuinely waterproof jacket. Many are only shower- or wind-proof and it rains a lot in New Zealand. If you don't want to go to the expense, while heavy yellow plastic coats may not be elegant bush wear, they're cheap and certainly keep the rain out. In wetter seasons, keep a few dry clothes in the car – if you do get wet, you have something warm to change into.

Security

An unfortunate fact of life is that car burglary is common in walk car parks, and some popular attractions have security guards. Short of leaving someone with the car there are a few things you can do to lessen the chances of having it broken into. Lock your car even on a short walk, double-check your windows are closed (it's easy to forget back windows). Make sure all valuables are out of sight, and if possible carry your most valuable items with you (wallet, camera, phone, video). Invest in an inexpensive steering lock: this won't stop your car being broken into, but will indicate to thieves you are security-conscious and almost certainly stop them stealing the car.

Mobile phones

Mobile phones can be very useful if you're lost, but be aware they don't always have coverage in more remote places.

Sandflies
New Zealand may not have snakes or dangerous animals, but sandflies can make a walk in the bush hell. Small and black, sandflies pack a nasty bite, which leave you scratching for some time. Sandflies are prolific in wetter bush areas, especially along the West Coast of the South Island, including Fiordland. The good news is that sandflies are deterred by insect repellent, readily available in supermarkets and chemists in roll-on or spray-on form. A citronella-based natural insect repellent called Bite Back is also available.

Giardia
Giardia is an invisible water-borne parasite common in New Zealand streams, and can ruin your holiday. Symptoms include diarrhoea, a bloated feeling in your stomach and a loss of appetite. No matter how clean or pure water looks, it can still contain giardia, so always boil or filter water before drinking it.

Kauri Die-back Disease
Kauri dieback disease was first noticed on Great Barrier Island as far back as the 1970s, but it wasn't until after 2000, that lone voices raised concerns about the spread of the disease. Where it came from, how it got here or even if the disease was always here, still remains unknown. It appeared the disease was spread by spores in soil on the bottom of visitors boots and shoes.

The pathogen causing the disease, *Phytophthora agathidicida* invades the tree's roots, and all affected trees will eventually die. By 2014, drastic action was needed. The greatest impact was around Auckland city and most tracks in parks and reserves with kauri were suddenly closed. Gradually a programme of upgrading tracks and a spraying programme at exits and entrance has allowed some tracks to reopen.

short walks in the
NORTH ISLAND

26
short walks in
Northland

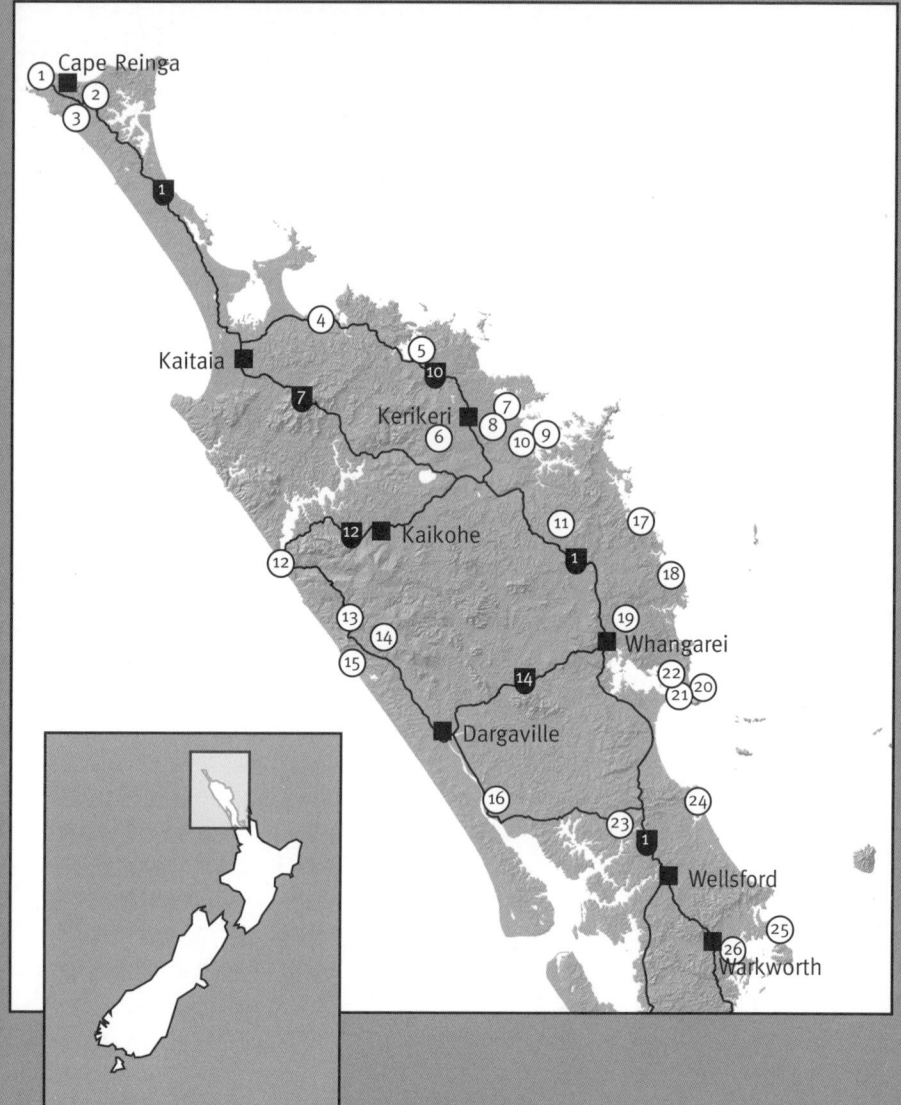

1 Te Werahi Beach, Cape Reinga
A clifftop walk to a magnificent empty beach.

Grade: Medium. **Time:** One and a half hours return.
How to get there: The track begins off the walk to the lighthouse at Cape Reinga located at the very end of SH1.

Often mistakenly described as the most northerly point (which is Surville Cliffs at North Cape), Cape Reinga is renowned for the spectacular seascapes of the Columbia Bank, where the Tasman Sea and Pacific Ocean meet. In Maori tradition this is the final departing point for the spirits of the dead on their journey to the underworld domain of Hine-nui-te-po, the goddess of death. The importance of this site to Maori has kept the area free from commercialisation, though it does become crowded in the middle of the day.

While the short walk (20 minute return) to the lighthouse (built 1941) attracts thousands of visitors, the more spectacular walk to Te Werahi Beach is almost totally ignored. This magnificent beach on the western side of the cape isn't far, and there's a good chance you'll have it to yourself. The walk begins along coastal cliffs, which drop steeply to the rocks. Salt-laden spray produces bonsai-like manuka and diminutive pohutukawa, while flax clings to the cliffs. From the cliff-top the track zigzags down an open hillside to a small cove and from there to the broad, sandy beach. This walk is part of the 53 km Cape Reinga Walkway leading to the Te Paki sandhills.

2 Bartlett's Rata Track
New Zealand's rarest tree.

Grade: Medium. **Time:** One hour return.
How to get there: Signposted to the right on the road between Waitaki Landing and Cape Reinga.

One of New Zealand's rarest plants, Bartlett's rata *Metrosideros bartlettii*, is found at Cape Reinga, with just 34 trees remaining in the wild. Discovered in 1975, unlike other species this rata has white flowers and flaky paper-like bark, supporting the theory these volcanic hills were once islands isolated from the mainland, allowing sub-species to develop.

Beginning as a 4WD track, after about 20 minutes a smaller track branches off to the right. At 300 m is a gate. Take the track to the left and follow the ridge steeply downhill. The track is muddy and not very well formed, ending in a single large kauri tree, behind which are two specimens of Bartlett's rata. Don't take seeds or cuttings.

3 Te Paki Sand Hills
Huge golden sand hills rise over 150 m above Te Paki Stream.

- **Grade:** Hard. **Time:** Allow one hour.
- **How to get there:** Te Paki Stream Road, off the Cape Reinga Road.

Like a scene from the Sahara Desert, massive sand dunes stretch from Te Paki Stream to Te Werahi Beach, in places as high as 150 m. The light gold sand blends with the yellowy-green dune-creeper, pingao, which in places manages a tenuous hold. Sand surfing on boogie boards is very popular, with a number of places hiring out boards, including right in the car park during summer months. The best way to walk the sand hills is to start from the car park, up the loose sand of the dunes. This is hard work – when you've had enough drop down to the Te Paki Stream, which is both flat and shallow and an easy walk back to the car park. As Te Paki Stream is also a major access to Ninety Mile Beach, keep an eye out for speeding vehicles.

4 Taumarumaru Scenic Reserve
Three historic pa sites overlooking Coopers Beach.

- **Grade:** Easy. **Time:** 1 hour.
- **How to get there:** 3 km west of Mangonui on SH10 with good carparking and information – at the time of writing the entrance sign had disappeared, but the reserve is directly opposite Coopers Beach Bowling Club.

At the western end of Coopers Beach/Koekoea, three historic pa are located within the Taumarumaru Reserve. The oldest and largest, Taumarumaru, occupies a high ridge in the centre. While the rectangular pa outline remains, the defensive ditches at either end have largely disappeared, though the ridge is lined with numerous rua, or kumara pits.

On the headland looking east along the beach to Rangikapiti is Ohumuhumu, built by Korewha and Puneka. An outstanding feature is two ditches protecting the land side, which are exceptionally deep, steep and difficult to clamber up. Topped with palisading, the trenches would have offered superb protection to the pa's living terraces on the seaward side.

The third pa, Otanenui, faces west. The name reflects the coastal location, 'the place of the huge old-man snapper' and was built by Tukiato after he was banished from Rangikapiti for killing a shark that was under the protection of his father, Moehuri.

You'll need to allow an hour to visit all three, along easy-walking grassy paths, though it's a scramble to get up onto Ohumuhumu. There's also a track to the reserve from the western end of Coopers Beach.

5 St Paul's Rock, Whangaroa Harbour
Spectacular views of Whangaroa Harbour.

 Grade: Hard. **Time:** One hour return.

How to get there: Take the road to Whangaroa, off SH10 north of Kaeo – Old Hospital Road is to the right, 500 metres past the Marlin Hotel and before the main wharf. The track begins at the top of this road.

The distinctive dome of St Paul's Rock, on the southern shore of Whangaroa Harbour, is impossible to miss, and the view from its peak is a pleasant surprise. Bush-clad, the fiord-like harbour stretches out to the narrow entrance, with Stephenson Island clearly visible.

Marine fossils in the area date back to the early Permian (approx. 270 million years ago), making them some of the North Island's oldest.

Whangaroa Harbour is an old river valley drowned over 5000 years ago by rising sea levels. Correctly spelt Whaingaroa, 'what a long wait', it's named for a woman whose husband went to war and was gone so long she lost patience. In Maori legend the rock is the head of Taratara, decapitated in a battle with a rival mountain over wives, while his headless body is the flat-topped mountain to the west. The barren rock is an old pa site, with evidence of middens everywhere, though it seems a long way to carry shellfish.

The track is a rough uphill climb; the last section is a rocky scramble, though chain handrails assist in the steepest places. Despite signs warning of limited parking and turnaround space, there's good parking and an easy turnaround 50 m beyond the beginning of the track.

6 Puketi Kauri Forest

An easy walk among magnificent mature kauri.

Grade: Easy. **Time:** 20 minutes.
How to get there: The forest entrance is 13 km along the Puketi Road between Okaihau and Kerikeri.

Together with the Omahuta Forest and the Manginangina Scenic Reserve, the Puketi State Forest is part of a 20,000-hectare kauri forest, home to kiwi, tomtits, kaka and Northland's largest population of rare kokako. While other forests contain larger trees, Puketi gives the visitor a better feel for the great kauri forests of the past. The short boardwalk loops among huge mature trees allowing visitors to get up close to this iconic New Zealand tree. The boardwalk is suitable for wheelchairs; longer tracks nearby lead deeper into the forest.

Of all the creatures inhabiting the kauri forest, the most unique is the kauri snail. Not only is it large, it's also carnivorous, feeding on insects, earthworms and other kauri snails. Despite its name, the snail avoids the immediate vicinity of kauri as the ground around their roots is often too dry to support insect life.

7 Ake Ake Point

Spectacular views over the Kerikeri and Te Puna inlets.

Grade: Easy. **Time:** 40 minutes return.
How to get there: The track begins at the end of Opito Bay Road.

This small headland pa, with spectacular views over the Kerikeri and Te Puna inlets and out to the Bay of Islands, is largely covered by regenerating bush, though the terraces and a deep defensive ditch are visible. The pa was home to the famous northern chief Tareha, renowned for his bravery and fighting skills. Allied with Hongi Hika, and supportive of the mission station, he was also famous for his physical size and great appetite. Invited to visit the ship *Dromedary*, his host, Samuel Marsden commented: 'There was not an armchair in the cabin on which he could sit.'

An easy loop track with a short flight of steps at the beginning leads to a small beach in Te Puna Inlet, then on to the pa site. The lookout itself is cleverly shaped, like a ship's prow. On the return trip the clifftop option provides excellent views along the Kerikeri Inlet, which emerges 300 m from the boat ramp. A short detour takes you down to a shingle beach.

8 Kerikeri River Walk
Attractive bush and rocky bluffs.

Grade: Easy. **Time:** 2 hours return.
 How to get there: Over the footbridge from Kemp House turn left, walk across the grass for 100 m to the beginning of the track.

Kemp House (1821), and the Stone Store (1835) are New Zealand's oldest buildings, sitting side by side in the Kerikeri Basin, as far upriver as boats could go before striking rapids. More important, they were adjacent to Koropito Pa, home of one of the most powerful northern chiefs, Hongi Hika, and without Hongi's partronage and protection, the mission had little chance of survival.

While thousands visit these important historical sites, few walk the easy track to Rainbow Falls, through attractive bush and rocky bluffs. Beginning in the car park just over the river, a point of interest is an old power station (1930), which supplied 17 households, now protected by a modern shed housing information and historic photos. A large partially buried intake pipe disappears uphill, where water was supplied from a weir above the falls.

Next stop is Wharepuke Falls, a picturesque waterfall dropping into a popular swimming hole, while further upstream are the Fairy Pools – two large swimming holes. At Rainbow Falls the Kerikeri River drops an impressive 27 m into a deep pool, with a large cave behind the falls.

Rainbow Falls is also accessible from Rainbow Falls Road, where a short track leads to the right from the car park to three lookout points high above the falls. A track to the left of the car park leads to the pool at the bottom of the falls. If you don't have someone to pick you up, you'll need to return the same way, though there's access to the road at Heritage Bypass Bridge.

9 Waitangi River Mangrove Walk
A boardwalk wends its way through an old mangrove forest.

> **Grade:** Easy. **Time:** One and a half hours one way.
> **How to get there:** The Waitangi end begins on the left by the golf course just past the Treaty House, while the Haruru Falls end is off Puketona Road.

The estuary of the Waitangi River is dense with mangroves and the long boardwalk is a highlight, snaking through an old mangrove forest. Although mangroves grow as far south as Opotiki, here in warm northern waters they attain maximum height. The estuary mud is thick with the aerial roots of these old trees with their white and grey bark and tough, small leaves. Mangrove swamps are now recognised as vital environments in maintaining water quality, providing a perfect nursery for young fish.

Unfortunately it's not easy to shorten this walk, so it's worth organising a pickup at the other end if you're not keen on a return walk.

10 Flagstaff Hill, Russell
An historic site with good views over the Bay of Islands.

> **Grade:** Medium. **Time:** 45 minutes return.
> **How to get there:** From the north end of the beach at Russell continue past the boat ramp and along the rocky shore to the beginning of the track.

Originally known as Kororareka, in the early nineteenth century Russell was nicknamed the 'hellhole of the Pacific'. Notorious for grog shops, brothels and general lawlessness, it was for nine months the capital of the fledgling colony.

Not long after the signing of the Treaty of Waitangi tensions grew between Maori and the British, mainly over trade and the imposition of duties and tariffs. Ngapuhi chief Hone Heke was aware of the symbolic nature of the British flag flying over Russell – and had gifted the flagpole in the first place. Inspired by talk of revolution by American Captain William Mayhew, on 8 July 1844 Hone hacked down the pole for the first time. When it was replaced, he cut it down again in January 1845 and flew the US flag from his waka.

After the third flagpole was also cut down, the fourth flagpole was partially clad in iron, which didn't deter Hone from cutting it down on 11 March 1845; for good measure, he sacked the town, burning down many buildings, including the Duke of Marlborough Hotel. In 1857, in an act of reconciliation, those involved in cutting down the pole erected a new flagstaff; and in January 1858 a British flag was raised, on a flagpole named Whakakotahitanga, or 'Unity', which still stands.

The first part of the walk is tide-dependent so it's best to start from this point and avoid having to return uphill if cut off by the tide. Walk north along the beach and around the rocks to the beginning of the track winding up through regenerating bush. At Titore Way turn right, and take the track uphill to the summit, where the views are impressive. On your return, walk down to the car park and take the steps down to Wellington Street, which leads back to town. If the tide is unfavourable, walk up Wellington Street to the top.

11 Ruapekapeka Pa

A well-preserved pa site, both innovative and effective in Maori resistance to British military might.

 Grade: Easy. **Time:** 45 minutes return.
 How to get there: 35 km north of Whangarei on SH1, turn right at Towai into Ruapekapeka Road – the pa site is 4 km down this road, which is unsealed and narrow in places.

Late December 1845 saw the final battle in the northern war, when a British siege of Ruapekapeka (the bat's nest) began with a heavy artillery bombardment. The British, outnumbering the Maori three to one, were confounded by Te Ruki Kawiti's innovative defences, which – unlike traditional pa – featured underground bunkers and foxholes to protect the defenders from both cannon and musket fire.

On Sunday 11 January 1846, the British noticed the pa appeared very quiet, and when a small party of soldiers breached the palisades they found it virtually empty. As British reinforcements were called up, Maori warriors tried to recapture the pa, and after four hours of fierce fighting the Maori defenders finally abandoned the fight.

There are two possible reasons why the pa was almost empty. One story has it that the Maori defenders, believing the British would never attack on a Sunday, had gone to a Christian service and were caught off-guard; the other theory is that the pa was left deliberately empty to lure the British into a trap, but the plan went badly wrong.

The outline of the pa is very clear, complemented by good information boards with great views over the surrounding countryside. Note the car park is a little way from the site, and the British position is not to be confused with the actual pa, the entrance of which is marked by a fine carved gateway.

12 Arai te Uru Heritage Walkway
Spectacular coastal scenery on the South Head of the Hokianga Harbour.

Grade: Easy. **Time:** 30 minutes return.
How to get there: Signal Station Road, off SH12, 4 km west of Omapere.

Rising sea levels since the last ice age have slowly invaded this river valley and today the long finger of the Hokianga Harbour stretches over 30 km inland. The narrow entrance channel produces a strong tidal flow at the ocean outlet and has created a rough, wild bar just offshore. In direct contrast, the upper reaches are characterised by languid backwaters, mangrove swamps and numerous estuarine rivers. At low tide around half of the harbour's 115 square km is exposed, creating a rich environment for aquatic and migratory birds.

First discovered by the legendary explorer Kupe, the sheltered waters were a vital transport link for Maori and, later, for Pakeha. In Maori legend the harbour was created by a family of taniwha and today two taniwha live one on either side of the harbour entrance: Niwa on the high sandhills on the north head; and Araiteuru in a cave on the south head. These two have an important task: using their powerful tails, they stir the water at the harbour entrance, creating treacherous waves and strong currents, thereby protecting the people of the Hokianga.

This short walk wanders through wind-blasted manuka, flax and toetoe with lookout points offering expansive views over the Tasman Sea, the sandhills of North Head and inland along the harbour. The hard sandy soil has been moulded by persistent wind. A side track leads down to a beautiful sandy cove facing the open sea and pounded by wild waves.

13 Waipoua Forest
New Zealand's largest kauri forest.

- **Grade:** Easy. **Time:** Four Sisters – 15 minutes return; Te Matua Ngahere – 45 minutes return; Yakas Kauri – one hour 10 minutes return.
- **How to get there:** Three walks start from the same track from the car park, 1 km south of Tane Mahuta on SH12 – a small fee is charged for parking security.
- **Note:** Some tracks may be completely or partially closed to prevent the spread of kauri dieback disease. The duration of the closure is uncertain

Waipoua Forest, along with adjoining forests, now covers over 13,000 ha and is the largest and most important kauri forest in New Zealand. It also contains the largest individual kauri trees and encloses a diverse range of native flora and fauna. Saved from the axe by inaccessible terrain, in 1876 the forest was acquired by the government. Despite public pressure to protect the forest, trees were felled up to the end of World War II, with the 1952 decision to set aside 9105 ha as a reserve attracting considerable opposition from milling interests.

The forest is notable for very large trees, including the tallest surviving kauri, Tane Mahuta (over 51 metres high), and Te Matua Ngahere, with the largest girth (16.5 metres). Both are estimated to be over 2000 years old. While the kauri are the main attraction, the reserve also includes magnificent rimu, towai, northern rata and taraire, and important fauna including brown kiwi and the carnivorous kauri snail.

The Four Sisters are a rare example of a four-headed kauri sprouting from a single base. Although not all the trunks are the same size, all are impressive trees.

These interconnected easy walks all start from the same point and together take around two hours. Described as the seventh-largest, it might be tempting to give the Yakas Kauri a miss but this appealing walk passes through magnificent groves of huge kauri, giving a much greater appreciation of this beautiful forest.

14 Trounson Kauri Park Loop Walk
A mature kauri forest on a 'mainland island'.

- **Grade:** Easy. **Time:** 45 minutes.
- **How to get there:** Accessed by a 15 km loop road clearly marked off SH12, south of Waipoua.

The heart of this reserve was originally set aside by local landowner James Trounson, and now covers over 450 ha of virgin kauri forest. The loop walk is through impressive groves of mature kauri with an understorey of nikau, fern and kiekie, and with fewer visitors than nearby Waipoua, the forest retains a quiet and primeval feel. The forest is a 'mainland island' reserve and has seen a recovery of many species, including kiwi and kereru. The concept of a mainland island stemmed from the success of offshore island reserves, where birds and forest were isolated and protected from predators by water. In a mainland island a section of forest is initially ringed by traps or a predator-proof fence and then, within the protected area, all predators are removed. The outside ring of traps prevents unwanted invaders returning and allows birdlife to flourish.

Near the entrance is a 'weta hotel', a specially constructed box enabling visitors to view weta. Related to crickets, locusts and grasshoppers, these ancient creatures are even older than the tuatara and have hardly changed in the last 100 million years. New Zealand has over 100 species, though around 20 of these are endangered.

15 Maunganui Bluff
Rare coastal forest and dramatic coastal views.

- **Grade:** Hard. **Time:** Three hours return.
- **How to get there:** 8 km north of the southern turnoff to Trounson Kauri Park on SH12 turn left and drive a further 6.5 km to the beach (this last section is gravel).

Maunganui Bluff dramatically marks the north end of the marvellous sweep of Ripiro Beach, stretching for 100 km from Pouto on the Kaipara Harbour. Apart from the tiny bach settlement at the foot of the bluff, the beach is virtually empty and open to thundering swells off the Tasman Sea and a persistent westerly wind. Rising to 460 m, the bluff itself was formed by a lava flow from eruptions 11–15 million years ago, and is cloaked with rare coastal forest. It's a solid trudge to the top, but the expansive coastal views from the summit are reward enough.

16 Tokatoka Peak Walk and Maungaraho Rock Climb
Fantastic views over the Wairoa River from this old volcanic core.

 Grade: Medium. **Time:** 40 minutes return.

 How to get there: At Tokatoka Tavern north of Ruawai turn right into Tokatoka Road – the track begins about 1.5 km on the left by the 'Scenic Reserve' sign.

The distinctive shapes of Maungaraho Rock and Tokatoka Peak are impossible to miss on the road from Ruawai to Dargaville. The cores of old volcanoes, they are all that remain after the outer volcanic material has eroded away over millions of years.

From a distance Tokatoka Peak looks difficult to climb, but the track from the eastern side isn't that hard, though not well formed and a bit of a scramble near the top. However, it's worth the effort, as the views are superb. To the south, the languid Wairoa River snakes through the flat landscape to the Kaipara Harbour, while to the east the views are inland to rugged bush-clad ranges. Right below, sitting on a bluff alongside the river, is the distinctive shape of an old pa site.

To get to Maungaraho Rock, just northeast of Tokatoka Peak, continue north on SH12 from Tokatoka for 6 km, then turn right into Mititai Road, following the signs for 7 km to the end of Maungaraho Rock Road. Maungaraho Rock is a more challenging climb. From the car park, the solid wall of rock rising 222 metres from the surrounding farmland looks unclimbable, but a rough track circles the rock, with the track to the top beginning from the other side. There is a short difficult section at the base of the rock, made easier by cables. Once past this tricky bit, the climb to the top isn't that hard. The views and the satisfaction of reaching the top make it all worthwhile.

17 Mimiwhangata Regional Park
Remote beaches and old pa.

 Grade: Easy. **Time:** Allow 2 hours.
How to get there: From Helena Bay take Webb Road for 5.5 km and turn left into Mimiwhangata Road – continue 5 km along this narrow, winding gravel road to the car park.

Mimiwhangata is a beautiful but isolated park, and the perfect place to get away from it all. Two long sandy beaches flank the peninsula on the north and south, so no matter where the wind blows from, you can find shelter.

Mimiwhangata was the site of a great battle between Ngapuhi and Ngati Manaia. In the dead of night Ngapuhi simultaneously attacked all three Ngati Manaia pa on the peninsula: Te Rearea, Taraputa and Kaituna. Caught by surprise, Ngati Manaia suffered a devastating defeat and huge loss of life, though their rangatira and some people managed to escape. Kaituna is still considered tapu.

Today a sprawling farm park covers the peninsula. There are official tracks, but the signage is erratic, although you won't get lost, as it's open farmland. Long sandy beaches make this an ideal destination for walking, but there's a long drive to get there. The only facilities at the park are toilets and some good DOC accommodation.

18 Whale Bay, the Tutukaka Coast
A small sandy bay overhung with pohutukawa with views looking out over Woolleys Bay.

 Grade: Easy. **Time:** 30 minutes return.
How to get there: Well-signposted to the right at the top of the hill, just north of Matapouri.

Whale Bay is everything you wish a beach to be – a small cove of fine, white sand perfect for swimming, overhung with old trees and ideal for a shady picnic on a hot summer's day. The short walk leads down through beautiful old puriri, pohutukawa and a fine grove of nikau, with both the track and beach having excellent views along the wide sweep of Woolleys Bay to the north.

There is a track out to the headland, and Whale Bay can be accessed by foot from the northern end of Matapouri Bay.

19 A.H. Reed Memorial Park, Whangarei
A well-preserved reserve of mature bush, including kauri.

- **Grade:** Easy. **Time:** 40 minutes.
- **How to get there:** The reserve is on Whareroa Road, which is off the end of Mill Road.

Bordered by the Hatea River within the city of Whangarei, this park contains several large kauri, some up to 500 years old. Named after pioneer publisher Alfred Reed, the park also contains fine stands of totara and a small waterfall.

20 Bream Head/Te Whara
A secret radar station and an old pa with magnificent views.

- **Grade:** Medium. **Time:** One hour 45 minutes.
- **How to get there:** The track entrance is from the beach access car park at Ocean Beach, 40 km from Whangarei and 3 km from Urquharts Bay.

Whangarei Heads is an example of outstanding coastal beauty, with sandy beaches, dense bush and rugged peaks rising to 476 m at Bream Head and 420 m at Mt Manaia. Bream Head is part of a massive volcano that erupted 20 million years ago, with the other remaining sections being Mt Manaia, Mt Lion and the Hen and Chicken Islands.

The Bream Head Scenic Reserve is the largest remaining area of coastal forest in Northland and contains rare flora and fauna, including kiwi, kaka and red-crowned kakariki.

Named Te Whara after Manaia's principal wife, the peak was renamed Bream Head by Captain Cook when he mistook tarakihi for bream. During World War II, in response to the sinking of the RMS *Niagara*, which struck a German mine off Bream Head in June 1940, a top-secret surveillance station was established with radar to scan the waters to the north and warn of any possible attack.

From the car park by the beach it is a steady uphill climb to the old radar station, also the location of a very old pa, though today very little remains of either. The views are sufficient reward for the solid climb – Ocean Beach below the head is a magnificent sweep of sandy beach renowned for its surf, ideal for a swim after a hot uphill walk.

21 Smugglers Cove

A stunning sandy beach, World War II gun emplacements, an old pa and views to the outer islands of the Hauraki Gulf.

Grade: Easy. **Time:** One hour return.
How to get there: The track to the cove begins at the car park at the very end of Urquharts Bay Road.

Smugglers Cove isn't just a colourful name – this beautiful sandy bay is a genuine smugglers' hideout where early Scots settlers smuggled crates of whisky ashore to avoid paying duty. On Busby Head overlooking the bay is an ancient pa site, and on the headland on the harbour side, are the remains of a gun emplacement built during World War II.

To get to Busby Head, the track is well marked from Urquharts Bay. From the car park take the track to the right around the gun emplacements and continue past them to a junction where the track to the pa leads along the ridge to the right. After visiting the pa, return to the junction, then turn down to the right and go back along the beautiful Smugglers Cove beach.

22 Mount Manaia

The distinctive rocky outcrops of Mount Manaia offer great views.

Grade: Hard. **Time:** Two hours return.
How to get there: From the city take Riverside Drive out towards Whangarei Heads – the track begins from the Mt Manaia Club car park, 30 km from the city.

This distinctive mountain (460 m) is easily recognised by the numerous volcanic outcrops which define the peak. As usual, a lively Maori legend is associated with Mt Manaia.

Manaia was a proud rangatira who had his pa on the summit. However, he was envious of the chief Hautatu, who lived across the harbour. Hautatu was married to a very attractive woman, Pito. Consumed with jealousy, Manaia connived to send Hautatu on a raiding party and while he was gone, raided his pa and kidnapped Pito. Hautatu was furious and attacked Manaia's mountain-top pa, forcing Manaia to escape with his two children and Pito. Hautatu quickly caught up with Pito and was about to strike her with a club when they were all turned to stone by a lightning bolt from the god of thunder – and there they remain.

It's all uphill, but not as hard as it looks, as the track is excellent and the grade steady for the most part. Take your time as the views are spectacular – keep an eye out for kaka in the bush leading up to the peak.

23 Piroa Falls, Waipu Gorge Scenic Reserve
A picturesque waterfall and cooling swimming holes

  Grade: Easy.   **Time:** 15 minutes return.
  How to get there: Well sign posted off SH 1, 8 km south of Waipu. The 6 km road is gravel, winding, narrow in parts and parking is limited.

While this walk is very short, this beautiful waterfall, just a short distance from SH1, is too attractive to miss. Winding down a steep hillside, this short zigzag tracks with steps, drops down to the rocky Ahuroa River. From there it is a short scramble upstream to the very picturesque Piroa waterfall. Here the river drops 20m over a bluff, where the water splashing on the rocks below which has a marked influence in cooling the air. Adding to the appeal is the picnic area under the tall totara trees and the numerous small swimming holes along the river.

24 Mangawhai Heads Walkway
Huge pohutukawa trees and spectacular coastal views

  Grade: Easy.   **Time:** Two and a half hours.
  How to get there: The beginning of the track is clearly marked from the beach 1 km north of the Mangawhai Heads Surf Club at the end of Wintle Street.

Forming a broad shallow estuary, the tidal Mangawhai River empties sluggishly into the ocean below a high bluff, protected from the open sea by a long sandspit. Now part of the 245-hectare Mangawhai Wildlife Refuge, the area attracts shorebirds including Caspian and fairy terns, oystercatchers and New Zealand dotterel. The fairy tern is one of New Zealand's most endangered birds with fewer than ten breeding pairs in existence. They breed only at Mangawhai, Waipu and at Papakanui on the Kaipara Harbour. In 1984 only three pairs remained.

North of the river is Mangawhai Heads, rising to 167 m and noted for massive pohutukawa trees and pockets of native bush. The well-formed loop track climbs steadily along the heads and affords spectacular coastal views from a viewing platform. If the tide's out you can drop down to the shore and return that way, otherwise return the way you came.

25 Tawharanui Regional Park
Beautiful sandy beaches combine with magnificent vistas of the Hauraki Gulf and Little Barrier.

- **Grade:** Medium.   **Time:** Tokatu Point – three hours return.
- **How to get there:** 26 km from Warkworth, the directions to the park are clearly signposted from SH1 – the last 5 km is unsealed, narrow and winding.
- **Note:** Some Tracks may be completely or partially closed to prevent the spread of Kauri dieback disease. The duration of the closure is uncertain

Tawharanui Regional Park covers almost 600 ha of rolling farmland and bushy gullies, at the very end of the Tawharanui Peninsula. To the north looms Little Barrier Island, with wooded Kawau Island to the south. Protected by a predator-proof fence, the park is home to a large number of native birds.

When travelling along the coastline, Maori used distinctive landmarks to guide them. Tawharanui was known to travellers as Takatu (or gannet, now incorrectly spelt Tokatu on the park signage), the name of the rock formation at the very tip of the peninsula. The name Tawharanui refers to the edible flower bract of the kiekie vine, which grew abundantly there.

A mixture of farmland and bush remnants, the park has a maze of excellent tracks. The magnificent sweep of Anchor Bay, north-facing and sheltered from southwesterly winds, is an ideal base for a loop walk round the park, though there's plenty of scope for shorter walks. Tokatu Point Lookout Walk starts from the eastern side of the car park at Anchor Bay. The views of the gulf are spectacular, with rare prostrate manuka on the way to the point. This manuka isn't a separate species, but a form which has adapted to exposed environments by growing parallel to the ground, rather than its usual upright habit. From Tokatu Point take the South Coast Track back to Maori Bay, from where there's a short walk to the car park.

26 Parry Kauri Park
A superb forest with two ancient kauri trees

Grade: Easy. **Time:** 30 minutes.
How to get there: South of Warkworth turn off SH1 into McKinney Road and after 2 km turn right into Wilson Road and the entrance to the park is well signposted to the left.

Large kauri are not uncommon in Auckland though in most places it is just one or two big trees and many much smaller ones. Parry Kauri Park is tiny (just 2 hectares) but still manages to be the best example of kauri forest in the Auckland area. The highlight of the reserve is the massive McKinney kauri, named after the original European landowner, the local Presbyterian minister Reverend McKinney. Reaching a height of 38 m, it is almost 12 m to the first limb and over 7½ m in circumference. The McKinney kauri is estimated to be approximately 800 years old and the largest kauri tree on the east coast.

In addition to kauri there are numerous kahikatea and good examples of rewarewa, rimu, tanekaha, kohekohe, taraire, karaka and totara, many of which are marked to assist in identification. In the carpark by the museum are relics of the early saw-milling operations.

The easy loop track, mainly on boardwalks to protect the delicate roots, meanders through small gullies thick with nikau and ferns.

22
short walks in
Auckland

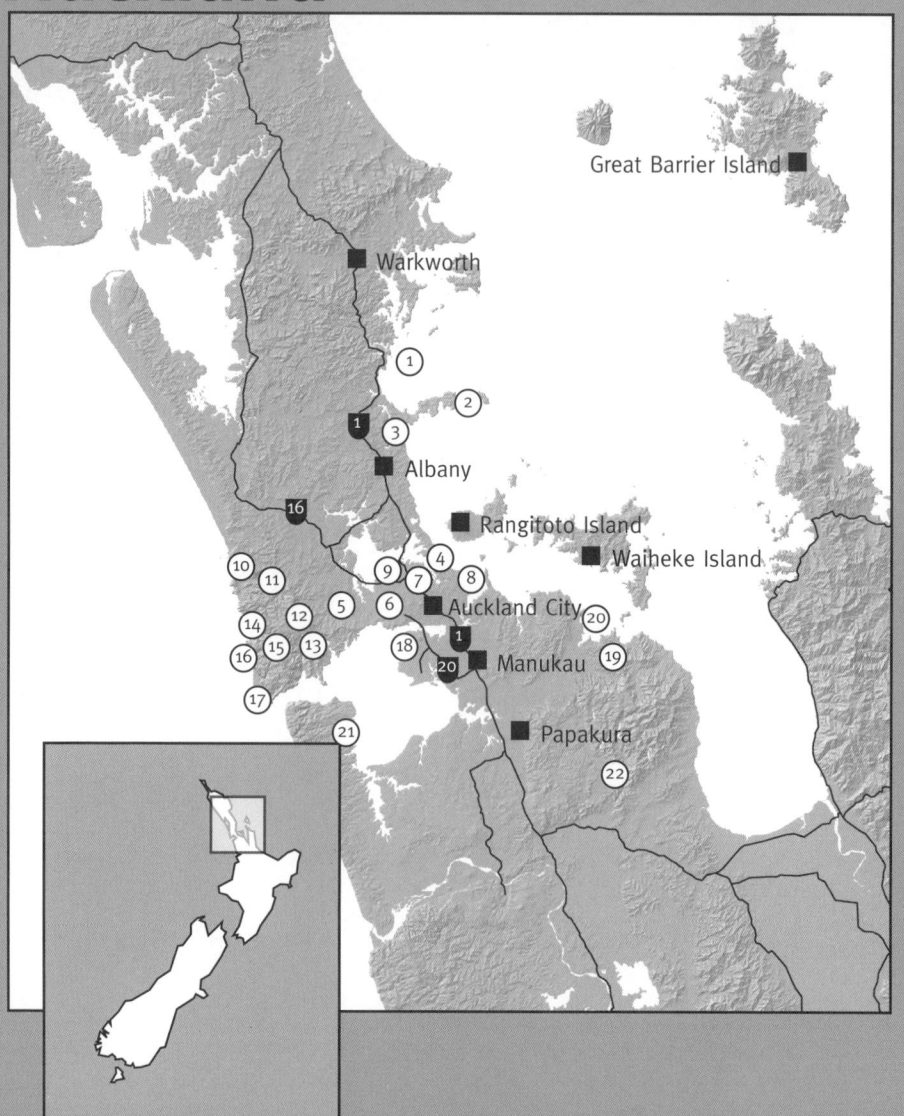

1 Wenderholm Regional Park
A beautiful, pohutakawa-lined beach and bush walk.

Grade: Medium.   **Time:** 45 minutes to the lookout and two hours for the perimeter.
How to get there: 1 km north of Waiwera on the Hibiscus Coast Highway.

Wenderholm Regional Park, between the Puhoi and Waiwera rivers, is an ideal family destination for a day out, combining a fine sandy beach, pohutukawa trees, an historic homestead and a bush walk. Wenderholm is Swedish for 'winter home' and an earlier name of the historic house (1857) now known as Couldrey House (open to the public). Walking tracks lead from beside the house up through a stand of native bush to a great viewpoint over the Hauraki Gulf.

The track to the lookout is well formed but a steady uphill climb with lots of steps through mature native bush where there are a surprising number of native birds, including tui, kereru and fantails. Beyond the lookout a rough section of track drops steeply to the Waiwera River, then continues along the river to the road and back to the park entrance. Another alternative which avoids the noisy road section is the track through the middle of the park up to a fine lookout over Puhoi and Waiwera, then steeply downhill back to the beach.

Near the junction of the Couldrey House and the Maungatauhoro Te Hikoi tracks are the remains of a pa, though it takes a little detection work to make out the earthworks.

2 Shakespear Regional Park
Views of the gulf, sandy beaches and old gun emplacements.

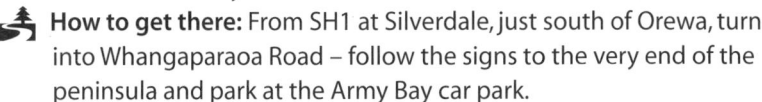

Grade: Easy.   **Time:** Two hours for the loop walk via the Lookout and Te Haruhi Bay.
How to get there: From SH1 at Silverdale, just south of Orewa, turn into Whangaparaoa Road – follow the signs to the very end of the peninsula and park at the Army Bay car park.

An attractive combination of bush, beach, history and great views over the Gulf, Shakespear Regional Park occupies the very end of the Whangaparaoa Peninsula. The area just north of the park is still Ministry of Defence land, but within the park are a number of historic pillboxes constructed as part of an elaborate defence network north of Auckland. Pillboxes were low concrete structures, often partially dug into the ground and designed to house machine guns or anti-tank guns. The park's name is not a spelling mistake, but recalls an early farming family with the surname Shakespear.

The walk begins at Army Bay, a north-facing sandy beach ideal for swimming, and climbs steadily uphill through a deep bush valley to open farmland and on to the lookout. The views are superb along the coast to the north, out to the islands of the gulf, and south to downtown Auckland. From here the track continues downhill to Haruhi Bay, lined with pohutukawa. The return track passes an old shearing shed built around 1900, finally leading through a wetland populated with water-loving birds.

3 Okura Bush Walkway

A very fine grove of mature puriri and an historic cottage.

- **Grade:** Easy. **Time:** 45 minutes return to the grove, one and a half hours to the sandspit in the river. Two hours return to Dacre Cottage.
- **How to get there:** Drive north on East Coast Bays Road from the intersection with Oteha Valley Road; after 4.5 km turn right into Haigh Access Road – the track begins at the end of the road.
- **Note:** This track may be completely or partially closed to prevent the spread of Kauri dieback disease. The duration of the closure is uncertain

This walk follows the Okura River to Karepiro Bay and historic Dacre Cottage. Built sometime in the early 1850s by Henry Dacre, the tiny cottage is highly unusual – constructed from brick, not timber. The track begins over a small tidal creek, plunging into a fine stand of native bush dominated by mature puriri, a very handsome native tree with glossy leaves, a broad spreading habit, and attractive small purple-red flowers which often carpet the forest floor.

After passing through the puriri grove the track winds through bushy gullies of mature trees with regenerating kauri on the ridges before descending to the Okura River, habitat of wading birds including oystercatchers, stilts and plovers. If the tide is right, at this point it's easier to walk along the water's edge. Finally the track turns to the left, climbing over a steep headland to Karepiro Bay and Dacre Cottage. The beach here is swimmable at high tide. At this point the track follows the Weiti River to Stillwater, but unless you have transport arranged you'll need to return the way you came.

4 North Head Historic Reserve
Wide views over the Waitemata Harbour from this sea-fringed volcanic cone, with fortifications including tunnels and gun emplacements.

- **Grade:** Easy. **Time:** 15 minutes return from the car park to the disappearing gun, but allow at least an hour to explore.
- **How to get there:** Main vehicle entrance is at the end of Takarunga Road, Cheltenham; North Head is about a 20-minute walk from Devonport Wharf.

Standing sentinel over the Waitemata Harbour, this prominent cone (Maungauika) was never fortified by Maori in pre-European times. While there is evidence of cultivation of the rich soil at the base of the head at Torpedo Bay, nearby Takarunga/Mt Victoria was the main pa for the area. When the great ocean-going waka *Tainui* explored they found people living here; over the centuries the area, valued for its fertile soil and excellent fishing grounds, was occupied by numerous iwi.

As early as 1836 a pilot station was established at the foot of North Head, and in 1885, in response to Russian expansion into the Pacific, three gun batteries were built. The underground tunnels and a cookhouse and barracks still remain, the oldest buildings on the summit. Further fortifications were added during World War I and World War II and the reserve's excellent signage includes photos of the defence positions. The south battery features one of the few Armstrong disappearing guns left in the world, designed to be loaded underground, raised and fired, protecting the men servicing the gun. The cookhouse on the summit (open 8.30 am to 4 pm) has a collection of old photos and a short video, while there are extensive tunnels on the eastern side. A track around the base of the cone leads to small sea caves and a sheltered sandy cove suitable for swimming.

5. Opanuku Walkway
Superb native bush in the heart of suburban Henderson

Grade: Easy. **Time:** 50 minutes
How to get there: There several entrances to the walkway but the main one is Henderson Park on Wisher Crescent.

Without a doubt it is one of the finest remnants of native bush in the Auckland urban area, the Opanuku walkway begins in Henderson Park and then follows the course of the Opanuku Stream south to Henderson Valley Park. The eastern side of the stream is a traditional park, with large grassy areas from which a wide concrete footpath and cycleway heads south through grass swathes and recent native plantings. Part of this track maybe closed to prevent the spread of kauri dieback disease. The duration of the closure is uncertain.

Across the stream the park couldn't be more different. An easy path begins over a bridge at Henderson Park and then wends its way upstream and along short boardwalks through stunning native bush. Dominated by massive totara and enormous kahikatea, there are also old titoki, karaka, a huge cabbage tree, kowhai overhanging the stream, groves of silver fern and several large kauri. It is just a small glimpse of what lowland forest in the region must have been like before the arrival of people.

The best section of this walkway is between Henderson Park and Border Road forming an easy loop that will take around 50 minutes.

6 Oakley Creek/ Te Auaunga
An appealing waterfall is the highlight of this bush walk.

Grade: Easy **Time:** 45 minutes
How to get there: There are numerous access points to the creek, though it is easier from the eastern side of the creek, especially from the Phyllis Street Reserve off Springfield Ave where there is off-street parking.

Oakley Creek begins life in Hillsborough, draining a wide valley between the volcanoes of Mt Roskill, Three Kings and Mt Albert before flowing north to join the estuary of the Whau River at Waterview. East of New North Road the creek is essentially a large ditch; part of a drainage plan from the 1930s when this area was a vast swamp. The lower section is by far more interesting and attractive.

While the water quality has been severely compromised, in recent years the creek below New North Road has undergone a radical transformation with an extensive restoration and replanting of native plants. Today the water runs much cleaner and the walk along the creek attracts locals and visitors alike. The big drawcard, the Oakley Creek Waterfall is the largest waterfall in the Auckland urban area. Here the water cascades 6 m over a basalt lava flow and the pool below the waterfall attracts many local swimmers during the summer months. Above the falls there are several small rapids, also over old lava flows and throughout the regenerating bush are lava boulders, a constant reminder of the area's dramatic volcanic past.

Despite the intensely urban surroundings with houses pushing close to the water, the bush along the creek is home to native birds such as tui, piwakawaka, and in the creek itself can be found eels, inanga, kokopu and freshwater mussels. The creek becomes tidal near the motorway where it joins the Waitemata Harbour by the Waterview Reserve and a walkway connects Oakley Creek to the Waterview Reserve /Howlett Esplanade and to the north crosses under the motorway to pass through a small wetland to join up with the Eric Armishaw Park and Walkway in Point Chevalier.

7 Parnell Historic Walk
Historic building and hidden parks.

 Grade: Easy. Time: One hour.
 How to get there: Start at St Mary's by Holy Trinity Cathedral on Parnell Road, then walk down St Stephens Ave.

Parnell is one of Auckland's oldest areas and this walk combines several of the city's most important historic buildings and hidden parks. Start at St Mary's, which was built entirely of timber between 1884 and 1897 by Benjamin Mountfort, in the Gothic style. Described as one of New Zealand's finest wooden churches, St Mary's was originally on the other side of the road and in 1982 was moved to its present site. Next stop is Bishopscourt, 8 St Stephens Ave. Designed by Frederick Thatcher and constructed between 1861 and 1863, these beautiful wooden buildings around a central courtyard were originally built for Bishop Selwyn. Bishopscourt is the Bishop of Auckland's residence and not open to the public. Continue to the very end of tree-lined St Stephens Ave and go down the steps towards the waterfront. Halfway down, turn left just before the bridge over Tamaki Drive, through the Parnell Baths. Originally a tidal swimming pool enclosed by a rock wall, this is Auckland's only saltwater pool. The building was awarded a Gold Medal in 1958 by the New Zealand Institute of Architects. A stylish stone and glass mosaic graces the front of the building.

Continue along the edge of Judges Bay and on the left, on a small rise, is St Stephen's Chapel. This picturesque chapel was built for the signing of the Constitution of the Anglican Church of New Zealand in June 1857. Designed by Fredrick Thatcher, the wooden building was used as Bishop Selwyn's semi-private chapel and today functions as a local church. From Judge's Bay take the steps up the hill through Dove Myer Robinson Park to the lookout over the sea and the city. From here turn around and walk through the Parnell Gardens, famous for a spectacular display of summer roses.

Walk up Gladstone Road for about 500 metres, turn right into Alberon Street, and right again into Alberon Place. At the end of this short street take the flight of steps straight ahead, leading down through dense nikau bush to Alberon Reserve. This lovely park edged with palm trees is almost unknown to anyone but locals, and is a peaceful haven. Take the path out of the park to the right and climb up to St Georges Bay Road. Turn right, then left into Scarborough Reserve, another pretty park hidden below Parnell Road. Take the exit to the right out of this park, up to Parnell Road. Turn left up Parnell Road to return to St Mary's. On the left, at 350 Parnell Road, is Hulme Court. Built in 1843, in the Regency style, this is reputed to be Auckland's oldest building on its original site. Later purchased by Colonel Hulme after whom the house is named, it was used as Government House during the 1850s and was also at one time the home of Bishop Selwyn. The bluestone walls have since been plastered over, but the hipped slate roof is original.

8 Tahuna Torea Nature Reserve, Glendowie
A haven for waterbirds in the Tamaki River.

- **Grade:** Easy. **Time:** One hour.
- **How to get there:** The main car park is at the end of West Tamaki Road.

Tahuna Torea Reserve falls into two distinct parts. The first area by the car park is a mix of coastal vegetation, tidal creeks, lagoons and saltmarsh, and is home to a wide range of birds including ducks, shags and pukeko.

In complete contrast, the other part of the reserve is a long tidal spit of sand and shell jutting far out into the Tamaki Estuary, the preserve of wading birds such as stilts, godwits and oystercatchers.

Initially the walk is a combination of track and boardwalk, providing easy dry walking at any tide. However, most of the spit is underwater at high tide, so if you want to walk this section check the tides, with the walk best planned on an outgoing tide. If the tide is low you can cut directly from the car park to the spit, but you'll need good footwear as the tidal flats are muddy and littered with sharp oyster shells.

9 Meola Reef, Point Chevalier
An old lava flow almost cuts the Waitemata Harbour in half.

- **Grade:** Easy. **Time:** 20 minutes.
- **How to get there:** The track is clearly marked on Meola Road between Westmere and Point Chevalier.

Waitemata Harbour is centred on two drowned river valleys, Riverhead to the west and north and the Tamaki River to the east and south, and is characterised by sandstone cliffs, sandy beaches, volcanic craters and estuarine rivers. Virtually cleaving the harbour in two at low tide is Meola Reef, an ancient lava flow from the Three Kings eruption.

In Maori tradition Meola Reef is Te Tokaroa (long rock), built by patupaiarehe (fairies, but not cute ones). Two patupaiarehe iwi who lived in the Waitakere bush clashed one night just west of Te Rae (Point Chevalier). The losing side was pushed back to the shore and decided to make their escape by building a bridge of rocks to the other side. Covered by water at high tide, this causeway would confuse their enemies as to how they escaped. Busy hauling heavy rocks as their stone bridge crept deeper into the harbour, the patupaiarehe forgot about the dawn. Suddenly the sun rose over the eastern horizon. With the bridge incomplete, the patupaiarehe were turned to stone by the sun's rays and trapped forever.

This is an easy, flat loop walk through open fields and regenerating coastal vegetation. Towards the exposed reef the track ends and mangroves give way to oyster-covered rocks. You'll need good, strong footwear to walk any distance onto the reef. This is best done at very low tide and is much more difficult than it looks.

10 Lake Wainamu, Bethells Beach
A massive sand dune creating a deep lake.

Grade: Easy. **Time:** One hour return.

How to get there: The track begins to the left once you cross the bridge about 1 km from Bethells Beach.

Just inland from Bethells Beach, sand driven up from the beach by westerly winds has formed a huge sand dune blocking the Waiti Stream, creating a small freshwater lake. From the road the track initially follows the shallow stream, then climbs the massive dune to the lake. The dune is much bigger than it first appears and in a strong westerly wind the sand is whipped across, reminiscent of a desolate desert movie scene. The lake at the edge of the dune is particularly deep and an ideal swimming spot. To return follow the lake edge to the left, then stroll back to the car park via the shallow stream. A good track encircles the entire lake and the circuit will take a further hour.

11 Auckland City Walk, Cascades Kauri Regional Park
A stroll along the Waitakere Stream, overhung with fern trees and nikau palms, leads to two massive kauri trees in a fine area of native bush.

Grade: Easy. **Time:** One hour.

How to get there: The track begins at the end of Falls Road, off Te Henga Road between Scenic Drive and Bethells Beach (drive right through the golf course).

Note: This track may be completely or partially closed to prevent the spread of Kauri dieback disease. The duration of the closure is uncertain

Cascades Kauri Regional Park is one of the best and most accessible native bush areas in the region. The walk begins by crossing the swingbridge below the car park and initially follows the Waitakere Stream, which at this point flows gently through jungle-like vegetation thick with ferns and palms. The Cascades themselves, accessed by a side track, are difficult to see as they are tucked away in a narrow cleft in the rock. The highlight of the walk are two giant kauri, which somehow survived early milling. Keep an eye out for sulphur-crested cockatoos, which have established a colony in the large kauri on the ridge above the stream. You'll hear these noisy birds before you see them.

While birdlife is notable by its absence, the Ark in the Park project, which covers 1000 hectares of the Cascades Kauri Park, has seen the reintroduction of whitehead, North Island robin and hihi (stitchbird) in the predator-controlled area. From the kauri trees the loop track then returns to the car park.

12 Waitakere Dam Walk

A water reservoir sits on top of a high bluff overlooking the Waitakere Valley.

Grade: Easy. **Time:** One hour return.
How to get there: Scenic Drive 7 km north of the intersection with Piha Road.

In the early part of the twentieth century, part of the rugged Waitakere Ranges was set aside as a water reserve to replace the city's water supply at Western Springs. Built between 1905 and 1910, this was the first reservoir constructed in the Waitakere Ranges and the area around the dam formed the nucleus of Waitakere Ranges Regional Parkland, which now covers over 17,000 ha. To assist in the construction of the dam, which at the time was in an isolated part of Auckland, a small tramway, which still operates, was built to bring materials to the site. Today the park is laced with walking tracks, ranging from sedate beach walks to demanding tramps in thick bush and steep terrain. Much of the park was milled for timber in the nineteenth century and large areas were cleared for farming, but today the bush is regenerating, covering old scars.

The dam is built across the Waitakere River on top of a high bluff, with extensive views over the bush and the valley far below. While access to the dam is by sealed roadway, the drop down to the dam is steep, and it's a solid climb back to the car park. On the way back up take a break and visit the large kauri two minutes off the main track. For those wanting a longer walk, there's a track along the tramway, as far as the tunnel.

13 Fairy Falls, Waitakere

A series of attractive cascades before a 15 m drop.

Grade: Medium. **Time:** One and a half hours return.
How to get there: On Scenic Drive 4.7 km north of the Piha intersection – parking is opposite the beginning of the track.
This track may be completely or partially closed to prevent the spread of kauri dieback disease. The duration of the closure is uncertain.

Set in attractive bush with large kauri and rimu, the track along Stoney Creek to the Fairy Falls is a dense jungle of kiekie, supplejack and nikau. The falls themselves begin as a series of cascades before a final 15 m drop into the pool below. The track to the top of the falls is excellent, but to reach the bottom is a bit of a scramble down steep steps, uneven ground and wet rocks. Good footwear is necessary. Think twice about taking young children all the way to the bottom of the falls, as it's quite an uphill slog on the way back.

14 Whites Beach, Piha

An isolated beach, surrounded by steep bush-clad hills.

Grade: Medium. **Time:** One and a half hours return.
How to get there: The track begins at the very north end of Piha Beach.

Whites Beach will appeal to those who enjoy the wild windswept nature of Auckland's west coast. The track to the beach, only accessible by foot, leads over a headland of regenerating manuka, flax and pohutukawa.
It will take 15 minutes to reach the top of the ridge, from where a short track leads off the left to a lookout with views over both Whites and Piha beaches. There's a really rough track from the lookout down to the beach, but it's best to return to the main track and continue on to the beach from there. As with all the beaches on this coast, the surf is rough and unpredictable even on a good day, and great care should be taken when swimming.

15 Kitekite Falls
A series of cascades into a bush-lined swimming hole.

Grade: Easy. **Time:** One hour return.
How to get there: Take the road to Piha and at the bottom of the hill, turn immediately right into Glen Esk Road, where the track begins from the car park at the end of the road.

The Kitekite Falls, on the Glen Esk stream, are situated at the head of a long valley thick with luxuriant bush. The traditional name is Ketekete and the valley Whatiwhati – both placenames closely connected to a battle in the seventeenth century. In a revenge attack for the death of Tawhiakiterangi, his son Taimaro ambushed a group from the South Kaipara who were visiting the falls. The attack was signalled by Taimaro clicking his tongue: 'ketekete'. Most of those from the Kaipara died in the attack but a few survivors escaped down the Whatiwhati valley.

This is the quintessential Waitakere walk. From the car park a broad track climbs steadily uphill to the falls. The Kitekite Falls themselves are three cascades, and the entire waterfall is best seen from a viewpoint above the valley, just before the end of the track. The track also offers views back down the valley over regenerating kauri. The lower falls are three drops into a small pool suitable for swimming, and the broad rocky area right by the falls is a good, if lumpy, spot for a picnic. The return track is down the other side of the stream.

16 Te Ahua Point
Dramatic cliffs drop into the wild Tasman Sea.

Grade: Easy. **Time:** 40 minutes return.
How to get there: The track begins at the end of Te Ahuahu Road/Log Race Road, which turns left off Piha Road.

Te Ahua Point is a superb lookout atop towering volcanic cliffs that drop hundreds of metres into a wild sea. To the south the view is along the coast to the dangerous bar marking the entrance to Manukau Harbour. On 7 February 1863, HMS *Orpheus* struck the Manukau Bar and of 259 men aboard, only 70 survived New Zealand's worse maritime disaster.

Jutting out to sea far to the south is Mt Karioi near Raglan, while to the north are Piha Beach and the Muriwai coast.

Maori legend tells of Hinerangi, who loved a chieftain from Karekare. One day Hinerangi's husband and two companions were swept off the rocks and drowned at the southern end of Te Unuhanga o Rangitoto (Mercer Bay). Searching for her husband, Hinerangi climbed to the top of this headland to scan the sea. She refused to leave, and eventually died of a broken heart. Her sad face is outlined in the rocks below, now known as Te Ahua o Hinerangi (the likeness of Hinerangi).

The track begins on the northern side of the car park and is well marked and well formed. Gradually dropping downhill, it skirts the tops of huge cliffs before reaching a grassy knoll. The views are spectacular, though in windy weather it's very exposed. For those wanting a longer walk, the track continues downhill to Karekare Beach.

17 Caves Walk, Whatipu
Large sea caves huddle behind sand dunes.

Grade: Easy. **Time:** 30 minutes return.
How to get there: Take the road through Titirangi to Huia on the northern side of the Manukau Harbour – from Huia the road to Whatipu is narrow, winding and unsealed. The track starts from the northern side of the car park.

Shaped by years of wave action, these large caves are now a considerable distance from the sea, as the marshy area between the cliffs and the ocean has built up naturally. The largest of the caves was once used for dances, though sand has raised the floor level by five metres. Although the caves are substantial, torches aren't necessary. The wetland between the caves and the beach is an important habitat for waterbirds, which can be viewed from the dunes in front of the caves.

The walk begins on the same track as the Gibbons Track, but branches off to the left and skirts the bottom of the cliff face, leading to the caves and a small camping area. Don't try to cross the wetlands – aside from disturbing the birds, the vegetation is surprisingly dense, and the water deeper than it looks. Return to the car park to access the beach.

18 Mangere Mountain, Mangere Bridge
Auckland's largest volcanic cone.

Grade: Easy. **Time:** Allow up to one hour.

How to get there: Main entrance at end of Domain Road off Coronation Road, Mangere Bridge.

The broad Manukau Harbour, with its narrow entrance to the Tasman Sea, is a huge tidal basin 20 km wide, covering almost 400 square km. Very shallow, a large proportion of the harbour bed is exposed at low tide. Despite an international airport and the concentration of industrial sites on the eastern shoreline, it's an important aquatic bird habitat.

Overlooking the Manukau, Mangere is the largest and least modified of Auckland's 50 volcanic cones, but attracts fewer visitors than other better-known volcanoes. This sprawling mountain has two separate craters, and in the middle of the larger one is a distinctive lava dome. The area's rich volcanic soils sustained a large Maori population in pre-European times, growing kumara and taro, and with easy access to seafood in Manukau Harbour. Maori land boundaries indicated by low stone walls fan out from the base of the mountain, with kumara pits and house sites visible inside the crater. There are excellent views from the top. The track follows the rim of the crater, but as the whole park is open grass, you can stroll anywhere.

19 Clevedon Scenic Reserve

Expansive vistas of South Auckland from the summit of this bush-cloaked hill.

Grade: Medium. **Time:** One hour return
How to get there: Thorps Quarry Road, off North Road, just east of the Clevedon-Kawakawa Road intersection, Clevedon.

Set aside as a reserve in 1930, the 100 ha Clevedon Scenic Reserve includes fine stands of puriri, totara, taraire, kahikatea, kohekohe, rimu, karaka and kauri. Birdlife includes kereru, tui, riroriro, piwakawaka, shining cuckoo and even the occasional kaka.

Near the carpark the Taitaia stream runs through a small wetland from where a number of tracks rise up to a summit of 225 m. The views from the top are stunning; east to the Hauraki Gulf and the Coromandel Peninsula, south over the Clevedon Valley and the Hunua Ranges, west over the Manukau Harbour and north to Auckland City and Takapuna Beach. There are two tracks to the summit which together form a loop – the Totara track to the left is shorter, but steeper and the Puriri Track to the right is a more gradual climb. A short side track leads into a small wetland in the old quarry, abandoned in 1957, with water trickling down the rock face thickly encrusted with mosses.

20 Duder Regional Park
Magnificent views and an historic landing site.

Grade: Medium. **Time:** One and a half hours.

How to get there: From SH1 travel towards Whitford and on to Maraetai, then follow the coast south to Umupuia Beach – from the southern end turn right into North Road. The entrance to the park is on the left, a short distance down this road.

While travelling north from Waihihi around 1300 AD, the waka *Tainui* anchored at the end of this peninsula, sheltering from an easterly storm. The crew gathered food in the bush, in particular the edible parts of the kiekie (whara), and the peninsula became known as Whakakaiwhara, 'to eat whara'. The *Tainui* continued on to the Waitemata, where some onboard decided to settle, over time occupying the Whakakaiwhara Peninsula. Whakakaiwhara pa was located at the very tip of the peninsula, where terraces, kumara pits and a defensive ditch are visible.

The Duder family purchased the land in 1866 and farmed it up to 1994, when it was sold to the Auckland Regional Council and became a park. Only a few small patches of bush remain, though these are expanding.

The Farm Loop Walk is best undertaken anticlockwise, following the south coast of the peninsula. This is a comfortable steady climb to the trig, with views over the Firth of Thames, the gulf islands of Waiheke, Ponui, Browns and Rangitoto, and to the east the blue-tinged Coromandel. A further track leads out to the point and the remains of the pa, adding another 50 minutes.

21 Awhitu Regional Park
An historic homestead on the shores of the Manukau.

Grade: Easy. **Time:** One hour.

How to get there: From Waiuku drive north along the Awhitu Peninsula to Matakawau – 2 km past Matakawau turn right into Brook Road.

Nestled on the sheltered eastern side of the Awhitu Peninsula, this attractive park is a lovely combination of natural and human history.

At its heart is the nineteenth-century Brook homestead, typical of comfortable farm villas of the day and set among fine old trees on a rise above the beach.

Just in front of the homestead is a small, roughly built cottage, which initially housed the family until sufficient money was available to build a more substantial home.

The area is tidal and much more attractive closer to high tide, though the tidal flats provide an important feeding ground for birds. Within the park substantial wetlands are home to shy and elusive fern bird, bittern and banded rail.

22 Hunua Falls and Cosseys Reservoir Walk
An impressive waterfall and bush walk.

Grade: Easy/Medium. **Time:** Two and a half hours return.

How to get there: From Hunua village drive north, turn right into White Road after 1 km, turn right again into Falls Road and the car park is another 2 km.

Lying to the southeast of Auckland, the Hunua Ranges cover 14,000 ha, most of which is a water catchment area for Auckland City, at the same time preserving important native flora and fauna. Rising to 688 m at Kohukohunui, the ranges are rugged with dense bush, though the area was milled in earlier times. Over 450 native plants have been recorded, with fine stands of rimu, kauri, matai, kahikatea and rata. Hunua is home to Auckland's only kokako population, and North Island robins, long extinct here, have been successfully reintroduced.

Especially impressive after heavy rain, the 28 m Hunua Falls flow over basalt rock, the rim of an ancient volcano. There's a good picnic ground. Two short walks on either side of the pool lead to lookout points.

The longer walk to Cosseys Reservoir begins on the Massey Track, climbing steadily uphill to an impressive kauri grove before dropping down to the reserve, from where there's a lookout point with views over the reservoir. From the reservoir, walk back along Cosseys Gorge track, notable for its very fine bush.

8
short walks in
Hauraki Gulf

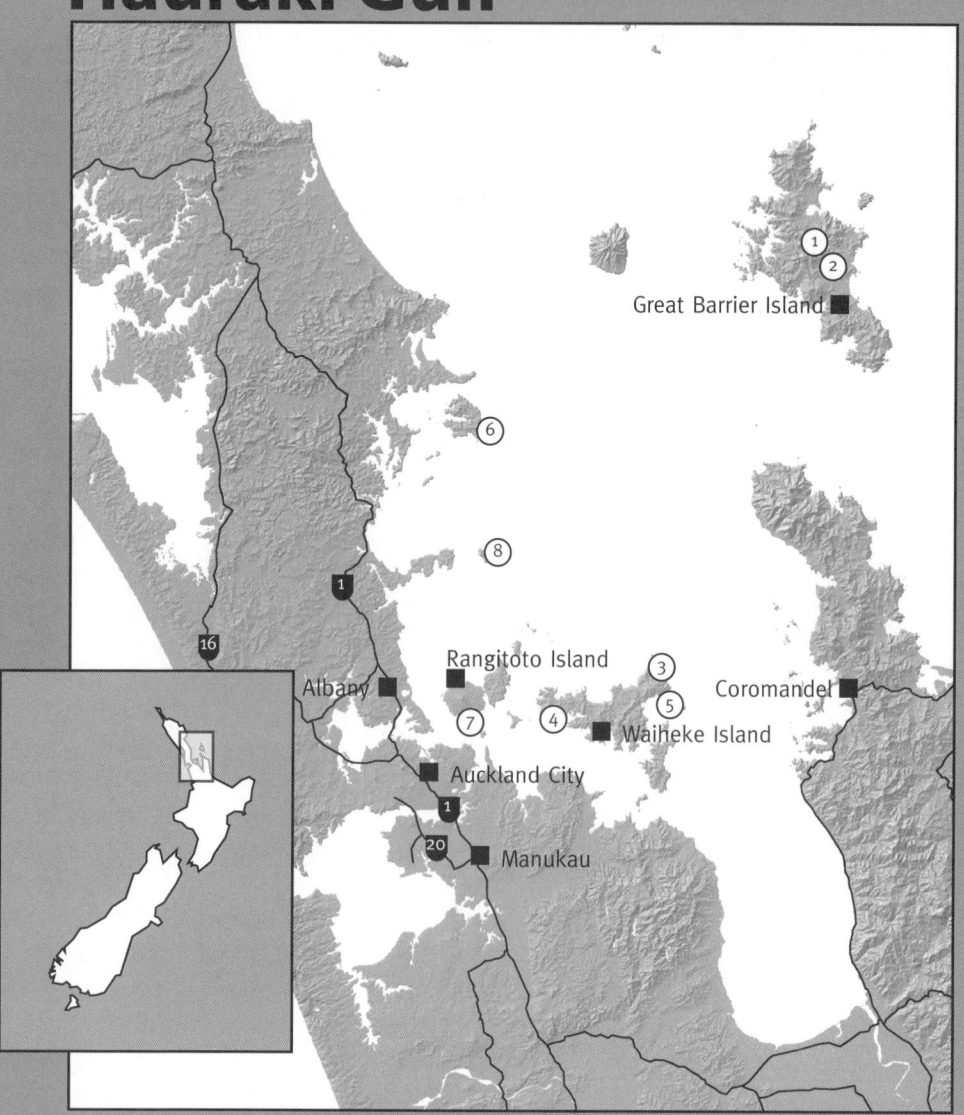

1 Mount Hobson, Great Barrier Island
On a clear day you can see forever.

Grade: Medium. **Time:** Three hours return.
How to get there: Signposted from the summit of Whangapoua Hill, on Aotea Road between Awana and Okiwi.

Lying 100 km to the northeast of Auckland, Great Barrier Island/Aotea is the largest island in the Hauraki Gulf. When sea travel was more common, the island was readily accessible and has a long history of Maori and Pakeha occupation. No untouched wilderness, having been ruthlessly stripped of its timber, today 60 percent of the island is conservation land. Having never had goats, stoats, deer, hedgehogs or possums, the island is a stronghold of several rare birds including the kaka, brown ducks and New Zealand dotterels.

Tradition holds that the discovery of this island gave this country the name Aotearoa, 'land of the long white cloud'. Kupe's wife (or daughter) on the *Aotea* waka, after the long journey from their Pacific homeland in Hawaiki, saw a long cloud on the horizon and cried out 'He ao, he ao', 'a cloud, a cloud'. From her call, Kupe named the island Aotea. Later when the mainland was discovered, the name was extended to Aotearoa.

It's far more likely both the island and the mainland were named after the *Aotea*. Maori never applied Aotearoa to the whole country, having no single name encompassing all the islands we now call New Zealand. For Maori and early settlers alike, if Aotearoa was used at all, it applied only to the North Island.

Hirakimata (Mt Hobson) in the centre of the island is the highest peak at 627 m, and on a clear day a trip to the summit is well worth the effort. The first part of the track to Windy Canyon is easy going, with the rugged outcrops testament to the peak's volcanic origins, eight to nine million years ago. Keep an eye out for glass-like obsidian embedded in the rocky walls and the Great Barrier tea-tree and daisy, both found only on the island. The walk to Windy Canyon is 45 minutes return.

It becomes more difficult after the canyon, though the track is well formed. The last section to the summit is more challenging – steep, narrow and rough in places, though at the summit boardwalks protect the fragile landscape. The views are exceptional, with the Coromandel Peninsula to the south and Auckland and the mainland stretching along the western horizon.

The top of the mountain is the unusual nesting ground of a rare seabird, the black petrel/taiko, which breeds only on the highest parts of Great Barrier and Little Barrier islands. Like their close relatives the Westland petrel, they are entirely black, including the tips of their beaks. While their breeding locations are confined to the Hauraki Gulf, they range as far as Australia and the coast of Peru in search of food.

2 Kaitoke Hot Springs, Great Barrier Island
A gentle soak in hot water is the reward for this easy walk.

- **Grade:** Easy. **Time:** Two hours return.
- **How to get there:** Signposted from the Whangaparapara Road, 5 km from Whangaparapara.

The Kaitoke Hot Springs well up from deep below the surface, and are a favourite destination for locals and visitors alike. The track begins over a shallow stream then meanders through regenerating bush to a clearing by the stream. The stream is quite shallow at this point, but often you'll find previous visitors have created people-sized rock pools deep enough to provide a pleasant soak.

3 Stony Batter Walk, Waiheke Island
Excellent views of the Hauraki Gulf from this extensive and well-preserved World War II fortification.

- **Grade:** Easy. **Time:** Allow one hour.
- **How to get there:** 6 km from Onetangi at the end of Man o' War Road.

One of the most impressive remains of New Zealand's coastal defences, this complex was begun in 1942 to protect the northern approaches to Auckland from the Japanese, though not completed until 1948, well after the war was over.

While very little exists above ground, the underground rooms are largely intact and surprisingly fresh in appearance. The walk is along a gravel road past olive groves, grapevines and small patches of bush, and the distinctive boulders from which the complex takes its name. The open and lofty location gives excellent views over the Gulf, and a track leads down to Hooks Bay for those wanting a longer walk.

Stony Batter is at the less-developed eastern end of the island. It is only a 20-minute walk from the end of the road, but getting there can be tricky, with no public transport. If you're planning to cycle, the road beyond Onetangi is very hilly and the last 6 km is gravel. There is a small charge for entrance to the underground tunnels to support the maintenance of the area.

4 Matiatia Historic Reserve Walk
Coastal views and a close-up peek at some amazing houses.

> **Grade:** Medium. **Time:** One hour 10 minutes.
> **How to get there:** Beginning and ending at Matiatia, the main wharf – while not marked, the start of the walk is via the shoreline beyond the Matiatia Reserve sign to the left of the car park.

No one knows where the name Waiheke, 'cascading water' originated. Some say it's a joke – no rivers or waterfalls remotely qualify. Others say a surveyor asked a local Maori, who thought he was asking the name of the stream by which they were standing. Taimoana Turoa, in *Te Takoto o te Whenua o Hauraki*, says when Kahumatamomoe came ashore from Te Arawa, he desperately needed to urinate – take your pick.

The walk begins to the north of the wharf car park. At mid to low tide follow the shore, but if the tide is high, scramble over rocks and tree roots for about 100 m. From the small bay beyond the wharf, the walk passes a large red shed, then follows markers around the coast, winding through open grass and rocky headlands with small beaches. Wide views include downtown Auckland, and the islands of the inner gulf.

In the early nineteenth century the Maori population was 1000, but halved following the 1821 Ngapuhi invasion. Fifty pa sites have been identified; the walk passes four headland pa within a short distance.

At Cable Bay, turn right uphill until you hit the road, turn left and continue down to the track leading to the right, just past the locked road gate, which takes you back to Matiatia. For a longer walk continue up the steep track at Cable Bay and on to Owhanake Bay. Turn inland, where the track takes you back to the road to the wharf – about two hours.

5 Rotoroa Island
A new wildlife sanctuary in the Hauraki Gulf.

Grade: Easy.   **Time:** Two hours
How to get there: Fullers 360, runs ferries to the island from downtown Auckland stopping at Waiheke Island (Orapiu) and Rotoroa on the way to Coromandel. Sailings are such that you will need to plan to spend the best part of a day on the island. Winter and summer sailings may vary. Phone 0800 8355377 www.fullers.co.nz.

For over 100 years Rotoroa was the Salvation Army's alcohol and drug rehabilitation centre for men (the women were on Pakatoa Island). Intensely farmed and developed, very little of the island's native vegetation survived but today Rotoroa Island today is a very different place. Now a wildlife sanctuary run by the Rotoroa Island Trust, together with the Auckland Zoo and the Department of Conservation, over half the island has been replanted with more than 400,000 native plants, and although most are just a few metres high, common and rare native birds are making a comeback in this predator-free environment.

Weka were one bird to survive the earlier bush clearances and a very common sight on the island, roaming the lawns around the administration buildings or on the beach feeding on sandhoppers. Tieke, kiwi, pateke and a pair of takehe have been reintroduced to Rotoroa, a small gannet colony is being encouraged and New Zealand dotterel nest on the beaches.

Two circuits, one going north and the south are easy walking and offer endless panoramic views over the Gulf, the long rugged hills of the Coromandel Peninsula and nearby Ponui and Waiheke islands. Both circuits take around an hour each. Several beaches are ideal for swimming, the best of which are Ladies Bay and Mens Bay, neither far from the wharf.

An excellent information centre details the history of the island as an alcoholic and drug treatment refuge under the auspices of the Salvation Army.

6 Coppermine Walk, Kawau Island
Romantic ruins of an old coppermine.

⋔ **Grade:** Easy. ⏲ **Time:** One and a half hours return.
🚶 **How to get there:** Kawau Cruises run regular ferries (summer and winter timetables) from Sandspit wharf and takes about 30 minutes. Phone 09 425 8006, kawaucruises.co.nz.

Copper mining began on the island as early as 1844, with the original house on Kawau Island built in 1845 for the mine manager. In 1862 George Grey (twice Governor, then Premier of New Zealand 1877–79) purchased Kawau Island for £3500 and greatly expanded the house, planted exotic trees and stocked the island with animals including monkeys, zebras, kookaburras and wallabies. The Parma wallaby is now extinct in Australia, and wallabies from the island (where they are a pest) have been shipped home. It's a relaxing walk to the site of the old mine. The 20 m engine room chimney is all that remains; shafts went deep under the sea below. The rocks around the chimney are a distinct green, the colour of copper in its natural form.

7 Rangitoto Island
An island volcano and the world's largest pohutukawa forest.

⋔ **Grade:** Medium. ⏲ **Time:** Two hours return to the summit.
🚶 **How to get there:** Fullers ferry runs from downtown Auckland with a stop at Devonport (www.fullers.co.nz Ph 09-367 9111). Don't miss your return ferry – there is no overnight accommodation.

Rangitoto is the region's largest and youngest volcano, erupting 600–700 years ago. The crater and summit (259 m) are covered in large trees. The last eruptions occurred further down the western slope, where lava fields are extensive and plants are slowly colonising the scoria.

The full name is Te Rangi i totongia a Tamatekapua, 'the day the blood of Tamatekapua was shed', referring to a battle in 1350, when crews of the waka *Te Arawa* and *Tainui* clashed and Tamatekapua, the captain of *Te Arawa* was injured.

The flora, which has had to adapt to barren lava fields, includes the world's largest pohutukawa forest, and the kidney fern. Usually glossy and fragile-looking, this fern shrivels up in the heat, returning to normal only when there is sufficient moisture. The rocky shore is a perfect habitat for little blue penguins, while near the wharf there are colonies of black-backed gulls.

The walk to the summit is a steady climb on an excellent track, with a magnificent view over Auckland and the Hauraki Gulf. A side track just below the summit (20 minutes return) leads to lava caves, where it's possible to scramble through.

Return the way you came, or take another option. One is to the east, via Islington Bay, close to Motutapu Island from which Rangitoto is separated by a few metres. Another is to the west, via McKenzie Bay where the track passes Rangitoto's famous baches, of which most have been removed but around 30 have been kept. Both routes take around 90 minutes.

8 Tiritiri Matangi Island
New Zealand's most accessible bird sanctuary.

Grade: Medium. **Time:** Allow two hours.
How to get there: Fullers 360 run a ferry from downtown Auckland with a stop at Gulf Harbour. Plan to spend the best part of the day on the island. www.fullers.co.nz, Phone 09-367 9111

In Maori legend, Tiritiri Matangi is one of the floats of a huge fishing net. Its name meaning 'tossed by the wind'. Maori occupation goes back to the fourteenth century. In 1821 local tribes were no match for Ngapuhi raiders from the north carrying muskets, and the people of Tiritiri Matangi, like those of all the islands of the Gulf and along the coast, abandoned their lands. While small numbers returned in the 1830s, Europeans found this coastline largely empty.

Stripped of its native bush, the island was farmed from 1850 to 1970, with only a few coastal remnants. The Department of Conservation embarked on a programme to replant the island and develop it as an open sanctuary. There is hardly an Auckland schoolchild between 1984 and 1994 who wasn't involved in the massive operation, planting a quarter of a million trees. Overwhelmingly successful, this has led to a haven for endangered birds and the island becoming a model reserve.

Once predators were removed and cover was established, recovery of birdlife was spectacular, with over 70 species of bird sighted here, including takahe, hihi, little spotted kiwi, brown teal, kokako, saddlebacks, bellbirds and kakariki. The island has a maze of tracks. The walk from the wharf to the lighthouse will take 50 minutes return, while a walk around the island can take up to three hours. None of the tracks is difficult.

16
short walks in
The Coromandel

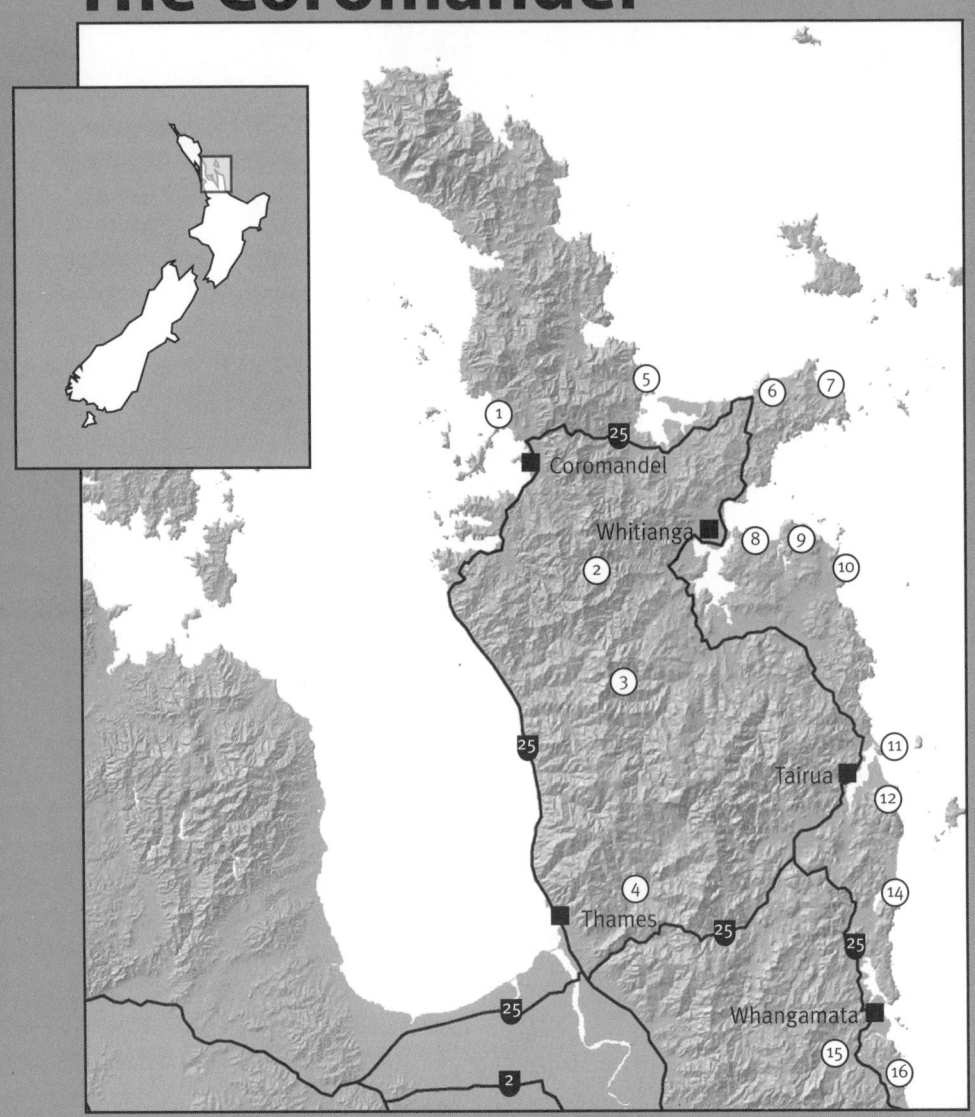

1 Coromandel Pa
An ancient pa site with spectacular views.

Grade: Easy. **Time:** 25 minutes return.
How to get there: The track to the pa is off Wharf Road, about 300 m from the main intersection in town – there's no parking down the driveway leading to the track but plenty across the road.

The history of this pa is obscure and even the name is forgotten, but the site is so impressive and the views so spectacular it is absolutely worth the short walk from town. The track is in excellent condition and while it's all uphill, the grade is reasonably gentle. At the top few signs of the old pa remain, but the strategic value is obvious with a 360-degree view encompassing the Hauraki Gulf and its islands and back across the town to the ranges.

2 Waiau Kauri Grove and Waterfall
Mature kauri, including a tree with a double trunk.

Grade: Easy. **Time:** 20 minutes return.
How to get there: Just south of Coromandel town turn onto the 309 Road, which is narrow, winding and unsealed. The Kauri Grove is on the left, 8 km from the turnoff.

When early timber millers began extracting kauri from the Coromandel, they were nothing if not thorough and few large trees escaped. This rare patch of mature forest deep in the ranges is now accessible via an excellent short track. The boardwalk at one point entirely surrounds the trunk of a kauri so it's possible to feel the texture of the bark. A short loop walk leads to an unusual double-trunked tree – two seedlings which grew together and fused at the base. A short distance down the road, and just a two-minute walk from the road, is the small but pretty Waiau Falls, with a pool.

3 Square Kauri Walk
A magnificent kauri with a distinctive square shape.

- **Grade:** Medium. **Time:** 20 minutes return.
- **How to get there:** 9 km from Tapu on the Tapu/Coroglen Road.

This huge kauri, over 41 m high, is estimated to be 1200 years old and has a squarish-shaped trunk. The short track is all steps up to the tree, but an extra bonus for your hard work is a great lookout over the ranges and across the valley to the Maumaupaki, or Camel's Back (822 m).

4 Edward's Lookout, Kauaeranga Valley
Marvellous views deep in the Coromandel Range.

- **Grade:** Medium. **Time:** 45 minutes return.
- **How to get there:** Just south of Thames shopping centre turn into Kauaeranga Valley Road – the visitor centre is 14 km down this road, which is mostly sealed. The lookout is another 5.4 km on.

Timber, not gold, first attracted Europeans to this valley, which leads deep into the hills behind Thames. From 1871 to 1928 magnificent kauri forests were milled virtually to extinction and, while the scars remain, the bush has reclaimed much of the land. Old pack tracks, and tramlines used to haul logs out of the bush, now form part of the extensive track system. Take time to check out the visitor centre, which displays information and photographs of the valley's natural and human history. A short distance away is a model kauri dam. Huge wooden dams were used extensively here until the 1920s, and the remains of two still exist. One dam trip, involving several dams, brought a staggering 28,000 kauri logs down the valley. Using the design of the Tarawaera dam, this model is one-third the size of the original, with excellent information boards showing exactly how it worked.

The track to Edward's Lookout is a steady uphill walk on an excellent track (all metal, no mud) leading to a rocky outcrop high above the river. From here there are fantastic views deep into the ranges with Table Mountain to the left, and the Pinnacle to the right. Below the road slices through the upper reaches of the Kauaeranga Valley, now entirely bush-covered with no visible traces of the substantial timber industry which stripped the hills of their kauri forests.

There are also several excellent camping areas along the river.

5 New Chums Beach

An unspoilt stretch of sandy beach overhung with old pohutukawa.

Grade: Medium.   **Time:** 50 minutes return.
How to get there: Follow the beach from the northern end of Whangapoua Beach, cross over the stream then pick up the track just above the high-tide mark.

Just a short walk over a low headland from Whangapoua Beach is a wonderful long stretch of white sandy beach, lapped by clear water. The beach is backed by handsome native bush and overhung with old pohutukawa trees, providing shade on a hot summer's day.

Few visitors are aware of the pa site on the peninsula between New Chums and Whangapoua. Built by Ngati Huarere, Motuto is a typical headland pa with steep cliffs providing defence from an attack by sea. A narrow isthmus connecting the pa to the mainland was easy to fortify and defend. The track leads off to the right from the main track to New Chums and it's a tricky scramble to get to the top. The main part of the pa faced the sea and today the well preserved terraces are clearly visible. As with most coastal pa, there are spectacular views.

6 Otama Beach

An undeveloped beach with a dune reserve.

Grade: Easy.   **Time:** 30 minutes one way along the beach.
How to get there: From Kuaotunu take the Black Jack Road – Otama Beach is 5 km along this narrow, unsealed and winding road.

Otama Beach is a long stretch of white sand with a few houses at the southern end. The whole length of the beach and the dune behind it is now protected from further development by a nature reserve. Common along the dunes is the creeping native grass pingao. Endemic to New Zealand, these plants favour open dune country above the high-tide mark and play an important role in binding loose sand with an extensive root system, crisscrossing the dunes with long, rope-like rhizomes. The beach looks out over the Mercury Islands, with the best access from the northern end, at the bottom of the Black Jack Hill. There is a basic camping ground at Otama (water, but no toilets).

7 Opito Pa, Opito Beach
A steep climb to a headland pa with outstanding vistas.

Grade: Medium. **Time:** 1 hour.

How to get there: At Kuaotunu take the Black Jack Road to Otama Beach and then to Opito – follow the road, parts of which are winding and gravel, to the very end.

This magnificent pa occupies the whole of the headland sheltering the southern end of Opito Beach. Steep slopes made attack difficult from the north, and sheer cliffs made it impossible from the south, while a steep bluff protected the landward side, further enhanced by several defensive ditches. The headland has numerous broad terraces and is pitted with rua (for storing kumara) and house sites. Views across the beach and along the coast are spectacular.

The walk begins at the southern end of the beach, with a long flight of stairs up the steep hill to the pa. Once at the top of the steps, walking around the huge pa is much easier.

8 Shakespeare Cliff and Lonely Bay
Great views over Mercury Bay, and a small sandy cove.

Grade: Easy. **Time:** 5 minutes to the lookout; 20 minutes to Lonely Bay; one and a half hours from Ferry Landing.

How to get there: Located between Cook's Beach and Flaxmill Bay.

In November 1769 Captain James Cook landed at Cook's Beach (promptly naming it after himself), remaining in the area for 11 days to observe the transit of Mercury across the face of the sun, thereby accurately calculating his longitude and latitude (hence Mercury Bay). The headland has extensive views over the bay, and a plaque commemorates Cook's visit, also indicating features around the bay. Cook fancied he saw a likeness of an orator reciting Shakespeare outlined in the cliff, and named the area after the bard.

A steep track from the car park leads down to quiet, pohutukawa-lined Lonely Bay, one of Coromandel's loveliest small beaches, and perfect for swimming. The lower section of the steps was designed by Akio Hizume, and is a project of the Japanese Society of Mercury Bay. Tracks lead to the headland from both Cook's Beach and Flaxmill Bay. From Whitianga township cross by ferry and walk to Flaxmill Bay, which will take around 25 minutes. The track to the lookout is marked at the far end of the bay.

9 Cathedral Cove, Hahei
A stunning sandy cove backed by pohutukawa.

- **Grade:** Medium. **Time:** One and a half hours return.
- **How to get there:** From Hahei Beach Road turn left into Grange Road South and continue to the car park – in summer the car park is overwhelmed and a shuttle bus runs from town.

Fringed with pohutukawa trees, backed by limestone cliffs and bounded by clean clear water, Cathedral Cove is the quintessential Coromandel beach. The two parts of the beach are linked by a sea cave, and the coastline is protected as part of the Te-Whanganui-a-Hei Marine Reserve. Cathedral Cove featured in the film *The Chronicles of Narnia: Prince Caspian* when the Pevensie children discover the ruins of Cair Paravel. Anna Popplewell, who plays the character Susan Pevensie, commented: 'The water shimmered so clearly audiences won't believe it's real water.'

Beach access is along a well-formed track which takes around 45 minutes each way, and there are toilet facilities at the beach itself. Very crowded in the height of the holiday season, the beach is best avoided during January and summer weekends.

10 Te Pare Historic Reserve, Hahei
A coastal pa site with great views over Mercury Bay.

- **Grade:** Easy. **Time:** 30 minutes return.
- **How to get there:** The track to the pa site begins at the end of Pa Road, or leads up from the southern end of the beach.

A stronghold of Ngati Hei, who arrived in the area on the waka *Te Arawa* in 1350, this reserve includes two pa sites: Hereheretaura on the headland and Hahei on the high ridge to the right. Hereheretaura is one of the most beautifully situated pa in the country, with broad terraces occupying a rocky headland, the sea on three sides and a magnificent outlook over Mercury Bay and Hahei Beach.

Hahei is quite different and less accessible, but easily recognised by north-facing terraces which fan out down the hillside, though there are no visible signs of defence earthworks. Hereheretaura, on the other hand, has both a defensive ditch and steep banks to protect the pa.

11 Paku Peak, Tairua
Marvellous coastal views from this old pa site.

Grade: Medium. **Time:** 30 minutes return.
How to get there: From the shopping centre on SH2 turn into Manaia Road, then into Paku Drive, following the road to the car park at the top.

Discovered by Kupe around 1000 AD, both coasts of the Coromandel Peninsula have a long history of Maori settlement, attracted by the now extinct moa and abundant kai moana, or seafood. In 1964, the only known artifact linking Aotearoa to Eastern Polynesia, a fish lure, was found in the sand dune behind Tairua Beach. The lure is made from a type of black-lipped pearl oyster shell not found in New Zealand, and given the location of the find, must have been brought to the area by an immigrant from Eastern Polynesia.

Originally a Ngati Hei stronghold, Tairua succumbed to Ngati Maru invaders in the seventeenth century, although their tenure didn't last. In the 1820s, heavily armed Ngapuhi with muskets swept down the coast. Ngati Maru escaped inland to take refuge with their Tainui relatives, where most settled permanently. Few ever returned.

A short rocky scramble leads to the top of the volcanic peak Paku, with dramatic coastal and inland views. Once an island, it's easy to see why this was an ideal position for a major fortified pa.

12 Mount Pauanui
Great views over Pauanui, Tairua and the rocky coast to the south.

Grade: Hard. **Time:** One and a half hours return.
How to get there: The walk is clearly marked from the southern end of Pauanui Beach.

It's a solid, steep, uphill climb to the 387 m summit of Mt Pauanui, but the track is very good, with any sweat rewarded by fantastic views north over Pauanui and Tairua, and to the south as far as Mt Maunganui. For the truly fit an annual race to the top and back is held over summer.

13 Broken Hills
Tunnels, ruins and an old jail in a bush-clad valley.

Grade: Easy/Medium **Time:** Up to two hours.
How to get there: Take Morrisons Road opposite the Pauanui turnoff on SH25 – after 1 km turn left into Puketui Road.

Gold was discovered at Broken Hills in 1893 and, until the 1930s, a flourishing town existed. Today a maze of short walks leads to an array of old mine shafts, battery sites and tunnels. The Tairua River meanders through a valley of attractive regenerating bush and this is a great place to bring children and explore. There's also a camping ground beside the river.

From the bridge car park two short walks each take about 20 minutes. The first is the Gem of the Boom loop walk, leading to the old Broken Hills jail, a gloomy cave dug into the hillside. The other is the Golden Hills Battery walk, with some fascinating ruins. Built in 1899, and now hidden in the bush, the jumble of arches and concrete walls from old cyanide tanks look more like a monastery than a gold-mine battery.

The most substantial walk is the Collins Drive Walk, taking two hours and beginning at the car park at the end of the road. On the north bank of the river, several tracks zigzag up an old water race to Collins Drive. The water-race track follows an old waterway, in places cut deep into the contour of the hill and including a number of low tunnels. Much further up is the impressive Collins Drive, a 500-metre tunnel created as an access tunnel through steep country. A torch is necessary, and there are some great lookout points.

14 Opoutere Beach
A wide sweep of empty beach and an important wildlife sanctuary.

Grade: Easy. **Time:** 20 minutes return to the beach.
How to get there: The turnoff to Opoutere is 10 km north of Whangamata; beach access is a further 5 km.

The long, wide sweep of Opoutere is one of the few undeveloped beaches on the Coromandel. Even at the height of summer, few venture here. Access to the beach is over a mangrove-lined tidal stream, then through dunes. Once on the beach, walk south to the harbour entrance and Wharekawa Harbour Sandspit Wildlife Refuge. This is an important breeding ground for several endangered birds, including the New Zealand dotterel, with nesting grounds roped off during spring and summer. Although the nests are mere scrapings in the sand, the eggs blend perfectly with the environment, and are easy to miss. What isn't easy to miss is the aggressive parent birds, which make it very clear when you stray into their territory.

15 Wentworth Falls Walk
An attractive waterfall deep in the bush.

Grade: Easy. **Time:** Two hours.
How to get there: Wentworth Valley Road is off SH25, 2 km south of Whangamata.

Wentworth Falls are a popular destination for day trippers from busy Whangamata. Here the Wentworth River tumbles over a 50-metre rocky bluff into a good-sized pool ideal for swimming on a warm summer's afternoon. Once a bustling gold-mining settlement and a major access track across the Coromandel to the Maratoto Valley, the track to the falls is now through thick native bush with little remaining sign of the area's early mining activities.

A viewing platform overlooks the falls, with a tricky, narrow track to the swimming hole at the bottom. The track continues beyond the platform to a viewing point at the top of the waterfall.

16 Waimama Bay, Whiritoa
A secluded white sand beach overhung with old pohutukawa trees

Grade: Easy   **Time:** 40 minutes return
How to get there: 13.5km south of Whangamata on SH25. The track begins at the northern end of the beach.

This tiny cove is reached by an easy track over a headland from the northern end of Whiritoa beach. Protected by rocky headlands at either end of the beach, this small stretch of white sand is overhung by ancient pohutukawa trees, ideal for lounging in the shade on a scorching hot day. The beach drops steeply into the water here and the surf can be surprisingly powerful, so take extra care swimming. At the southern end at low tide are bath-sized rock pools perfect for cooling off while the waves crash on the rocks below.

27
short walks in
Waikato and King Country

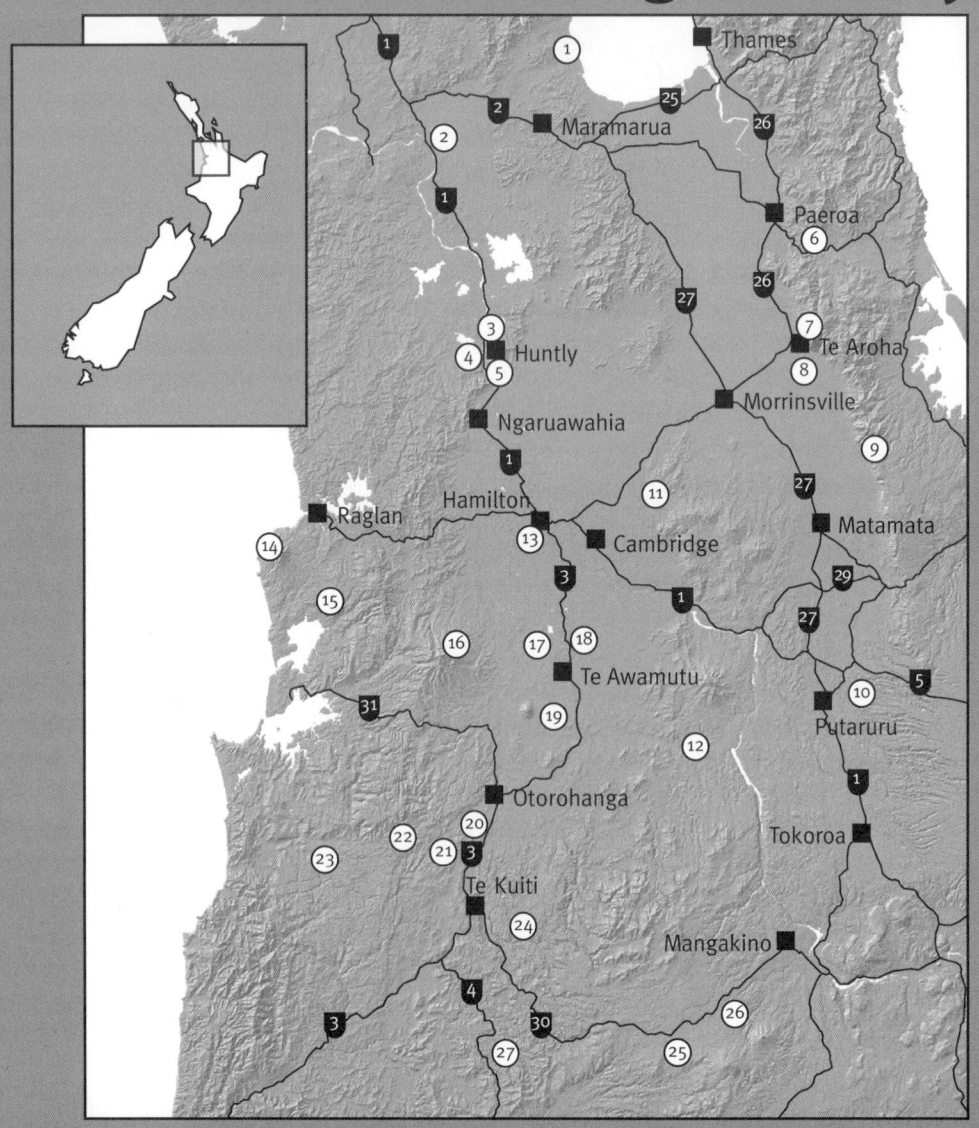

1 Miranda Shorebird Centre
One of New Zealand's most important wading and migratory bird habitats.

- **Grade:** Easy. **Time:** Allow one hour.
- **How to get there:** The walk begins opposite the visitor centre at 283 East Coast Road, Miranda, just south of Kaiaua.

Each year thousands of birds from the Arctic tundra, as well as New Zealand-breeding shorebirds, converge on the rich tidal feeding grounds at Miranda recognised by the Ramsar Convention as a wetland of international significance.

There are wading birds all year round, but large flocks (7000–10,000) of bar-tailed godwits arrive about September and stay until March. The bar-tailed godwit make the longest non-stop flight of any migratory bird, flying 11,000 km from Alaska in less than week. The birds time their September departure to coincide with strong northerly storm winds, travelling south over open ocean to New Zealand, to feed during the southern summer. In late March/early April the birds gather to prepare for their flight north to breed, though unlike the flight south, they take a different route through Australia and east Asia, wisely stopping along the way.

Other common birds are wrybill, plovers, New Zealand dotterels, variable oystercatchers, black-billed gulls, pied stilts, curlews and sharp-tailed sandpipers, red-necked stints, eastern curlews, banded dotterels and ruddy turnstones.

The walk is over saltmarsh, shell banks and tidal mangrove creeks, hugging the edge of huge tidal flats. The best time for bird watching is two to three hours either side of high tide. Before heading off, it's worth spending time at the visitor centre, which has excellent information on the bird life. For serious birdwatchers, there's a bird hide.

2 Te Teoteo's Pa and the Whangamarino Redoubt
The first serious clash of the Waikato War.

- **Grade:** Easy. **Time:** 30 minutes return.
- **How to get there:** Oram Road, 2 km south of Mercer.

During the 1860s tensions grew between Maori and British over land, and during 1862 and 1863 the British prepared for war by building redoubts across South Auckland and pushing the Great South Road through to

Pokeno. Despite his efforts, Governor Grey couldn't provoke the Maori King into declaring war, and finally attacked by crossing the Mangatawhiri Stream, which Maori had declared their northern boundary.

The first serious clash occurred at Te Teoteo's pa, where Maori had hurriedly constructed a defensive position. In an attack by 500 British troops that left 30 Maori dead, the pa defenders retreated a short distance south to the Meremere pa. The British then quickly built the Whangamarino Redoubt, from where they bombarded the Maori position.

The pa site is now somewhat overgrown but the views are extensive along the Waikato River. The redoubt, however, is well preserved and Meremere is clearly seen to the south.

An easy track leads up from Oram Road across farmland. The redoubt is on the right and Te Teoteo's pa is on the left, overlooking the river.

3 Lake Hakanoa
Picturesque walk around a small lake.

- **Grade:** Easy. **Time:** 50 minutes.
- **How to get there:** The walk begins on the south end of the Huntly Park Domain on Taihua Street.

On the eastern side of Huntly, the Hakanoa Walkway encircles a small lake of the same name. The entrance is marked by a carved gateway and an excellent information board. Flat all the way, the walk takes in wetlands, grassy picnic areas and several formal gardens as well as informal plantings. While the lake is shallow and muddy, the excursion around it is very pleasant.

Once an important source of eels, the lake takes its name from the lifting of the tapu on fishing – noa – and the ceremonial dance – haka – performed to celebrate the lifting of the tapu.

4 Hakarimata Scenic Reserve
Massive kauri trees and a lookout with fantastic views.

Grade: Medium. **Time:** 40 minutes to the kauri, one and a half hours for the loop.
How to get there: From SH1 at Huntly cross the Waikato River at the traffic lights and turn left into Riverview Road. Follow the river for 5 km and turn right into Parker Road – the car park is 500 m from the turnoff.

The Hakarimata Range, west of Ngaruawahia, is near the southern limit of kauri's natural growing area, and somehow these magnificent specimens escaped the logger's axe. Standing out boldly from surrounding bush, the largest tree is over 600 years old. While the trees are worth a visit in themselves, it's also well worth the uphill grind to the Upper Lookout. From here there is a magnificent view of the lower Waikato Basin, with the river taking centre stage. To the north are clear views of Huntly, the surrounding lakes of Waahi, Rotongaro, Hakanoa, Kimihia and Waikare. In the distance are the Hunua Ranges. To the northeast, Moehau can be glimpsed at the top of the Coromandel Peninsula, and Mt Te Aroha lies on the horizon.

5 Taupiri Mountain Summit
Taupiri, the sacred mountain of Tainui.

Grade: Hard. **Time:** One hour 15 minutes.
How to get there: The tracks begins by the small marae just south of Taupiri township where SH1 crosses the Mangawara River. Park by the marae and walk to the beginning.

The importance of Taupiri to Tainui cannot be overstated. As 'beloved' or 'the close-clinging lover', in legend Taupiri is the wife of Pirongia – the smaller peaks Kakepuku and Te Kawa, near Te Awamutu, are their children.

A pa on the lower hill below the summit was home to Te Patu. In a clash with a rival iwi, the chief was killed on the riverbank. His mana was so great, his blood made the area below Taupiri tapu and the pa was abandoned. Early travellers remarked that when approaching Taupiri they had to cross to the other side of the river to avoid touching tapu ground.

After land confiscations in 1864, when Waikato Maori returned, they were dismayed to see a road had been built around Taupiri, with construction of a railway line and later a quarry as further desecrations.

Tainui allow access to the summit, with two tracks forming a loop, both marked by small wooden gateways. The first is by the car park and is steeper and rougher. The second is about 500 metres along the gravel road: not so rough, with a gentler grade, but taking longer. From the summit on a crisp sunny winter's day, snow-capped Ruapehu is visible to the south, while below, the Waikato River winds through fertile farmland.

The lower slopes are Tainui's principal burial grounds, where Maori kings and queens are buried. The cemetery is not a tourist attraction and casual visitors are requested to respect this area and not walk among the graves.

6 Karangahake Gorge
A river of tears.

Grade: Easy. **Time:** One and a half hours.
How to get there: 8 km east of Paeroa on SH2.

Karangahake, a bustling gold-mining town of 5000 people, once stood on the banks of the Ohinemuri River. To the east, the now defunct Paeroa to Waihi Railway ran through a dramatic river gorge. Across the river three batteries, the Woodstock, Crown Hill and Talisman, crushed gold-bearing quartz from mines under Karangahake Mountain. Maori named the river after the youngest daughter of Te Onekiteakua. When Hinemuri wanted to marry, her father refused until her older sisters had wed – and the heartbroken tears of 'the woman left behind' formed the river.

Flat and easy, the track runs from Karangahake to the Waikino Visitor Centre, with the most popular section a loop in the middle of the gorge. Beginning over the river from the parking area, this includes the battery ruins, a 1-km rail tunnel, the old rail bridge and the rugged gorge. While the tunnel is lit, a torch is handy, with lights at irregular intervals and the track rough underfoot.

After crossing the main swingbridge, cross the second bridge over the Waitawheta River, turning right into the substantial ruins of the Talisman Battery (1901–20), with its footings and rusting machinery. In 1914 the battery produced a quarter of a million pounds worth of gold. At the higher level, follow the tramline. To the left the line end overlooks the

Ohinemuri River and the site of Karangahake – whose main street was located in the car park. To the left is a series of short tunnels, with gaps in the wall providing dramatic views. You'll need a torch for the longer tunnel.

7 Mount Te Aroha, Whakapipi or Bald Spur
Great views over Te Aroha and the Hauraki Plains.

Grade: Hard. **Time:** One and a half hours return.
How to get there: The track begins behind the Mokena Bath House in the Te Aroha Domain.

Once a flourishing spa town, Te Aroha has successfully renovated its Edwardian Domain. Modern hot pools with family appeal complement historic buildings, including the Cadman Bath House (1898), housing the local museum, the No 2 Bath House, restored tearooms and boarding houses. At the back of the Domain is the world's only hot soda water geyser, erupting every 40 minutes to around 4 m, with the soda water reputed to have medicinal value.

The literal translation of Te Aroha is 'love', but those expecting romance and passion will be disappointed. Te Mamoe, the son of an Arawa chief, lived at Maketu. On an expedition west of the Kaimai Ranges, Te Mamoe became lost in the vast swamp then covering the Hauraki Plains. Climbing to the highest peak, he became homesick when he saw Maketu shining in the distance. As an expression of his love for his home, he named the mountain 'the love of Te Mamoe'.

The track to a lookout point at 350 m is a good alternative if a trek to the summit is beyond your reach (952 m, two and a half hours one way). The track zigzags up through regenerating bush to a lookout with excellent views over the town and Hauraki Plains. While it's a steep climb, the track is well formed and not too difficult, and you can reward yourself with a soak in the hot pools. If the uphill trudge doesn't appeal, there are a number of shorter walks directly behind the domain, including a 30 minute walk to a small waterfall

8 Waiorongomai Valley Lower Loop Walk
An easy walk along old gold mine workings tucked away in dense bush.

Grade: Easy. **Time:** Two hours return.
How to get there: Park at the end of Waiorongamai Loop Road, 5 km south of Te Aroha on the Te Aroha-Gordon Road

When gold was discovered in the Waiorongomai Valley in 1881, the southern slopes of Te Aroha mountain were the scene of feverish activity with stamper batteries, a tramway, pack trails and inclines, and a small town sprang up on the flats at the foot of the mountain. However, the optimism was not well founded, the yields proved disappointing and by 1930s the mines had ceased operation and the town had virtually disappeared.

The old trails and tramway now form a series of excellent tracks of all grades zigzagging up the mountainside right to the summit. Of these, the two lower level tracks form a loop that is an easy walk for all ages. What is especially appealing is that not all of the old tracks and equipment have been hauled away.

From the carpark take the Lower Level track up the valley, through thick bush and past three small waterfalls. This track passes through a short tunnel and eventually joins the Piako County Tramway track. Take the track to the left and it is along this section that you will find the old rail tracks, gold mines, mining equipment and the bottom of the dramatic Butlers Incline, an engineering feat designed to bring goldbearing ore down a very steep hillside. At end of the Tramway track is Fern Spur Incline from where is a great view over the Kaimai Ranges and the Hauraki Plains. From where there take the track to the right down the steps which leads to the bottom of the Incline and back to the car park. You can scramble up or down the Incline but it is hard work.

What adds to the pleasure of this walk is the fantastic signage all along the track which is both informative and enjoyable and features historical photos, newspaper clippings and diagrams. Especially useful is the map at the start of the walk which shows how all the tracks linked the mines, inclines and batteries.

9 Wairere Falls
One of the highest waterfalls in the North Island.

Grade: Medium. **Time:** One and a half hours return to the falls lookout.
How to get there: The track to the falls starts at the end of Goodwin Road off the Te Aroha–Okauia Road, 20 km south of the town.

The spectacular 153-m falls drop in two stages over the Okauia Fault in the Kaimai Ranges and are visible from a wide area of the Waikato. Following the stream, the track meanders through attractive bush with water trickling down moss- and fern-covered rock. The stream itself is a strong testament to the power of water, with huge boulders littering this small valley, some the size of a small car. The walk is a steady uphill grade until you reach a long flight of steps just before the viewing platform. The top of the falls is a further 45 minutes from this point.

10 Te Waihou Walkway
The clear headwaters of the Waihou River flow through a short gorge.

Grade: Easy. **Time:** From Whites Road, One and half hours one way. From Leslie Road, 30 minutes return.
How to get there: One entrance to the springs is on SH 28 between Putaruru and SH 5 to Rotorua and the other is 4 km down Leslie Road which turns off SH 28 to the right just beyond the bridge crossing the Waihou River.

In direct contrast to the muddy brown river which empties into the Firth of Thames, the Waihou begins as the most stunningly pure water, filtered down from the Kaimai Ranges after being underground for over 50 years. Crystal clear and a brilliant blue/green colour, the stream supports an incredible array of aquatic plants, which drift languidly in the transparent water while trout swim effortlessly in the swift current. Think twice before leaping into the water on a hot day, as it emerges from the Blue Spring at an even 11°C all year round.

Most of the walk is through farmland, with a small section of bush along the short gorge. Replanting of native trees is taking place along several sections. There is a picnic spot and toilet halfway along the walk.

If you don't have transport at either end, nor the time or inclination for the return trip, start walking at the Leslie Road end, as this is the most attractive part. From this point it will take 40 minutes return to the gorge and one and a half hours return to the two bridges.

11 Maungakawa Loop Walk
A loop walk through a bush remnant with views over the Waikato Basin.

Grade: Easy. **Time:** 30 minutes.

How to get there: From Cambridge take Thornton Road, which becomes Maungakawa Road. After 9 km turn right in Gudex Road and park at the first car park on the right.

Maungakawa, also known as Sanatorium Hill, rises 495 m east of Cambridge and was the site of one of the grandest houses in the Waikato, purchased by Daniel Thornton in 1868. In 1890 Thornton's widow built a magnificent house just below the summit. Huge and expensively furnished with beautifully landscaped grounds, it soon became a local attraction. In 1912 the government purchased the house, turning it into a sanitorium for those with tuberculosis. A few years later it became a convalescent home for World War I soldiers, but by 1922 had become too costly to maintain and the buildings were dismantled. Today all that remains is a small concrete building, said to be the old boiler room, and several exotic trees. Within the park is a stone memorial erected in 1968 to Michael Gudex, a well-known gardener and early conservationist.

Park at the first large grassy area by the small ruined concrete building and from here go to the right, where the track begins. Continue on a short distance to a small viewing platform with magnificent views to the west. Return to the track and walk through the bush, which is mainly tawa with some good-sized rimu. Plant identification signs help you brush up your knowledge of native trees.

The track eventually emerges onto another large grass area, in the centre of which is the Gudex monument. Cut directly across to return to the start point.

12 Maungatautari Ecological Island
An inspirational environmental success story

- Grade: Easy. Time: One hour.
- How to get there: End of Tai Road, Pukeatua, between Putaruru and Te Awamutu

Maungatautari is an extinct volcano rising to 797 m just south of Cambridge, and while cleared around the fringes most of the 3,360 ha is still virgin forest, a forest that includes silver beech, a tree usually found much further south. Like so much of New Zealand forest, predators took a toll on native birds and fauna, but locals under the auspices of the Maungatautari Ecological Island Trust and inspired by offshore island sanctuaries erected the longest predator-proof fence in the country. Over 47 km, the fence encircles two enclosures, one to the north of the mountain and the other just to the south.

Native birds, including northern kaka, takahe and kiwi have been reintroduced and in December 2007 the first kiwi chick hatched at Maungatautari. In 2004 it was discovered that a small colony of the rare Hochstetter's frog had survived on the mountain.

The larger southern enclosure has an information centre, rare birds and impressive large trees and there is an entry fee. It's a short but steep walk to the gate and while the tracks within the reserve are winding and undulating, there is nothing difficult. Ranging from 30 minutes to two hours there are numerous walk options all of which form handy loops.

13 Lake Rotoroa, Hamilton
An easy walk around a small wetlands lake.

- Grade: Easy. Time: One hour.
- How to get there: The main entrance is off Ruakiwi Road, near the intersection with Pembroke Street.

Affectionately known locally as Hamilton Lake, this shallow body of water is just 6 m at its deepest. It is home to numerous waterfowl. A dead-flat path, just short of 4 km, circles the lake and is one of the most popular walking and running tracks in Hamilton City.

All around the lake are small picnic areas, shady groves, sports fields and playgrounds. At the starting point is a large café and at Innes

Common, on the western side of the lake, there is a large fountain.

14 Te Toto Gorge Scenic Reserve
Spectacular coastal scenery below Mount Karioi.

Grade: Medium. **Time:** Up to 30 minutes.
How to get there: From Raglan follow Wainui and Whaanga roads around the coast. After Manu Bay the road becomes narrow, winding and unsealed – the car park is on the right, 1 km past the sign 'Te Toto Gorge Scenic Reserve'.

Stunted, almost prostrate manuka is testament here to fierce westerly winds, which sweep the lower slopes of Mt Karioi, an extinct volcano. It may therefore come as a surprise to learn that this steep, exposed coastline was once extensively cultivated by early Maori.

Despite the wind, the wide slopes are surprisingly sheltered and face northwest for maximum sunshine. The abundance of volcanic rocks allowed Maori to build walls and mounds, enhancing the sun's warmth by reflecting the heat off the stones. Maori also planted karaka trees to harvest their berries, and many of these are still growing. The name Te Toto is believed to mean 'blood' in Maori, with quiet whispers about the gorge being the scene of a grisly atrocity.

The views from the lookout high above the 100 m cliffs are superb to both the north and south, along the exposed Waikato coastline. The track begins in the car park; although not marked as such, it is reasonably well defined. How far you want to go is determined by how far uphill you want to walk on the way back, and the track eventually peters out in the long grass. The track to the Karioi lookout and summit starts on the other side of the road.

15 Bridal Veil Falls
A single fall drops into a fern-fringed pool.

Grade: Easy. **Time:** 15 minutes return to the top of the falls, 35 minutes to the base.

How to get there: On SH23, 7 km from Raglan, turn into Te Mata Road – the falls are 13 km down this road, 3 km beyond the Te Mata settlement. (The car park is notorious for car theft so be extra vigilant, even if there are plenty of cars and people about.)

One of the Waikato's most popular scenic attractions, the Bridal Veil Falls drop 55 m over a hard layer of basalt into a pool fringed by moisture-loving plants. The short flat walk from the car park follows the stream, with two viewing platforms at top of the falls, though the view from the bottom is more spectacular. The track to the bottom of falls has been upgraded, and although it involves a lot of steps, there is a lookout point halfway down. The base of the falls is thick with parataniwha, a low-growing native plant with wide nettle-like leaves, which in certain seasons turns from green through to shades of light pink and deep red.

16 Mount Pirongia
Fantastic views over the Waikato from a rocky peak.

Grade: Medium. **Time:** Two hours return to Ruapane.

How to get there: The track begins at the car park at the end of Corcoran Road, off the Te Pahu Road.

Dominating the skyline of the Western Waikato is the 959 m extinct volcanic cone of Mt Pirongia. The mountain is surprisingly rugged and the bush an unusual mixture of cooler and warmer climate plants. A stronghold of the wily patupaiarehe (fairy people with a nasty streak), Pirongia is a contraction of Pirongia te aroaro o Kahu, 'the fragrant pathway of Kahu', and relates to a journey the tohunga Rakataura made across the mountain, following the scent of his wife, Kahu. The full name of Mt Karioi, which lies just to the west – 'Maunga o karioi' meaning 'to linger' – relates to the same story.

The track to the summit is a slog, but a good alternative is the much easier walk to Ruapane, at 723 m. From the car park follow the sign 'Picnic Area and Lookout' and the Ruapane track peels off into the bush to the left, about 30 m away. The track is a gradual climb, some of it through fine tawa forest, but not far from Ruapane the track becomes steeper before arriving at a well-defined rocky outcrop with a fantastic view back over the lush Waikato. Beyond Ruapane the track leads to another rocky outcrop called Tirohanga, with even better views.

17 Yarndley's Bush, Te Awamutu
The largest remnant of kahikatea forest in the Waikato.

Grade: Easy. **Time:** 30 minutes.
How to get there: 4 km north of Te Awamutu turn left off SH 4 into Ngaroto Road – the reserve is 1 km on the left.

The kahikatea is New Zealand's tallest tree, with colonial sources recording trees up to 90 m. Even today a tree on the Kaniwhaniwha track on nearby Mt Pirongia is 66.5 m tall, making it New Zealand's tallest living native tree, 15 m taller than Tane Mahuta. Despite its height, the tree is relatively slender and seldom more than a metre in diameter, with broad spreading buttresses at the base, giving support in damp soils. The tree tapers toward the top, with small, narrow leaves, while the bark is rough and flaky.

The kahikatea has separate male and female trees, with the male producing pollen-bearing cones and the female trees bearing the seeds, a favourite food of kereru and kaka. At 14 ha this is the largest remaining lowland bush in the Waikato, and unusually consists almost totally of kahikatea. On entering the reserve the immediate impression is not of native bush but of a pine forest – easy to see why kahikatea was called white pine by early Europeans. A drop in the water table, through drainage of nearby farmland, has led to the kahikatea's distinctive roots being more exposed than normal. The walkway has extensive boardwalks to protect the fragile roots, and a viewing platform allows a partial bird's-eye view of the forest.

18 Lake Ngaroto
A small lake, the scene of New Zealand's greatest battle.

Grade: Easy. **Time:** One and a half hours.
How to get there: From the main street of Te Awamutu (Alexandra Street), head north 2 km and turn right into Paterangi Road. After 4 km turn into Bank Road; the lake is at the end of this road.

Lake Ngaroto is a small lake south of Hamilton, where the Battle of Hingakaka was fought. Said to be this country's largest, the battle (dates vary between 1790, 1803 and 1870) originated in tensions between coastal Tainui – allied with Taranaki, and their inland relatives, Ngati Maniapoto and Waikato. The issue came to a head over distribution of the fish harvest. Pikauterangi, a chief from Marokopa, gathered 7000–10,000 warriors and invaded Ngati Maniapoto territory.

Wahanui, a Maniapoto chief, called on his Waikato allies. With a force of 1600–3000, he confronted the invaders on a narrow ridge overlooking Lake Ngaroto. Pikauterangi's warriors made the first attack, but were confused by the defenders' clever tactics. The decisive point came when Pikauterangi was killed. Retreating towards the lake, the invaders were ambushed, and in full panic were trapped in the swamp. Thousands died, attempting to escape through unfamiliar terrain or swim the lake. Hingakaka means 'fall of the kaka' – so many chiefs died, it was compared to a hunt for kaka.

Lake Ngaroto was also known for its island pa, whose remains can still be seen. The walk around the lake is flat and easy, though vegetation obscures the water. Two island pa sites can be seen on the eastern side. As the water level is now lower they're little more than small hillocks on the shore. The battle took place on a ridge south of the lake, and Bank Road, leading to the lake, crosses the battlefield.

19 Kakepuku

An extinct bush-covered volcano rises from lush farmland.

Grade: Hard. **Time:** Two and half hours

How to get there: From Te Awamutu turn off SH3 into Fraser Street, which becomes Puniu Road and then Pokuru Road, travel 6.5 km and turn left into Te Mawhai Road. After 1 km turn right into Kakepuku Mountain Road – the car park is on the right.

Rising 449 m, Kakepuku's volcanic cone dominates the landscape south of Te Awamutu. The name is a contraction of 'Kakepuku te aroaro o Kahu', the swollen stomach of Kahu. The mountain was named by Rakataura, honouring his wife Kahu's pregnant stomach.

There are five pa in the reserve area protecting the mountain, settled around 1550 AD, and in pre-European times most of the bush had been cleared from the mountain. By the 1860s all the pa on the mountain were abandoned and the bush began to return. Today the bush is dominated by tawa, rewarewa, kohekohe, mangeao and pukatea, and in recent years North Island robins have been reintroduced.

The new track is a more gradually climb than the old track but the view from the top on the lip of the crater, though partly obscured by trees, is well worth the trip. The most obvious pa site is on the summit, which is ringed by wide terraces.

20 Opapaka Pa

A bush walk leads to an old pa site.

Grade: Easy/Medium. **Time:** One hour return.

How to get there: The entrance to the track is easily missed. It leads off the car park of the Waitomo Adventure Centre on the right 6.5 km from the Waitomo turnoff on SH3.

Ngati Hia built this long ridge pa in the eighteenth century to defend their lands in the valley below against incursions from Tane Tinorau, living to the south. The pa has very distinctive terraces and defensive ditches, but the kumara pits attract the most attention. In other pa sites the kumara pits are mere indentations in the ground, but here they are enormous, measuring several metres wide and the depth of an adult. Located just outside the central part of the pa, they were only lightly defended. Within the central part of the pa is an area known as the tihi, a special raised area where the chief lived. Only part of the site is accessible; the western end is overgrown with vegetation. Good information panels make this site worth visiting.

From the car park the walk is a steady uphill climb through mature bush, complete with tree identification information. After about 20 minutes the track emerges out of the bush onto farmland and from there it's a short walk up to the pa site, following the fenceline.

21 Ruakuri Walkway
Limestone caves, arches and caverns are interwoven with native bush.

 Grade: Easy. Time: 30 minutes.
 How to get there: 2 km from the Waitomo glow-worm cave next to the entry to Aranui cave.

The short 30-minute walk along the Waitomo River is crammed with fantastic limestone outcrops, caves and a huge natural tunnel. The unspoiled bush features luxurious growth, in particular ferns, mosses and lichens. Easy to miss is the fantastic underground cavern, which is about 5 m past the natural bridge viewing platform. Initially it appears to be just a hole in the ground, but let your eyes adjust and the short flight of steps becomes apparent. These lead to a lookout point in a huge cavern high above the river, as it disappears underground. The walkway was part of an old track Maori used to travel from the coast to inland villages.

The area has glow-worms at night, but don't forget your torch. The track is well formed, but walk it anticlockwise or the signs won't make sense.

22 Mangapohue Natural Bridge
Two natural bridges located in a bush-lined gorge.

 Grade: Easy. Time: 20 minutes return to the natural bridges; 30 minutes return via the fossils.
 How to get there: 26 km from Waitomo on the Te Anga Road.

Located a short distance from the road are two magnificent natural limestone arches, one on top of the other, created by the waters of the Mangapohue Stream. The walk to the arches is through a deep narrow gorge lined with ferns and mosses, lit at night by glow-worms (a torch is necessary if a night walk is planned). Beyond the bridges the track continues out into open farmland, and returns to the road via large rocky outcrops. These contain the fossilised remains of gigantic oysters, from a time when this area was submerged under the sea.

23 Marokopa Falls
A magnificent waterfall hidden in lush bush.

- **Grade:** Easy. **Time:** 20 minutes return.
- **How to get there:** 31 km from Waitomo on the Te Anga Road.

Not far from the sea, the Marokopa River plunges 30 m, creating a spectacular waterfall. Just a short 15-minute walk from the road through cool, lush bush, this waterfall, together with the Mangapohue natural bridge on the same road, is well worth a detour from a visit to the Waitomo Caves.

24 Mangaweka Gorge Scenic Reserve, Te Kuiti
A clear stream runs through bush along a limestone gorge.

- **Grade:** Easy. **Time:** 40 minutes return to the cascade, one hour 15 minutes return to the waterfall.
- **How to get there:** 2 km south of Te Kuiti on SH30 (the road to Mangakino).

Just south of Te Kuiti, this reserve centres on a deep gorge of towering limestone bluffs along a pleasant stream. The mature native bush includes large tawa, rimu and kahikatea and native birds are common, particularly kereru. The walk begins by crossing the swingbridge by the car park, and following the stream to an attractive cascade, then further on to a small waterfall. You need to return the same way as there is only a very rough track on the other side. As an added bonus, there are numerous swimming holes, ideal on a hot day.

25 Totara Walk, Pureora Forest
Huge native trees, hundreds of years old and absolutely magnificent.

- **Grade:** Easy. **Time:** 25 minutes return.
- **How to get there:** Pureora Forest Headquarters is located 3 km down the Barryville Road on SH30, 56 km from Te Kuiti, and 20 km from Mangakino.

This magnificent forest was saved from the axe by protesters, who in 1978 perched themselves on platforms in the trees. Logging was finally halted in the early 1980s, and the area is currently a mixture of forest park and commercial forest. This provides some interesting contrasts between pristine native bush and clear-felled pine forest.

The forest was destroyed in the Taupo eruption 1800 years ago, when this cataclysmic event blew out the western side of Lake Taupo, over 70 km away. Even at this distance the force of the blast was so strong it decimated the entire forest, knocking over huge mature trees, then burying them under a deep layer of ash and pumice. However, the ash provided a soil so rich in nutrients the trees here are among the biggest in the country.

The beginning of the walk is just 200 m from the Forest Field Centre and strolling through this forest it's easy to see what motivated both conservationists and loggers. A mixture of totara, maire, rimu and tawa, the height and size of these huge trees has to be seen to be believed.

26 Pouakani Totara
The world's tallest totara tree.

- **Grade:** Easy. **Time:** 40 minutes return.
- **How to get there:** The entrance to the track is 10 km from the Barryville Road turnoff towards Mangakino, and 12 km from Mangakino on SH30.

Pouakani is a giant totara tree, over 42 m tall and estimated to be 1800 years old. While thousands of visitors flock to Tane Mahuta, this tree is hardly known and rarely visited, yet is so impressive. Its rivals, the second- and third-largest totara trees, are both located in nearby Pureora Forest. The walk to the tree is through a handsome forest of wheki (tree fern) with a sprinkling of larger trees, and although the track isn't marked it is reasonably well defined.

27 Mapara Scenic Reserve
The most accessible and important stronghold of the kokako.

Grade: Medium.   **Time:** One hour return.

How to get there: Travel 26 km south of Te Kuiti on SH4 and turn left into Kopaki Road, then after 2 km turn right into Mapara South Road – the reserve is 5.5 km down this gravel road.

One of the last strongholds of the kokako, this 1400-hectare reserve is the most accessible if you want to hear or see this elusive bird. Between 1989 and 1995, stoats, weasels and ferrets were trapped here and between 1978 and 1995, 8200 goats were removed. As a result, kokako pairs rocketed from five to over 100, with birds now being transferred to other conservation areas.

Kokako are striking, notable for both their colouring and song. The feathers are a rich, glossy dark grey-blue, though lighter around the head with bright blue wattles and a distinct black mask across the eyes. A South Island subspecies with bright orange wattles is now considered extinct.

The song is noted for its melodious tone, and is very long and very clear. In the legend of Maui and the sun, when Maui traps the sun in his net in order to slow its crossing from east to west, the kokako brings water in its long wattles to the struggling and thirsty demigod. To reward it for its kindness, Maui gave the kokako long, nimble legs to more easily hop through the trees to find food.

A one-hour loop walk in the reserve leads through the territories of several birds so the chance of hearing them is high, but you'll need to be patient to see one. Your best chance is two hours after dawn, so you have to get up very early, especially in summer.

13
short walks in
Bay of Plenty

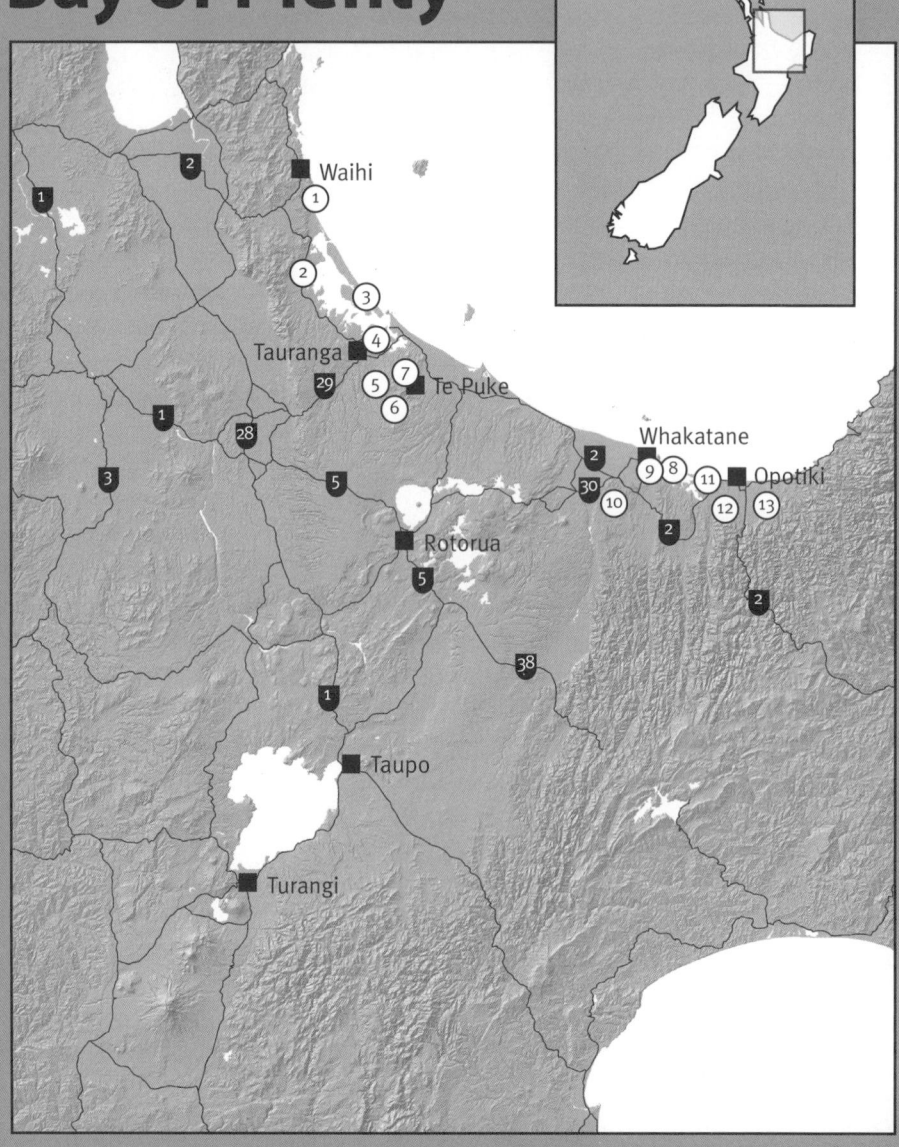

1 Orokawa Bay and Homunga Bay, Waihi Beach
Two beautiful sandy beaches, backed by old pohutukawa trees.

Grade: Easy/medium. **Time:** 2 hours one way, one and a half hours return to Orokawa Bay.

How to get there: At Waihi Beach the track begins at the northern end of the beach with the other end at the very end of Ngatitangata Road. From Waihi take SH25 towards Whangamata and, after 1.2 km, turn right into Barry Street, which becomes Golden Bay Road and then Ngatitangata Road, a distance of 9 km.

North of Waihi Beach a track follows the coast, winding its way through regenerating bush to two magical bays, which are as close to perfect as you can get. Crystal-clear water rushes on to a wide sweep of sand fringed with ancient pohutukawa trees, ideal shade on a hot day. The surf can be rough here, so take care when swimming – there are occasional stingrays in the shallow waters. Orokawa Bay is the first bay and from here a side track from the beach leads up to the 28 m high William Wright Falls (30 minutes return). At Homunga Bay small streams drop off a steep bluff onto the beach, creating an ideal shower to rinse off after a swim.

While most do the return trip to Orokawa Bay, the coastal stretch from Orokawa Bay to Homunga Bay is far more attractive – the track is in better condition and with fewer people.

The best way to do this walk is to start from the northern end, but that requires a cooperative person to drop you off at the start. This means you walk down the very steep hill to Homunga Bay then follow the coast, a pleasant and relatively easy two-hour walk. Failing that, this is a four-hour return walk.

2 Haiku Pathway, Katikati
A gentle stroll in a river park, contemplating haiku.

Grade: Easy. **Time:** As long as you need.

How to get there: SH2 Katikati – the entrance is well signposted next to Hammer Hardware in the main shopping centre.

Haiku is a form of poetry, specifically a 17-syllable poem consisting of five, seven and five syllables, usually arranged in three lines and read in one breath. The world's shortest form of poetry, it was established as a great literary form in Japan, expressing profound truths in the simplest natural images. Haiku finds a perfect home in this park.

Rather than establish yet another walk by a river, the residents of Katikati have been particularly clever. As well as providing a pleasant open space they have added haiku on rocks and stones in the riverside park behind the shops in the centre of town. This is believed to be the largest display of boulder haiku outside Japan, with writers ranging from ancient Japanese poets through to contemporary international writers.

3 Mount Maunganui/Mauao
Spectacular views of the Bay of Plenty.

Grade: Summit – hard, base – easy. **Time:** One hour, 15 minutes return to the summit, 45 minutes return to the base.
How to get there: The track begins in Mt Maunganui on the corner of Adams Terrace and Marine Parade.

Mauao/Mt Maunganui is a dormant lava dome, over three million years old and long since eroded, leaving dramatic rock formations. Once an island, the mountain is joined to the mainland by a tombolo, a long sandbar.

In Maori legend Mauao was a nameless slave in love with Puwhenua, who loved Otanewainuku. Unable to endure seeing her with another, he decided to fling himself into the ocean. Patupaiarehe dragged the lovesick mountain to the sea, a long slow haul. Fearful of the sun, the patupaiarehe fled, naming the hapless mountain Mauao, 'caught by the morning sun'.

The *Takitimu* waka made landfall here on its journey from Hawaiki. The people gave thanks for their safe journey by chanting karakia and planting their mauri, or life force, at the summit.

A steady climb to the 232 m peak, the tracks are mostly in excellent condition and not that difficult. After passing through the camping ground and through the gate, the track leads uphill to the left. At the junction there are two options, with the Oruahine track gentler than the steeper Waikorere. On the summit, which is surprisingly flat, the views are dramatic, with the remains of an old pa. The return down the mountain is via the 4WD track down the harbour side.

The broad, undulating base track following the coast is also popular. From the superb surf of the main beach the track winds around to the busy harbour entrance. Overhung with pohutukawa, it continues to Pilot

Bay, passing a statue of Tangaroa, god of the sea, and an historic stone jetty.

4 Waikareao Estuary Walk, Tauranga
An easy coastal walk around a wide estuary.

- **Grade:** Easy. **Time:** Two hours return.
- **How to get there:** There are numerous access points – from the city the easiest is via Tauranga and Wharepai domains on Cameron Road, then over the footbridge to the track. By car the best place to start is in the small park on the corner of Chapel and Maxwell's roads.

The Waikareao Estuary behind the Tauranga CBD is typical of the broad, shallow waterways characterising Tauranga Harbour. Waikareao means 'sparkling waters of the new day' though in reality the estuary is tidal and the walk more attractive at high tide. At low tide you'll see wading birds including herons, stilts, gulls and oystercatchers, and the fascinating aerial roots of the mangroves, with small crabs scuttling into muddy holes.

Circling the entire estuary, this track is definitely a walk of two halves. Along the northwestern side of the harbour, the flat walk includes a surprising variety of ecosystems. Sturdy boardwalks and a flat, wide track wander through flax and raupo swamps, saltwater marshes, mangrove wetlands, a bush remnant and small grassy parks. Just offshore is a tiny island, once a Maori pa and accessible only on a very low tide. The southeastern section runs alongside a busy arterial roadway into Tauranga and is not that picturesque. Fortunately this section is shorter.

5 Waterfall Track, McLaren Falls Park, Kaimai
A pretty waterfall hides in a bushy gully.

- **Grade:** Easy. **Time:** 20 minutes.
- **How to get there:** On the lower Kaimai road into Tauranga (SH2) turn into McLaren's Falls Road – the park is 1.4 km from the intersection, just over the falls.

In 1925 a hydroelectric dam on the Wairoa River created Lake McLaren, on the shores of which a 190-hectare park was established. Now a popular picnic spot, much of the park consists of open grassy areas intermingled with plantings of exotic trees. Easy short tracks weave through the entire park, but the most popular short walk is a loop track through a dense bush gully.

The Waterfall Track follows a small stream through native bush dense with ferns, mosses and some good-sized trees. The waterfall, while not large, drops into a pretty fern-shrouded pool. A short side track zigzags up a hill to a lookout point with pleasant rural views.

6 Otanewainuku
A wonderful outlook location in virgin native forest.

Grade: Easy/medium. **Time:** one and a half hours return.
How to get there: From SH29 at Tauranga take Oropi Road for 14 km, turn left into Mountain Road (part gravel) and continue for 7 km to the car park and shelter.

Rising to 640 m, bush-covered Otanewainuku is closely connected with two famous stories. Tutanekai, lover of Hinemoa, while being pursued by his enemies, leapt spectacularly from the summit of Otanewainuku to avoid capture. This is also the mountain which caused Mauao so much grief when Puwhenua rejected him, choosing Otanewainuku instead.

A loop track through magnificent virgin forest leads to the summit, where a lookout tower gives spectacular views. The tracks are in very good condition with surprisingly little mud, considering the dense, wet bush. The right-hand side of the loop following the ridge is a steady but not steep climb, while the left hand side to the summit is flatter, but much steeper at the end.

For a shorter walk, an easy 30 minute loop track that begins opposite the car park winds through attractive bush

7 Papamoa Hills Regional Park Summit Walk, Te Puke
Spectacular views over the Bay of Plenty from the impressive remains of an old pa.

Grade: Medium. **Time:** One hour 15 minutes return.
How to get there: 5 km east of Te Puke on SH2, turn left into Poplar Lane and drive 800 m to the car park.

A steady uphill climb begins through regenerating native bush after the clearance of old pine trees. Spectacular views to the west are revealed just before the summit (224 m). This is the site of Karangaumu, an impressive pa and one of seven in the park. A large pa covering the top of the hill, its ramparts, defensive ditches and terraces are all clearly visible. Even to the untrained eye, the strategic military advantage is immediately obvious. The whole bay is clearly visible and watchful lookouts would have missed nothing. The track is particularly well maintained and signposted.

8 Nga Tapuwae o Toi, Whakatane
Two popular and accessible walkways.

- **Grade:** Easy to medium. **Time:** While the whole walkway is 17 km long and takes 7 hours, the most popular section is from Whakatane to Ohope (2 hours 30 minutes one way) with part of the track tide-dependent. Kapu Te Rangi is 45 minutes return from Seaview Road and Otarawairere Beach is one hour return.
- **How to get there:** There is a bus service from Ohope to Whakatane – check the information centre for tides and the timetable. Kapu Te Rangi (Toi's Pa) and Otarawairere Beach are accessible from either end of the track. Kapu Te Rangi begins from the car park on Seaview Road. If walking up from town, take the steps in Canning Place behind Pohaturoa Rock. The track to Otarawairere Beach begins at the bottom of the hill just as the road from Whakatane enters Ohope – turn left into West End Road and go to the end. Walk along the beach towards the headland; the track starts at the base of the hill.

Toi was one of the greatest of Polynesia's legendary voyagers, exploring the coastline of New Zealand and repeatedly crossing the South Pacific. Kapu Te Rangi is one of New Zealand's oldest pa sites and the strategic value of its hilltop location obvious. The views are endless, and the steep drop on the river side of the pa makes it eminently defendable. The male crew of the *Mataatua* were visiting here when it slipped its moorings and was saved by Wairaka; and this is also the place where kumara came to Aotearoa. The track is in excellent condition with some stepped sections. At the very beginning the walk crosses the Wairere Falls.

Otarawairere Bay is a secluded beach accessible by foot from the western end of Ohope Beach. From a lookout point, Ohope Beach and the eastern Bay of Plenty stretch out in the distance, framed by native bush, the home of tui and bellbirds. The beach is a small cove of sand and shell, enclosed by rocky headlands and overhung by huge pohutukawa trees, making this the ideal destination on a warm day or for an early morning walk. In the distance White Island smoulders quietly.

9 Whakatane River and Historical Walk
Maori and Pakeha history intertwine on this attractive walk.

Grade: Easy. **Time:** One hour return.
How to get there: Start at the Visitor Information Centre in Kakahoroa Quay, Whakatane.

Before leaving Hawaiki, Toroa, captain of *Mataatua*, was told by his father Irakawa to look for three landmarks, which would mark the place to settle. These are still visible 800 years later in the centre of Whakatane. The first is Muriwai's Cave (partially collapsed) where Irakawa's daughter lived, and highly tapu until 1963, when the tapu was lifted. The second is Wairere Falls – while not spectacular, nonetheless attractive for a waterfall in the middle of town. And finally, Pohaturoa Rock contains a highly tapu cave where tohunga performed sacred ceremonies.

With the waka moored in the river estuary, the men climbed Kapu Te Rangi, leaving the women and children behind. An outgoing tide put the waka in danger but, in a breach of tradition, Toroa's daughter Wairaka picked up a paddle, exclaiming 'E! Kia Whakatane au i ahau' (let me act like a man), and brought the waka back to safety, with the other women. Her action is the origin of the name Whakatane.

Start by the information centre and follow the river towards the sea past Whakatane Wharf, home to commercial and pleasure boats, and on to the landing place of the *Mataatua* and a replica of the famous waka. Continue to the heads and the bronze statue of Wairaka, overlooking the narrow river entrance. Follow the road back to town, taking in Toroa's three landmarks – Muriwai's Cave, Wairere Falls and Pohaturoa's Rock.

10 White Pine Bush
A rare patch of lowland bush.

Grade: Easy. **Time:** 20 minutes return.
How to get there: Pine Bush Road (SH2), 20 km south of Whakatane.

A tiny reserve established in 1923 is all that remains of the dense lowland forest once covering this plain. Huge kahikatea dominate, some up to 600 years old, and it is from these trees that the reserve takes its name. Kahikatea were known to early European settlers as white pine, as forests of pure kahikatea have the distinctive feel of a pine forest, even though they don't belong to the pine family. Kahikatea is a very pale timber and was used in the past to make butter boxes as the wood was both light, readily available and – more importantly – didn't taint the butter.

11 Ohiwa Harbour Sandspit Wildlife Refuge
A birdwatcher's paradise.

Grade: Easy. **Time:** 90 minutes return.
How to get there: Follow Harbour Road right to the very end, just beyond the boat ramp, where a sign indicates the refuge.

Ohiwa Harbour is tidal, with over 70 percent of the seabed exposed at low tide, making it an important refuge for wading and migratory birds including the godwit, which flies non-stop from the Arctic each spring, New Zealand dotterels, and both the pied and variable oystercatchers. While there are reserves on both entrances to the harbour, this one is on the western (Ohope) side.

Unfortunately there is no signage or map and the only track is a 4WD access road through the middle of the dunes, which is not at all helpful if you are here to see the birds. The following walk is mainly coastal and will prevent you from getting too lost.

From the car park follow the grass track along the coast to a point about 500 m past the golf course, where the track splits. Take the right-hand track down onto the sand and follow the sand all the way round to the harbour entrance and the open sea beach. This area is the main bird-watching site, with wading birds favouring the tidal flats and nesting seabirds occupying the sand above high tide. On the ocean side continue around until you see an old fencepost on the dunes to your left. Just to the right of this fence post is the 4WD track leading back to the car park.

12 Hukutaia Domain/Burial Tree, Opotiki
A 2000-year-old puriri tree formerly used to hold the bones of the dead.

- **Grade:** Easy. **Time:** 30 minutes.
- **How to get there:** From Opotiki take the road to Whakatane and just over the Waioeka River bridge turn left into Woodlands Road – the reserve is on the left, 7 km down this road.

Established in 1918, this small reserve of low rainforest was set aside primarily to protect Taketakerau, an ancient puriri tree. The tree was used by the local Upokorehe hapu to conceal the bones of the notable dead from desecration, though after the tree was damaged the remains were buried elsewhere. Thought to be over 2000 years old, this huge tree is highly tapu.

From 1933 to 1970 local amateur botanist Norman Potts travelled throughout New Zealand to gather plants, creating one of the most extensive collections of native trees and shrubs in the country. His work was continued here by Mark Heginbotham, from 1970 to 1990.

The tracks are well marked on a map at the entrance and the puriri tree is easy to locate.

13 Marawaiwai Reserve, Opotiki
A fine remnant of virgin lowland forest.

- **Grade:** Easy. **Time:** 25 minutes.
- **How to get there:** From Opotiki take SH2 towards Gisborne and after 5 km turn left into Warringtons Road, then right into Harrisons Road – the reserve is on the right, 2 km down Harrisons Road.

Huge kahikatea dominate this rare reserve of lowland forest, which is easily accessible on this flat loop track, built by students from the local college. A small raupo swamp is also protected within the reserve. There's good interpretive signage to help identify native plants, and a very pleasant grassy picnic spot at the entrance to the reserve adds to the appeal.

17
short walks in Rotorua and Central North Island

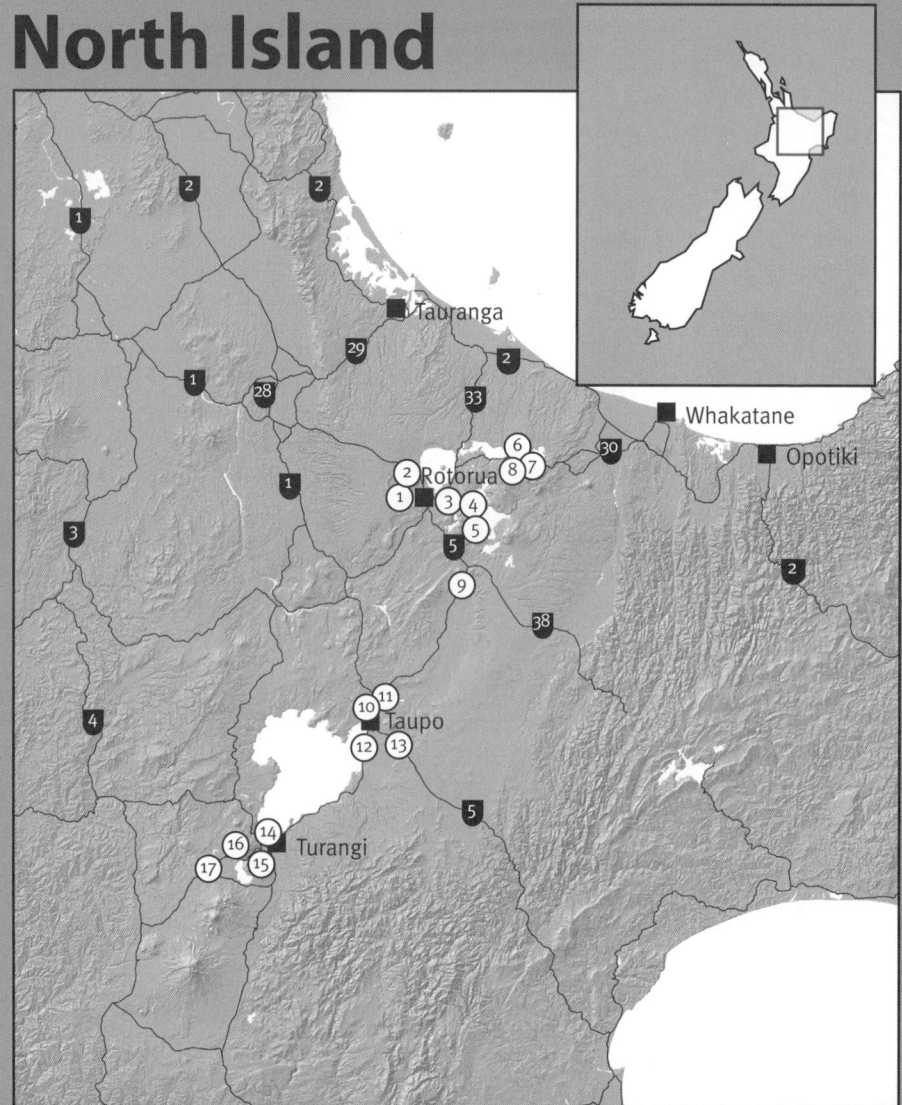

1 Rotorua City Walk
Rotorua's key historic buildings and thermal surprises.

Grade: Easy. **Time:** One hour return.
How to get there: Start in the Government Gardens, Fenton Street, Rotorua.

Start from the superb Government Gardens in Fenton Street, established on land gifted by Ngati Whakaue and developed at the end of the nineteenth century. The park contains formal gardens, historic sites and hot-water springs. Highlights are the Bath House, the Blue Baths and the Polynesian Spa. The distinctive totara arch at the eastern end of Arawa Street was built to celebrate the 1901 visit of the Duke and Duchess of Cornwall, and the genteel lawn bowls and croquet grounds complement the beautifully restored 1903 Edwardian tea pavilion.

Walk through to the lake front – thermal areas here are unpredictable and visitors must stay on the marked paths. Lake Rotorua covers an area of 80 sq km and is the North Island's second-largest lake. After the last major eruption, 140,000 years ago, the crater collapsed and partially filled with water. The whole Rotorua basin is part of a larger crater known as the Rotorua Caldera, of which the shallow lake (45 metres at most) is the lowest point. The area where Rotorua City is situated is the most geothermally active.

The lakefront is the starting point for trips onto the lake, including to Mokoia Island. It is also the base for floatplane excursions. Popular *Opera in the Pa* concerts are held in the park, which is also noted for over-friendly black swans.

Continue west along the lakefront to Ohinemutu Village, an important Ngati Whakaue settlement, and the centre of Maori Rotorua. Ohinemutu is a contemporary Maori community, not a tourist attraction, and while locals welcome visitors, every respect should be shown. The heart of Ohinemutu is the beautifully carved meeting house, Tama Te Kapua, on Te Papaiouru Marae, named after the captain of the *Arawa* waka, who brought the Arawa ancestors to Aotearoa around 1350 AD.

Overlooking the lake is St Faith's Church (1910), its interior decorated with fine weaving and paintings. Note the window showing Christ as a Maori chief, positioned so he appears to be walking on the waters of the lake. Sunday services are held in English and Maori. Behind the church the graves are above ground, as the area is too active geothermally for burial.

Continue west past fine carved meeting houses and left into Ariariterangi Street, where steam floats up from stormwater drains, and hot water bubbles in backyards, then along the lake. Turn left into Rangipahere Street, which leads to Kuirau Park.

Thermal activity is concentrated in the northeastern section, an area of increasing thermal activity, which varies dramatically from season to season. By the children's playground are two shallow pools, designed for soaking tired feet. From here, cross to Arawa Street, leading back to the Government Gardens.

When geologists describe the earth's crust as 'thin' here, they're not talking figuratively. The ground is a fragile layer over very hot subterranean water and can collapse at any time. Warnings to stay on the path must be taken seriously – even the smallest steam vents can inflict a painful scald.

2 Ngongotaha Summit
Dense bush is the home of the mysterious patupaiarehe.

Grade: Medium. **Time:** 2 hours return.
How to get there: The track begins from the Violet Bonnington Reserve located at the Rotorua end of Paradise Valley Road.

Ngongotaha was one of the strongholds of the mysterious patupaiarehe, also known as iwi atua, 'the godlike tribe'. Patupaiarehe shunned human contact, were known for trouble-making, and seldom showed kindness to humans. Patupaiarehe who occupied the mountain were known as Ngati Rua and numbered over a thousand, living close to the summit, then known as Te Tuaahu a te Atua (the altar of the god). The name of the mountain commemorates a rare act of kindness when Ihenga was given water by a patupaiarehe woman while exploring the summit. Ngongotaha means 'to drink from a calabash'.

This track has recently been extended and upgraded. It begins through fine virgin forest and gradually climbs to the summit through dense bush. The grade is steady rather than steep. Near the top it joins Mountain Road for the short section to the summit, which is bush-covered, with no views.

3 The Redwoods/Whakarewarewa Forest
Magnificent groves of redwoods.

> **Grade:** Easy. **Time:** Three loop tracks from 30 minutes to one hour 15 minutes.
>
> **How to get there:** From SH30 turnoff at Te Ngae and take the Tarawera Road – the turnoff to the redwoods is immediately to the right and the beginning of the walk is 500 m on the left.

Officially known as the Whakarewarewa Forest, but popularly referred to as the Redwood Grove, this forest stretches from Rotorua City right through to the Blue and Green Lakes, and is a complex maze of tracks, which can take from 30 minutes to all day. The highlight is an extensive grove of huge redwood trees planted as part of early forestry experiments, with areas of Douglas fir, larch and a grove of plane trees.

Three short loop tracks start from behind and to the right of the visitor centre – all are very well formed and easy walking, though the longest loop has slightly more of an uphill gradient. If you want to avoid the coachloads who pack these walks during the day, try to visit earlier in the morning or later in the afternoon. This is a particularly lovely place to visit on a quiet summer's evening, for a picnic on the grass in the old quarry. There are separate tracks for mountain bikes.

4 Okareka Walkway
An excellent lakeside wetland walk.

> **Grade:** Easy. **Time:** 30 minutes return to the end of the boardwalk, one and a half hours to the Okareka outlet.
>
> **How to get there:** From SH30 turn off at Te Ngae and take the Tarawera Road. Turn left on to Okareka Loop Road, and at the lake turn left into Acacia Road – the walk is signposted to the left.

The landscape around Lake Okareka is quite different from other Rotorua lakes. Most lakes are bush-fringed or at least ringed with trees, but the land around Okareka is largely farmed. On one side of the lake is an extensive wetland with excellent tracks and boardwalks. The track cuts through the marshland of sedges, rushes and raupo, home to a wide range of freshwater aquatic birds including black swans, pukeko, shags, ducks and stilts. A bird hide in the middle of the wetland is an ideal spot for birdwatchers.

5 Blue and Green Lakes
A lakeside walk around the Blue Lake with views over the Green Lake.

- **Grade:** Easy. **Time:** One and a half hours.
- **How to get there:** On the Tarawera Road the Blue Lake is 8 km from Te Ngae turnoff on SH30.

Obviously named for their colour and known respectively in Maori as Tikitapu and Rotokakahi, these are two old volcanic craters. On the northern shore of the Blue Lake is a sandy beach where a boat ramp adjoins a large picnic area. The track around the lake begins from the western side of this picnic area. The lake has no visible outlet, but drains underground into the Green Lake, which is 20 m lower. The water level rises and falls substantially from year to year – at times the lake is ringed by beautiful small beaches, while at others all but two of the beaches disappear.

When you reach the car park at the opposite end of the lake, take some time to view the Green Lake, which is tapu and not accessible. Return to the point where the track meets the car park, take the steps down to a lovely sheltered beach and continue around the shoreline, back to your starting point.

6 Hinehopu's Track, Lake Rotoiti
A walk combining lake scenery, native bush and history.

- **Grade:** Easy. **Time:** Two hours return.
- **How to get there:** At the eastern end of Lake Rotoiti turn off SH33 into Tamatea St and continue for 500 m to the car park where the track begins – there is limited car parking at the Lake Rotoehu end.

This excellent track through attractive bush links Lakes Rotoiti and Rotoehu and takes around two hours return. There are three entrances, none of which is particularly well marked, with the best starting point at the Lake Rotoiti end. The highlight is a famous matai tree under which the baby Hinehopu was hidden from enemies by her mother. It was under this same tree that she met her husband, Pikiao, and many of Ngati Pikiao iwi trace their lineage directly back to the couple. The tree is right by the main road, which detracts somewhat from the atmosphere.

Led by Hongi Hika, in 1823 Ngapuhi warriors dragged their waka along this same track, from Rotoehu to Rotoiti, and launched a devastating attack on *Te Arawa*, who thought they were safe on Mokoia Island.

7 Lake Okataina Walkway

A walk to an historic pa site on the Eastern Okataina Walkway.

- **Grade:** Easy. **Time:** 40 minutes return.
- **How to get there:** Turn off SH30 at Lake Rotoiti into Lake Okataina Road – the walkway begins 7.5 km away at the end of this road.

Okataina is a small, beautiful lake surrounded entirely by bush, dominated by high rocky bluffs. Although it has no visible inlets or outlets, water seeps through the rocks at Otangimoana Bay into Lake Tarawera, which is 20 m lower than Okataina. The level of Lake Okataina varies considerably, and in the past was 12 m lower than it is today. During the Hawkes Bay earthquake in 1931, the lake level abruptly dropped nearly 4 m.

The Okataina Walkway on the eastern shore of the lake is an easy bush walk of three hours one way, to the shores of Lake Tarawera, with a swimming beach and views to Mt Tarawera. A shorter option, and just as pleasant, is a return walk to Te Koutu, a pa located on a small peninsula jutting out into the lake.

The walk begins through the archway by the car park and follows the shoreline through the bush to the small peninsula where the pa is located. Te Koutu was the most important settlement on Lake Okataina, and easily defended. Today the pa is covered by regenerating bush, but all the earthworks are clearly visible. In particular, the pa is noted for its stone kumara storage pits and burial caves carved into the hillside.

8 Twin Craters/Ngahopua Track

A short walk leads to a viewing point over two small craters.

- **Grade:** Easy. **Time:** 40 minutes return.
- **How to get there:** Turn off SH 30 at Lake Rotoiti into Okataina Road and the walk begins 4 km on the left opposite the turnoff to the Okataina Education Centre – with limited parking, it's best to park on the road to the Education Centre.

Rotongata and Rotoatua are two small lakes in a crater formed over 3000 years ago. While the track begins through a grove of spectacular large totara, most of the trees on this walk are tawa, their light foliage giving the forest a soft filtered light. The steady uphill climb leads to a high ridge overlooking Rotongata, the first lake, then follows the ridge to a lookout over Rotoatua. There is no point going further, as the lookout points beyond are overgrown and the track quickly leads downhill.

9 Rainbow Mountain/Maungakaramea
An active crater lake nestles below coloured cliffs.

- **Grade:** Lookout – easy; summit – medium **Time:** Lookout – 20 minutes return; summit – two and a half hours return.
- **How to get there:** On SH 5 south of Rotorua on the road to Waiotapu, 500 m on the left past the Murupara/Waikaremoana turnoff.

Maungakaramea, or Rainbow Mountain, lies about 25 km south of Rotorua and is scarred and torn by a series of volcanic eruptions going back thousands of years. The lakes are old craters and the last eruption was believed to be around 1000 years ago. Plumes of steam rise from the mountain's steep slopes and the lake near the beginning of the track up the mountain is geothermally active. Above the lake tower cliffs of multi-hued red, orange and brown volcanic rock, discoloured by continual exposure to steam, which give this mountain its European name.

Many of the plants found on the mountain are peculiar to the area and specifically adapted to harsh geothermal conditions. The walk to the top is steady rather than steep. Lakes Tarawera, Rerewhakaaitu, Taupo and Rotomahana are all visible, as are the central North Island volcanoes, the Urewera and Kaimanawa ranges, and closer at hand, Mt Tarawera lies to the east. If you are short on time a quick walk up to the lookout over the lake will take 20 minutes.

10 Craters of the Moon
An active and changeable thermal area.

- **Grade:** Easy. **Time:** One hour return.
- **How to get there:** Travel 6 km north of Lake Taupo on SH5, then turn into Karapiti Road.

One of the most recent and most active thermal fields in the area, the Craters of the Moon is constantly changing. Over the years the thermal area has expanded considerably and activity is unpredictable – sometimes mass columns of steam rise from the entire area, while at others it is disappointingly quiet. The most common thermal activity is steam vents, though there is one major crater with furiously boiling mud, or water – depending on the water levels. The area is open, with intriguing low-growing plants, which have somehow managed to adapt to the inhospitable environment. An entrance fee applies.

11 Huka Falls Walkway
The Waikato River churns into a frothy mass over the Huka Falls.

- **Grade:** Easy. **Time:** Two hours return.
- **How to get there:** Either from Huka Falls off SH5 or from Spa Park off Spa Road, Taupo.

The best way to begin is from Spa Park in Taupo, without visiting Huka Falls beforehand. From here the track follows the river downstream from where a small hot-water stream joins the river, creating a popular swimming hole where hot water mingles with the cooler water of the Waikato River. The track follows the southern bank through a variety of vegetation, not all of it pristine, but with extensive planting of native trees along the track, this can only improve. The track is in excellent condition though there are some steep parts.

As it leaves Lake Taupo the river is a beautiful iridescent blue/green, but the tranquil waters become increasingly swift. Visitors who go directly to the falls won't appreciate how big the river is, and how much water is forced through the narrow gap. The sheer volume of bright clear water gushing through the narrow gap more than makes up for the falls' modest size – over 200,000 litres per second roar over the 3-m falls with impressive fury.

Recently extreme kayakers have attempted the falls, though this bravado is hardly new. An early Maori chief narrowly escaped death trying to negotiate the falls in a waka, giving rise to a proverb, 'A little water through the lashing hole wrecks the canoe.'

There's no return track on the other side of the river. If you haven't organised someone to pick you up, you'll need to retrace your steps.

12 Taupo nui a Tia
An easy pathway on the shores of New Zealand's largest lake.

Grade: Easy. **Time:** 2 hours one way.
How to get there: Begins on the corner of Ferry Road and Redoubt Street, where the Waikato River leaves the lake.

Lake Taupo is New Zealand's largest lake, covering an area of 616 square km, fed by melting snow from mountains to the south. The whole basin is an old caldera, created by a series of 30 eruptions over the last 27,000 years and 186 m at its deepest point. The last eruption, around 180 AD, known as the Hatepe Eruption, is believed to be the largest in recorded history and was observed in Rome and China. On the western side of the lake, this ejected over 100 cubic km of volcanic material, devastating the surrounding area. The buried forest at Pureora, 70 km away, is an area of flattened forest knocked over by the incredible blast. A wall of water was sent racing down the Waikato River and in swamps west of Huntly, huge kauri have been found buried, felled by the resulting flood. The area around the lake is still geothermally active, particularly around Wairakei, northeast of the lake, and around Tokaanu in the southwest.

The full name of the lake is Taupo nui a Tia, 'the cloak of Tia'. Tia was a tohunga aboard *Te Arawa* waka, and when the lake is rough, the whitecaps are said to be the white feathers adorning Tia's cloak.

A walkway extends along the lake from the yacht club by the Waikato River to Wharewaka Point, 7 km of easy walking.

13 Opepe Reserve
The historic site of a clash between Maori rebels and local cavalry.

Grade: Easy. **Time:** Allow 30 minutes return.
How to get there: On SH5, 14 km from the junction with SH1 in Taupo.

After the defeat by militia and their Maori allies in Poverty Bay in January 1869, the rebel Te Kooti escaped into the rugged Urewera country. The price his Tuhoe allies paid for sheltering Te Kooti became too much, and Te Kooti sought the protection of Tawhiao in the King Country. He started to make his way west, in the direction of Lake Taupo.

On 7 June 1869 an advance party of Te Kooti's men came across the camp of the Bay of Plenty Cavalry. This unit was scouting the area for signs of Te Kooti, but had failed to post sentries and was caught completely off-guard. Nine men died in the attack and five escaped, taking several days in bitterly cold weather to reach Fort Galatea.

The Opepe Reserve is cut in two by SH5 from Taupo to Napier. On the northern side of the road there is an easy 10-minute return walk through bush to the soldiers' lonely graves, which later became the burial place of local settlers. Across the road another 10-minute return walk will take you to the redoubt, of which very little remains apart from an old well. Deep gullies on three sides made this an easily defended spot, though it saw no further action as Te Kooti had already moved further west.

14 Tongariro National Trout Centre Walk
Trout and a pleasant riverside walk.

- Grade: Easy. Time: 30 minutes return.
- How to get there: SH1, 4 km north of Turangi.

Trout in the Taupo area are sustained by wild trout spawning in the rivers and lakes. While trout normally spend some of their life at sea, here Lake Taupo acts as a substitute ocean. The hatchery is a safeguard should a natural disaster seriously affect the trout numbers. The complex raises trout from eggs and at all times of the year there are usually trout in some growth stage on show. The visitor centre has excellent displays on all aspects of the trout fishery, including a fascinating collection of rods and flies.

A series of paths link the various pools and lead down to the Tongariro River, and an underground glass viewing chamber allows visitors to see the trout below water. While the paths are a little confusing to follow, it's impossible to become lost.

Open daily 10am to 3pm and there is an entrance fee.

15 Lake Rotopounamu

A small lake fringed by virgin forest nestles in the lee of Mount Pihanga.

Grade: Easy. **Time:** Two hours.
How to get there: Travelling on SH47 from Turangi, the track is located on the left, on the downhill side of the Te Ponanga Saddle.

Rotopounamu is a beautiful bush-fringed lake on the lower slopes of Mt Pihanga. The name means Greenstone Lake, referring to the colour of the water as no greenstone is found here, though the water isn't always green.

From the road it's a short but steady climb up to the lake, formed thousands of years ago by a giant landslide. There is no visible outlet. The track around the lake is largely flat, following the edge of the water through mature forest of red beech, kahikatea, rimu and matai. On the eastern side of the lake is Long Beach, an ideal picnic spot and a good place for a swim on a hot day.

16 Te Porere Redoubt

Two redoubts mark the final stand of Te Kooti.

Grade: Easy. **Time:** 45 minutes.
How to get there: 26 km from Turangi on SH47.

Government troops were desperate to capture Te Kooti Arikirangi Te Turuki, as he travelled west seeking the protection of the Maori King, Tawhiao. Aware of the price the Tuhoe had paid for sheltering Te Kooti, Tawhiao was reluctant to bring further bloodshed to his people, who had suffered badly at the hands of the British just a few years before.

With protection in the King Country denied him, Te Kooti had no choice but to make a stand, choosing Te Porere, southwest of Turangi, where he had two redoubts built. By this time the old-style defensive pa was redundant. What makes these fascinating is that while they resemble British-style redoubts externally, the layout inside is cleverly enhanced. The area is laced with deep trenches to protect defenders from rifle and cannon fire.

Led by Lieutenant Colonel Thomas McDonnell, 500 government soldiers and their Maori allies, armed with rifles and cannon, attacked Te Kooti and his Tuwharetoa allies on 4 October 1869 at Te Porere. The lower redoubt fell quickly. The defenders retreated to the upper redoubt, which was also overrun. Te Kooti barely escaped – of the 41 casualties, 37 of his men died and just four government soldiers.

Both redoubts are in an excellent state of preservation and well worth the short detour. The walking is easy and the experience enhanced by excellent information boards and an outlook over the upper redoubt.

17 Taranaki Falls, Tongariro National Park
Lava fields, beech forest and a dramatic waterfall.

- **Grade:** Easy. **Time:** One and a half hours.
- **How to get there:** The track starts in the small street behind the Chateau Tongariro, just below the visitor centre.

Tongariro National Park, gifted to the people of New Zealand in 1887 by paramount chief Te Heuheu Tukino IV on behalf of Tuwharetoa, was our first national park and the fourth such park in the world. Containing the volcanic peaks of Ruapehu (2797 m) Ngauruhoe (2290 m) and Tongariro (1968 m), the park covers 80,000 ha of stark volcanic lava and ash interwoven with vast expanses of golden tussock and flax, pristine streams, herb fields and untouched rainforest. The mainly beech forest has survived in pockets and sheltered valleys, protected from the Taupo eruption and more localised recent volcanic activity. The walk to Taranaki Falls is one of the best for those on a day visit, traversing a wide range of terrain from the subalpine to beech forest, with excellent views.

The lower section dips through tussock fields, following a valley which has escaped recent lava flows and is dense with beech forest and ferns. The falls burst through a narrow gap in an old lava flow, plunging 20 m over the cliff face. At the first entrance to the track, current signage doesn't indicate this is a loop track, and many return after viewing just the falls. However, at the falls continue uphill to the left and return via the upper track. This area has a more open, raw feel and has been subjected to more recent and obvious lava flows. Keep an eye out for tiny hebes, alpine daisies and other delicate flowering mountain plants.

21
short walks in
East Cape, Gisborne and Hawke's Bay

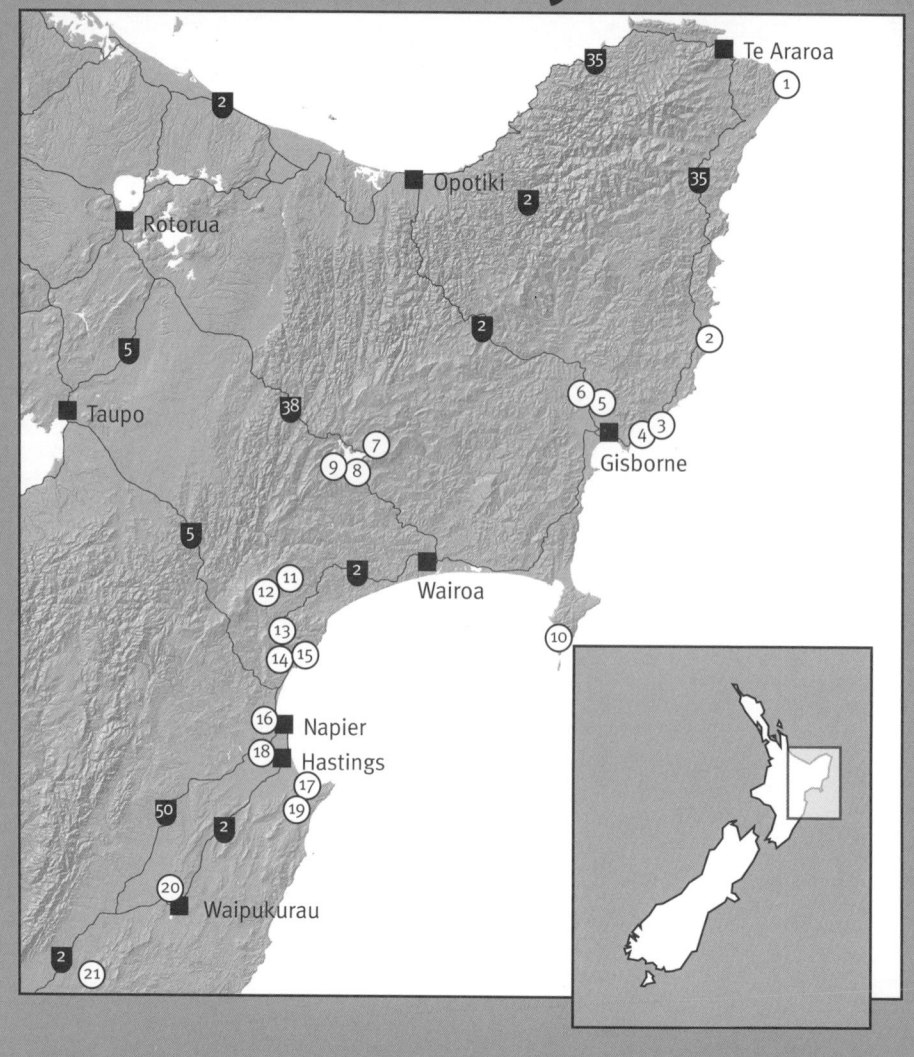

1 East Cape Lighthouse

An historic lighthouse above the most easterly point of mainland New Zealand.

- **Grade:** Medium. **Time:** One hour return.
- **How to get there:** 20 km from Te Araroa.

Lighthouses were vital for local shipping, and as early as 1875 a lighthouse was needed at East Cape. Authorities chose a small island 2 km offshore, now called East Island, but known locally as Whangaokeno or Motu o Kaiawa. Work began in 1898, despite difficult access and warnings that the island was highly tapu. Four men drowned when the boat they were using to transport material from the steamer *Hinemoa* overturned, and were buried on the tiny island. Just one month after the light was lit in August 1900, heavy rains washed away the winch and ropeway used to haul supplies up to the lighthouse, and a small tramway.

Trouble continued, and by 1906 three of the lighthouse keeper's children had died. In February the same year an earthquake toppled their gravestones, followed by a severe storm in July which cut the telephone link to the mainland and washed the ketch *Sir Henry* onto the island's rocky shore, with the loss of three more lives. When slips threatened the lighthouse in 1921, the decision was made to move the light to the mainland, where it is today; once the lighthouse was removed, the slips and earthquakes stopped.

This is a beautiful location, though somewhat lost and lonely. The track climbs 150 m to the lighthouse and includes a long flight of stairs. The road from Te Araroa is unsealed, winding and slow going.

2 Cook's Cove, Tolaga Bay

A walk across farmland to Captain James Cook's historic landing.

- **Grade:** Medium. **Time:** 50 minutes return to the lookout, 3 hours return to the cove.
- **How to get there:** Wharf Road, signposted off SH35 at the southern end of Tolaga Bay.

Captain James Cook's first landing at the Turanganui River (modern-day Gisborne) was an uncharacteristic disaster, through a series of misunderstandings. In October 1769 and in desperate need of water and firewood, the *Endeavour* sailed north to this cove.

The ever-observant Cook and his crew left one of the rare detailed descriptions of Maori life in the eighteenth century. Surprisingly few of the pa were occupied, indicating a period of peace, though locals demonstrated haka for the men of the *Endeavour* and told stories of war and conflict. Tupaea, the Tahitian who acted as the expedition's translator, particularly impressed the local people, who renamed several localities after him, including the cave where he slept. The well dug by Cook's men was called Te Wai Keri a Tupaea.

The walkway to the cove takes three hours return and is through open farmland. Beginning as an easy uphill walk to a wooden platform looking down on Cook's Cove, from there the track winds downhill to the cove. The track is closed for lambing from 1 August through to Labour Day weekend.

3 Makorori Point, Wainui Beach
Coastal views over the splendid Makorori and Wainui beaches.

Grade: Easy. **Time:** 30 minutes return.
How to get there: The track is off SH5 at the north end of Wainui Beach, just as the road climbs uphill.

Makorori Point lies between Wainui and Makorori beaches, with spectacular coastal views to the south beyond Young Nicks Head to the Mahia Peninsula, while to the north lies the magnificent and undeveloped Makorori Beach.

It's best to park down by the beach and walk the short distance up the hill to the start of the track, as there's no parking at the beginning of the walk. The initial section is up steep steps to a lookout point over Wainui Beach, then wanders along a wide grass track to the lookout point over Makorori Beach.

There is a track down to the road from the Makorori end, but this means walking back along SH35, not a pleasant option, as there's nowhere to walk off the road. A walk back the way you came is recommended. Just across the road and up the hill is Okitu Bush, a small coastal forest remnant, where it takes around 20 minutes to walk the loop track to a lookout.

4 Titirangi/Kaiti Hill, Gisborne
Beginning from the historic Cook Memorial, the track leads uphill to wide views over the Gisborne district.

- **Grade:** Medium. **Time:** Plane Table Lookout: 35 minutes return
  Cook Plaza/Princess Diana Pohutukawa: 40 minutes return
  Titirangi: One hour return.
- **How to get there:** Follow the road to the Port and Cook Memorial. The track starts opposite. There is limited parking.

Titirangi/ Kaiti Hill at the mouth of the Turanganui River has always been a point of arrival beginning with the early Polynesian immigrants on board the two great voyaging waka, Horouta and Te Ikaroa a Raura. Many centuries later, this was also the first landing point of James Cook in 1769.

For such a popular destination, there is very little helpful signage. To complicate things further, there is not one, but four lookout points and there is an easy way and a hard way. All that said, while you might be confused, you won't get lost.

From the road start the walk on the wide track heading up hill until you get to Y junction. Take neither of the tracks, but instead climb the set of steps in the middle to the first lookout. Here there are excellent views inland over the city, Waikanae Beach and across Poverty Bay to the headland known as Young Nicks Head or Te Kuri-a-Paoa. A directional Plane Table helpfully indicates important landmarks. A little further along is Cooks Plaza with a pohutukawa tree planted by Diana, Princess of Wales, in 1983. From this point walk up the road to the summit of Titirangi. It is quite safe on the road as cars travel slowly it's an easy walk to the top.

If the views aren't enough attraction, there is also a substantial WWII gun emplacement and an excellent display detailing the Polynesian discovery and exploration of Aotearoa. From the summit carpark take the track (unmarked) by the rubbish bins which winds down hill back the lower lookouts. Just to the left below the Plane Table lookout are a long flight of steps down hill. Near the bottom of the steps is another lookout to the left which looks directly over the port.

Now the hard option for those much fitter and that is to take the steps up rather than the path. The steps are easy to find and lead up to the right about 50 metres from the start.

5 Gray's Bush
Beautiful bush with an unusual mixture of puriri and kahikatea.

- **Grade:** Easy. **Time:** Short loop 20 minutes; long loop 40 minutes.
- **How to get there:** 10 km from Gisborne on the Back Ormond Road.

Gray's Bush is an impressive subtropical forest with massive kahikatea and puriri and a dense understorey of nikau palms, the only remaining lowland bush on the Poverty Bay plain. Early recognition of this unique forest combination saved the tiny bush from being felled. Puriri tend to favour well-drained soils, while kahikatea thrive in wet conditions, and this combination of kahikatea and puriri is highly unusual. Furthermore, the height of the kahikatea has resulted in the puriri growing much taller and straighter than their usual spreading habit. The tracks are not clearly marked, but the reserve is so small it is impossible to get lost.

6 Waihirere Domain
An easy walk to a small waterfall.

- **Grade:** Easy. **Time:** 45 minutes return.
- **How to get there:** 12 km from Gisborne, on the Back Ormond Road, turn into Waihirere Domain Road.

A pleasant short drive from Gisborne City, Waihirere Domain is a popular picnic destination with large grassed area with tables, a playground and toilet facilities. The walk begins over a small footbridge and continues along a tree-shaded valley to a small waterfall with a pool suitable for swimming.

7 Lou's Lookout
A rocky clamber to a viewpoint over the lake.

- **Grade:** Medium. **Time:** 45 minutes return.
- **How to get there:** 8.5 km south of the Aniwaniwa Visitor Centre, Lake Waikaremoana.

Named after Tuai policeman Lou Dolman, who helped build the tracks around the lake in the 1960s, the track to Lou's Lookout is a steady but not hard uphill walk which weaves through massive limestone boulders. These huge rocks are a startling reminder of the scale of the landslip which occurred over 2000 years ago, blocking the Waikaretaheke River and forming Lake Waikaremoana. The boulders now form arches, caves and overhangs along this track. At the top the reward is an expansive lake view, which includes the dramatic Panekiri Bluff to the south.

8 Onepoto Caves
A scramble through huge boulders, caves and arches.

Grade: Medium. Time: 1 hour return.
How to get there: Onepoto, 12 km south of the Aniwaniwa Visitor Centre.

Onepoto is a complex of caves, rock overhangs, arches and tunnels, used by local Maori in time of trouble as a refuge, known as Te Ana o Tawa. In one famous story the chief Tuwai protected the people sheltering there by standing at the narrow entrance to the cave and killing five attackers, one by one, as they tried to enter.

This is a great walk to explore the jumble of rocks from the giant landslide, which according to geologists formed the lake. The track is convoluted with numerous side tracks and caves and you'll need to wear shoes with good tread, as the rocks are often slippery. A torch will be handy if you want to explore the caves, while around halfway there's a good lookout point over the lake.

The track terminates at the road, with a short 15-minute walk back to the car park.

9 Panekiri Bluff
Magnificent views over the lake.

Grade: Medium. Time: 2 hours return.
How to get there: This is the first section of the Lake Waikaremoana Great Walk at Onepoto, 12 km south of the Aniwaniwa Visitor Centre.

The massive bulk of Panekiri Bluff dominates the southern end of the lake, rising to 1100 m at the summit, known as Puketapu (five hours one way). However, the more modest first trig point can be reached after an hour of steady uphill walking and has magnificent views over the lake. The track begins at the far end of the flat grassed area, which was once the

Armed Constabulary parade ground. Government forces clashed with the supporters of Te Kooti near here in 1866, but by the time the redoubt was built Te Kooti was long gone. Very little remains, apart from an old historic cemetery and a limestone rock carved with the names and dates of soldiers stationed here in the 1860s and 1870s.

Once you enter the bush, the track is uphill all the way, though the grade is steady rather than steep and it's not until you near the top that the lake comes into view.

From the old parade ground another short track leads off to the left to Lake Kiriopukae. More pond than lake, Kiriopukae lies in a wetland, which expands and shrinks with the seasons. Weathered limestone outcrops and boulders are scattered around the lake.

10 Mahia Peninsula
A loop walk through bush with wide coastal views.

- **Grade:** Medium. **Time:** 2 hours return.
- **How to get there:** The reserve is located 7 km south of Mahia Beach on Kinikini Road, a narrow, winding, gravel road.

In the Maori legend of Maui hauling up his great fish (the North Island), Mahia is known as Te Matau a Maui, the fishhook of Maui. In the fourteenth century the great waka *Takitimu* landed here. Ruawharo, tohunga on the waka, decided to end his voyaging and settled on the peninsula. Tradition also has it that Ruawharo brought whales to the bay, and the wharenui at Opoutama is named in his honour.

Most of the peninsula has been stripped of vegetation, but the Mahia Peninsula Scenic Reserve protects 374 ha of coastal bush. Steep in places and with some stream crossings, the loop track has a lookout with great views to the south.

Left: Te Werahi Beach is a short walk from Cape Reinga, at the tip of the North Island.
Above: The Mangawhai Heads walkway has superb coastal views.
Below: Smugglers Cove was once used by locals avoiding tax on imported whiskey.

Left: The Arai Te Uru Walkway has superb views over the entrance to the Hokianga Harbour.

Below: Wharepuku Falls is one of the highlights on the walk along the Kerikeri River in Northland.

Opposite above left: Superb views of Whangaroa Harbour from the summit of St Paul's Rock.

Opposite above right: The kauri Te Matua Ngahere in Waipoua Forest on the west coast has a girth of 16.5 metres.

Opposite below: Mansion House on Kawau Island was the home of Governor Sir George Grey.

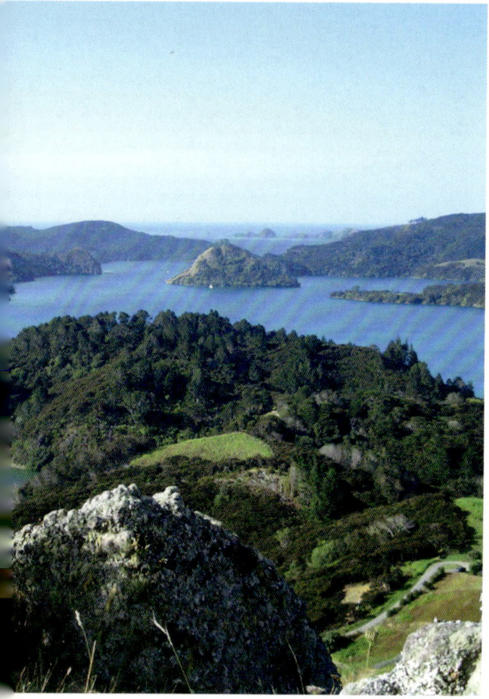

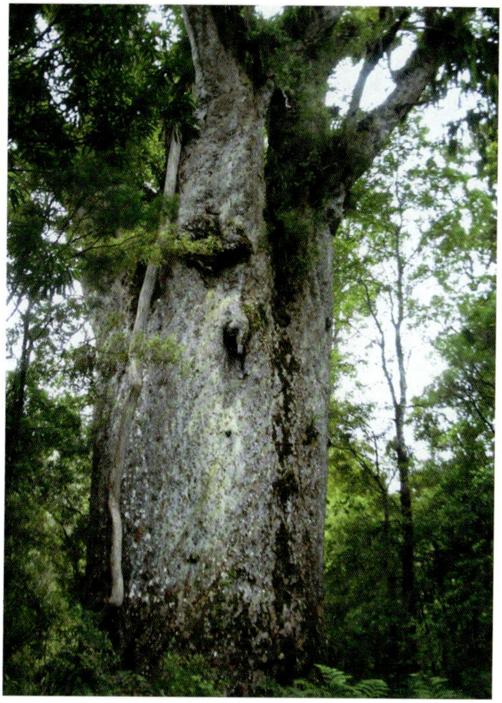

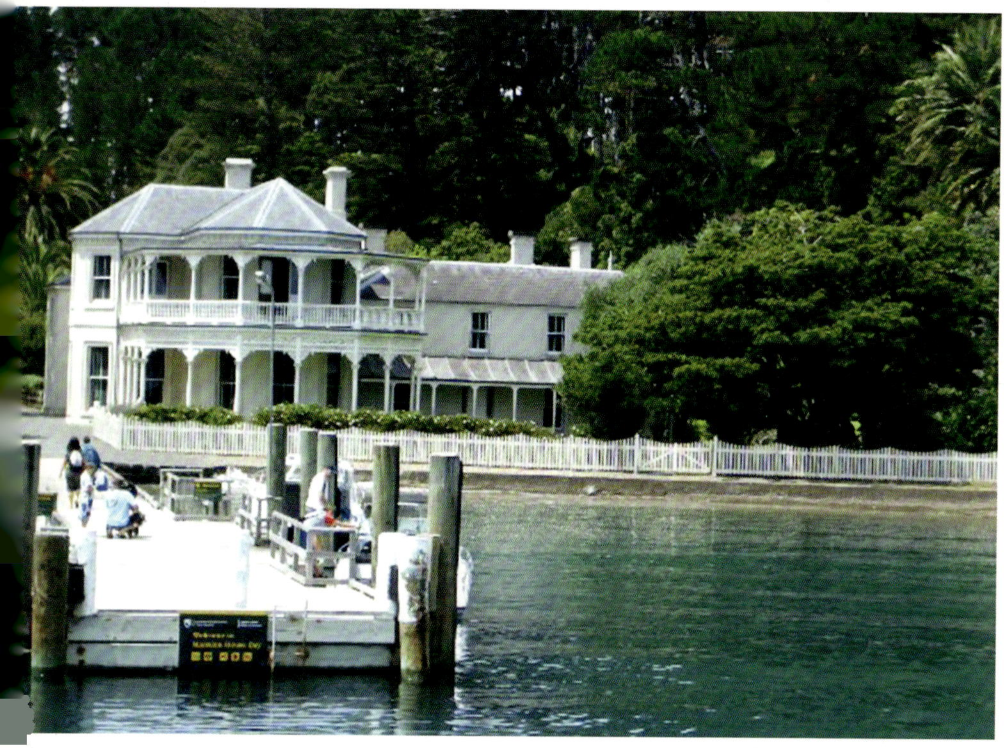

Above: Even the local cattle enjoy the views at Tawharanui Regional Park, outside Warkworth.
Left: Wenderholm is a wonderful combination of beach, bush and an historic homestead.
Bottom: Te Hauri Bay at Shakespear Regional Park on the Whangaparaoa Peninsula.
Opposite above left: Kitekite Falls near Piha on the west coast is an easy walk through lush bush.
Opposite above right: Waitakere Dam commands extensive views over the bush and valley below.
Right: The Gap at Piha, a popular black sand beach west of Auckland, was once the lair of the legendary taniwha, Kaiwhare.

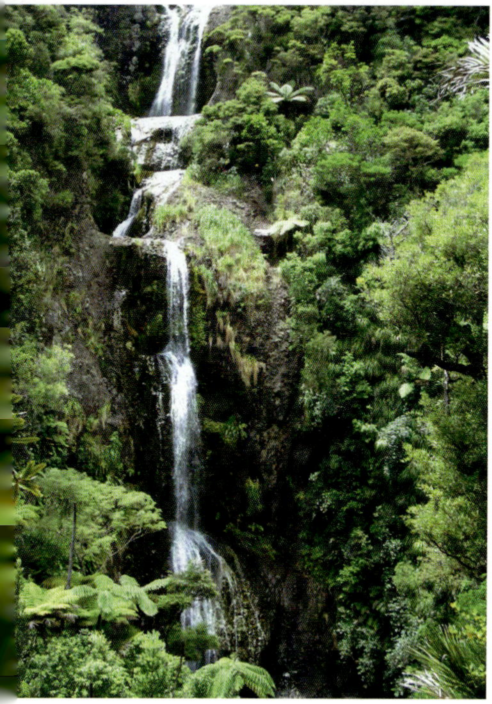

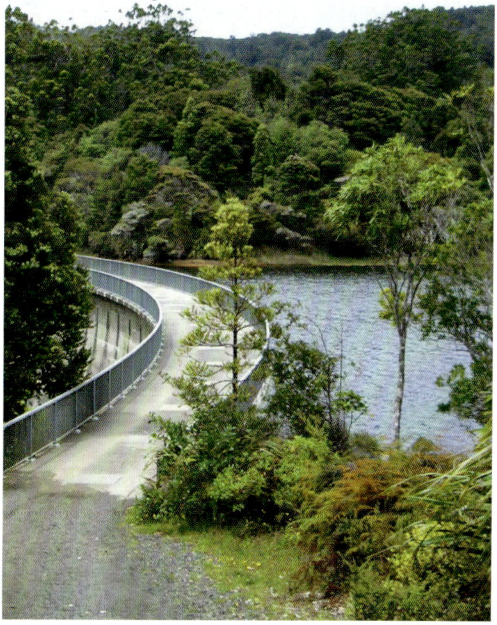

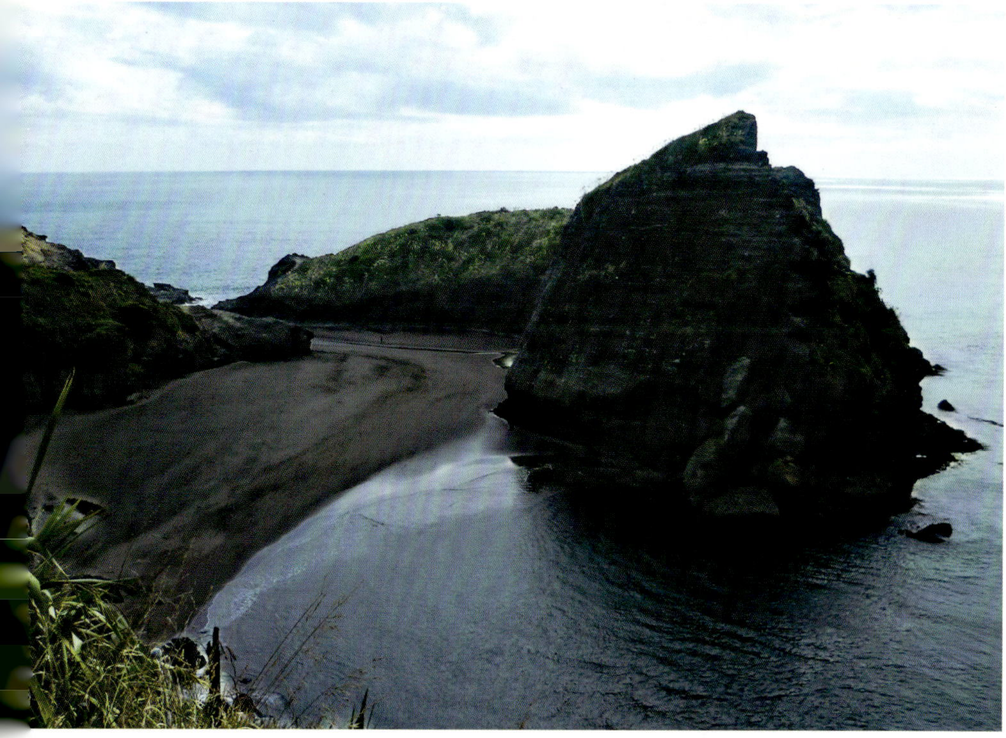

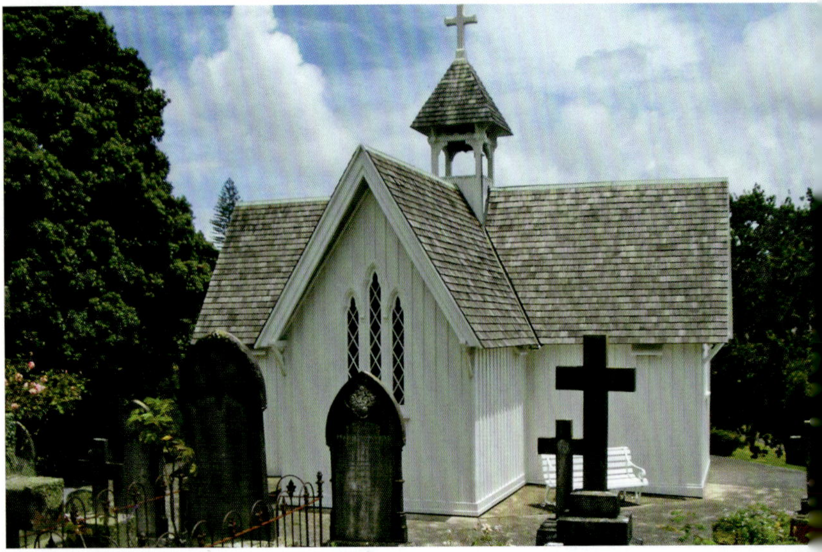

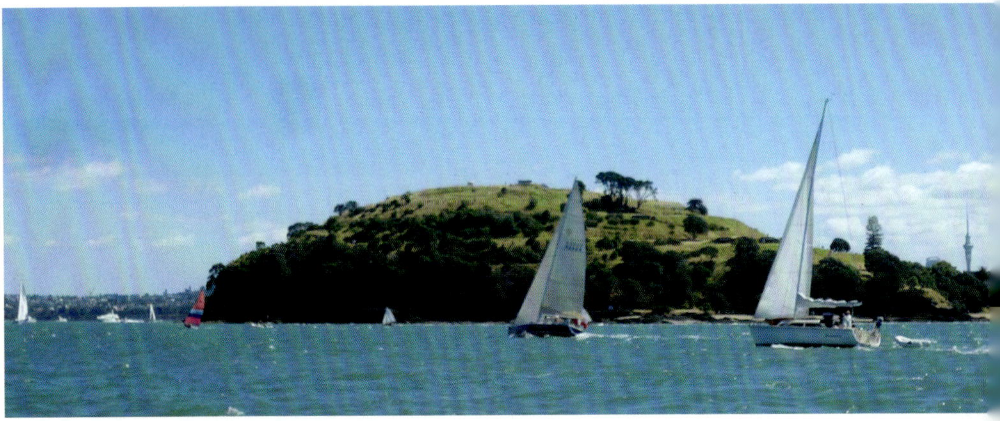

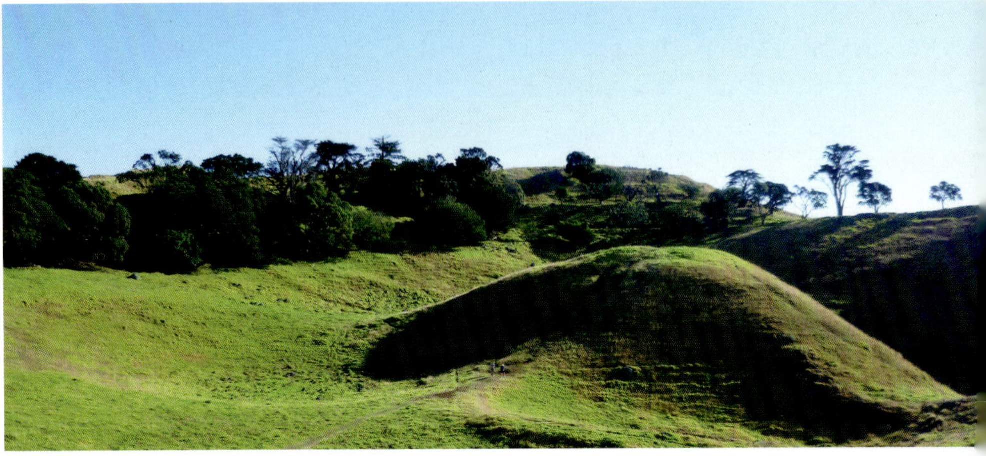

Opposite left: Built in 1857, St Stephen's Chapel overlooks Judges Bay, in Auckland's Parnell.

Opposite below: North Head in Devonport was fortified in 1885 to protect Auckland from a Russian invasion.

Opposite bottom: A lava dome takes centre stage in the crater of Mangere Mountain.

Right above: Hulme Cottage in historic Parnell is said to be the oldest building in Auckland.

Right below: The sea caves at Whatipu, near Titirangi were once the scene of local dances.

Bottom left: Duder Regional Park offers great views over the Hauraki Gulf.

Bottom right: Test your fitness on the steep sandhills at Lake Waimanu, near Bethells Beach on Auckland's west coast.

Above left: Bridal Veil Falls near Raglan is one of the Waikato's most popular attractions.
Above right: It is a steep walk up to where Wairere Falls tumbles down the Kaimai Ranges, just south of Te Aroha.
Right: Dense bush lines the Mangaoweka Gorge near Te Kuiti.
Below: The railway bridge over the Ohinemuri River is now part of a walkway through the Karangahake Gorge, between Paeroa and Waihi.

Above: The Victoria Bridge spans the Waikato River at Hamilton.
Right: The Windows Walk overlooks the Waitawheta River near the Karangahake Gorge.
Below: Te Toto Gorge near Raglan is exposed to constant fierce winds.

Above: The peak of Paku at Tairua affords spectacular views over Pauanui on the Coromandel Peninsula.

Left: Even in summer the beautiful beach at Opoutere can be largely deserted.

Below: New Chums Beach is a short easy walk from Whangapoua Beach.

Above: The walk around Lake Rotoroa in the centre of Hamilton is flat all the way.
Left: The meeting house at Ohinemutu is one of the highlights of a walk around central Rotorua.
Below left: Over 200,000 litres of water per second pour over the Huka Falls.
Below right: The Craters of the Moon is an active geothermal area near Taupo.

Above left: Pohutukawa-fringed Orokawa Bay is a short walk from Waihi Beach.
Above right: Papamoa Regional Park in the Bay of Plenty has no fewer than seven historic pa sites.
Left: Take a peaceful stroll along the Haiku Walk in Katikati.
Below: The steep climb to the top of Mauo/Mt Maunganui is well worth the effort.

Above: Panekiri Bluff dominates Lake Waikaremoana.
Right: Otatara Pa near Taradale is one of the largest pa sites in New Zealand.
Below left: Te Mata Peak has expansive views over the Hawkes Bay.
Below right: The Masonic Hotel is one of Napier's many Art Deco buildings.

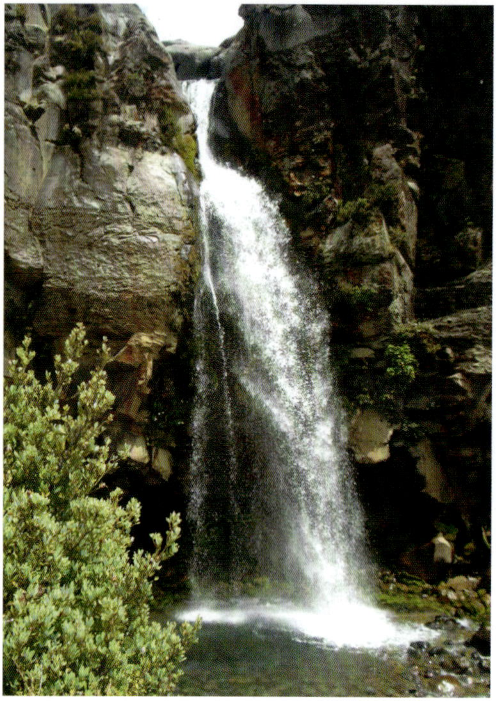
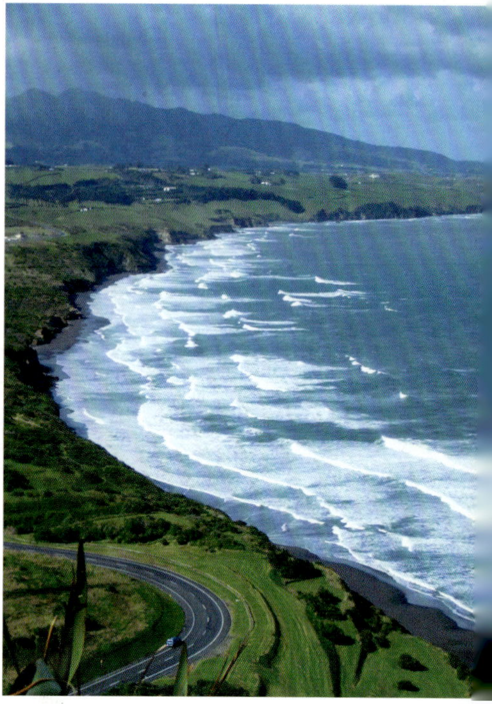
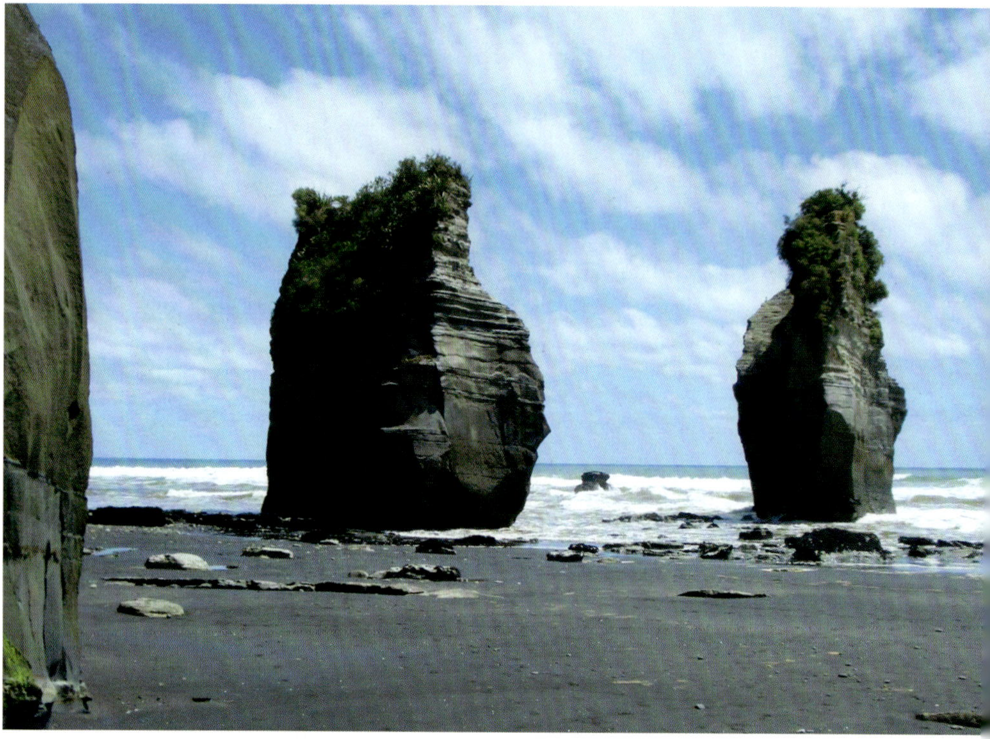

Opposite above left: Taranaki Falls lies in the dramatic volcanic landscape of Tongariro National Park.
Opposite above right: Spectacular coastal views from the top of Paritutu in New Plymouth.
Opposite bottom: The Three Sisters stand in the endless surf at northern Taranaki.
Above: Kapiti Island from the dunes at Queen Elizabeth Park between Paekakariki and Raumati, near Wellington.
Right: Deep gullies are a feature of the 'badlands' at the Putangarua Pinnacles.

Above: A long flight of stairs lead to the storybook lighthouse at Cape Palliser.
Right: Native plants star at the Otari-Wilton's Bush gardens and reserve in Wellington.
Below left: Korokoro was New Zealand's first gravity-fed dam, built in 1903.
Below right: A stroll along Wellington's waterfront reaps rich rewards.

11 Shine Falls
The highest waterfall in Hawke's Bay.

Grade: Easy. **Time:** One and a half hours return.
How to get there: At the Tutira store, on SH2, 45 km north of Napier, turn into Matahorua Road. At the junction with Pohokura veer to the right (still Matahorua Road) and after 5 km veer to the left into Heays Access Road – the track begins on the left 7 km down this road.

At 58 m Shine Falls are the highest waterfall in Hawke's Bay, and certainly one of the most attractive in the North Island, with two streams breaking into a myriad of rivulets spreading over a broad rockface into a wide, deep pool. The falls are located in an 800-hectare 'mainland island', and intensive predator management has resulted in an obvious recovery of both bird and plant life. Recently both kokako and kiwi have been reintroduced.

The first section of the track leads through farmland, along a limestone gorge with rocky bluffs towering above the stream. The second section is through recovering bush, the floor of the forest thick with regenerating seedlings; unlike much New Zealand forest, the bird life is conspicuous by its presence.

The sudden appearance of the waterfall at the very end of the track increases the appeal of the walk. It's a bit of journey to get to Shine Falls, and much of the road from Tutira is winding and gravel, but it's well worth the effort.

12 Opouahi Lake
A short walk around a beautiful small bush-fringed lake.

Grade: Easy. **Time:** 30 minutes return.
How to get there: At the Tutira store, on SH2, 45 km north of Napier, turn into Matahorua Road. At the junction with Pohokura Road turn left and the reserve is a further 4 km on the right.

Formed by a massive landslip in times long gone, Opouahi Lake is surprisingly deep at 24 m and is ringed by attractive bush, including some fine old kowhai trees. One of the few intact wetlands in Hawke's Bay, the lake supports a wide range of both bush and aquatic birdlife, including the rare spotless crake and brown kiwi. The track is well formed and flat all the way and a small jetty gives access to the lake for kayakers and swimmers.

13 Lake Tutira Refuge and Country Park
Waterbirds abound on this lake, once part of the famous Tutira Station.

Grade: Easy. **Time:** 20 mins return for the Lake Waikopiro Walk, and one and a half hours return for the combined Kahikanui and Galbraith tracks.
How to get there: SH2, 44 km north of Napier.

This popular walking and picnic spot was originally part of Tutira Station, owned by farmer and author Herbert Guthrie-Smith. Guthrie-Smith, who very early on recognised the need for conservation of native plants and birds, published his massive book, *Tutira: The story of a New Zealand sheep station* in 1921, based on years of painstaking observation. Today Lake Tutira is alive with waterbirds including ducks, pukeko, swans, herons and teal.

Adjoining Lake Tutira to the south is tiny Lake Waikopiro. The narrow strip of land running between the two lakes was the site of a very unusual pa, called Te Rewa. Taking advantage of the location, the pa was built up with tree trunks and protected by a moat. Even in 1882 few signs of the pa remained, and today a raised mound is the only trace. A number of other pa sites can be found on the eastern side of the lake.

The picnic area at the southern end of the lake was the site of the station's woolshed, and is now the beginning of several tracks in the Tutira Country Park. The walk around Lake Waikopiro takes about 20 minutes, while for a longer walk the Kahikanui and Galbraith tracks together form a loop on the eastern side of the lake. This walk begins at the very far end of the picnic area, and the track passes through regenerating native bush, taking in an old headland pa.

14 Te Ana and Tangoio Falls
Two waterfalls in Tangoio Falls Scenic Reserve.

- **Grade:** Easy. **Time:** 30 minutes return to the Te Ana Falls and one hour return to the Tangoio Falls.
- **How to get there:** Well signposted on SH2, 7 km north of Napier.

Not one but two attractive waterfalls are tucked away in the 550-ha bush reserve north of Napier, both very different. The Te Ana Falls plunges out of a gap in a rock face and into a small swimming hole, while the Tangoio Falls spreads gracefully over a wide rock face in a fern and moss-clad basin.

There is no signage indicating the track at the start of the walk, but if you cross the small bridge by the car park, and head right past the picnic tables, the wide track is obvious. A bit muddy in places, the gentle track leads through bush following the Kareaara Stream, first to the Te Ana Falls, at which point the track to the Tangoio Falls leads off to the right. This section is a bit rougher and muddier than the first half.

15 Waipatiki Reserve
A lowland nikau forest near a sandy beach.

- **Grade:** Medium. **Time:** One hour 15 minutes return.
- **How to get there:** From Napier take SH2 for 20 km and then turn right into Tangoio Road (follow the signposts to Waipatiki Beach). After 6 km turn into Waipatiki Road and the reserve is clearly marked to the left.

Dense with mosses, ferns and nikau palms, the subtropical nature of this reserve is so striking even locals claim this bush as unusual, when in fact the 64-hectare Waipatiki Reserve is a sad reminder of what is now lost. So little lowland forest remains in Hawke's Bay, yet even this small reserve with its dense nikau groves and 400-year-old trees bears scars of past logging, made obvious by the scarcity of very large trees and the presence of enormous stumps.

Part of the track within the bush was originally an old Maori trail linking the plains to the south with settlements around Wairoa. This was developed into a bridle trail in 1860, but by 1900 the inland road to Wairoa had been opened and the track fell into disuse.

The initial part of the track is a steep uphill climb to a junction with a sign referring to an 'upper' and 'lower' track – it doesn't matter which route you take as this part of the track is a loop. If you want to do the steep bit first, take the 'upper' track.

It's worthwhile taking some time to visit the very attractive, sandy Waipatiki Beach, which is just a few kilometres down the road at the bottom of the valley.

16 Art Deco Napier
Well-preserved art deco buildings.

Grade: Easy. **Time:** Allow one hour return.
How to get there: Begin the walk at Napier's Deco Centre at 163 Tennyson St.

On 3 February 1931 a massive earthquake caused widespread damage from Wairoa in the north to Dannevirke in the south, killing 258 people and devastating Hasting and Napier. Napier suffered particularly badly when fire broke out in the city centre. Large sections of Bluff Hill collapsed and the surrounding lagoons all but disappeared when the land rose 2 m. The city was rebuilt in what was then the most fashionable style – art deco, Spanish mission and stripped classic. As all the new buildings had to be built in concrete and low-rise, the resulting effect is surprisingly uniform and appealing. The area with most of the art deco building is concentrated on Tennyson, Hastings, Emerson and Herschell streets and Marine Parade.

Key buildings include the Scinde Building, the Daily Telegraph Building, State Insurance Building, Bank of New South Wales, Masonic Hotel, the Colonnade, the Soundshell, ASB Bank and the shop facades on Emerson Street.

Art Deco week is a popular event, celebrating the 1930s lifestyle. Held over a three-day period on the third weekend in February, the festival includes over 80 events ranging from picnics and themed dinners to jazz concerts, culminating in a huge street parade.

Just to the south of the city centre is Clive Square, with formal flower beds, a huge Moreton Bay fig tree and immensely tall Washingtonia palms. Set out as a garden in 1884, the square became a temporary shopping centre after the earthquake, affectionately known as 'Tin Town'.

17 Maraetotara Falls Heritage Walk
A great swimming hole and an old power station.

Grade: Easy. **Time:** 20 minutes return.

How to get there: Take the Waimarama Road out toward Ocean Beach – after leaving the Tukituki River the Maraetotara Road turns off to the right, with the falls entrance 2.5 km down this road, clearly marked by white painted fencing.

In 1922 the Havelock North Borough Council built a concrete weir on top of the existing falls to provide water for a small power station downstream. The power station is long gone, but today large trees shade the crystal-clear waters of the Maraetotara River, making this short walk particularly appealing. Below the falls is a large, deep swimming hole very popular in summer, and complete with a rope swing to drop swimmers deep into the cool waters.

While the walk is easy, at one point there is a stainless steel ladder down the side of the weir which needs a bit of careful negotiation.

18 Otatara Pa Historic Reserve
Two ancient pa high above the Tutaekuri River.

Grade: Medium. **Time:** One hour return.

How to get there: Springfield Road where Gloucester Street crosses the Tutaekuri River.

Situated high above the Tutaekuri River, the superb views from Otatara at the top of the hill encompass the Heretaunga Plain and far inland. The pa were established around 1400, and over time various iwi occupied this site. In the seventeenth century both came under attack by Ngati Kahungunu, under the leadership of Taraia. While Hikurangi fell, Taraia was unable to take Otatara and built a new pa at Pakowhai. A short time later he besieged and captured Otatara, which was then abandoned.

The pa are perfectly situated to take advantage of the resources of the shallow lagoons between the pa and the ocean, while the river gave access to inland forest resources. A large tidal lagoon, Te Whanganui a Orotu, an extension of the enormous Ahuriri Lagoon, originally came to the foot of the pa, but the 1931 earthquake effectively drained the land.

The site is huge, covering almost 100 ha, with terraces, house sites, kumara pits and defensive earthworks. Hikurangi occupies the summit while Otatara is more of a headland pa and has been partially destroyed by quarrying.

The addition of a carved gateway, palisades and tall pou give this reserve an ancient air, and the open site allows a clear view of terraces, defensive ditches, house sites and kumara pits. There is no single defined track, but the site is mostly farmland.

19 Te Mata Peak, Havelock North
Fantastic views of the rugged Te Mata Range.

- **Grade:** Medium.
- **Time:** Allow one hour return.
- **How to get there:** Te Mata Peak Road, Havelock North.

The legend of Te Mata arose from conflict between Waimarama on the coast and those living on the Heretaunga Plains. Heretaunga gathered at Pakipaki and came up with a plan involving Te Mata, chief of Waimarama, falling in love with Hinerakau, daughter of a Heretaunga chief. Te Mata had to complete a series of herculean tasks, one of which was to eat his way through the hills separating the coast and the plain, creating a path. On his very last bite, Te Mata choked and died; his body now forms the hills. The gap he created with his final mouthful is known as Pari Karangaranga or 'the echoing cliffs'. Hinerakau, consumed with grief, covered her dead husband with a blue cloak before leaping to her death from the peak.

The rugged, barren peak of Te Mata, 399 m above the Tukituki Valley, has spectacular views in every direction, from Mahia to the north to Ruapehu on a fine day. While it's easy to drive to the top, it's worth spending some time walking in this wonderful countryside. The hills are laced with a network of tracks, so it pays to check the information board at the park entrance.

An easy walk begins at the second car park just past the restaurant. This steady uphill track follows the escarpment overlooking the Tukituki River to Te Mata Peak. From here you can return down the road or continue past the main car park and along the ridge to the Redwood Grove, returning via the Te Mata Walk.

20 Lindsay Scenic Reserve, Waipukurau
A remnant of lowland bush alongside the pretty Tukituki River.

Grade: Easy. **Time:** 25 minutes return.

How to get there: After crossing the Tukituki River north from Waipukurau turn left into Lindsay Road, and after 2 km turn left into Scenic Road. At the stopbank turn right and park in the picnic area on the left.

Kahikatea dominates the treescape in this small reserve alongside the Tukituki River and this bush contains some very impressive specimens of New Zealand's tallest tree. Although the tracks are not well marked, it is impossible to get lost. There is also access to the river. While not really deep enough to swim, it's a pleasant spot to cool off on a hot day.

21 Mangatoro Scenic Reserve
A fine stand of totara and kahikatea.

Grade: Easy. **Time:** 30 minutes return.

How to get there: From Dannevirke take the road to Weber and after 11 km turn into Ngapaeruru Road – the reserve is on the right.

An easy walk through the 8-hectare reserve alongside the Mangatoro Stream passes through, including some very fine ones: tall kahikatea, rimu, matai and one especially impressive totara. One of New Zealand's iconic trees, totara is also one of the tallest, reaching up to 40 m, though in open country the crown will take on a more rounded, spreading appearance. Totara are easily identified by their shortly prickly dark leaves and flaking bark, which pulls away from the tree in long strips. Common throughout the country (though not found on Stewart Island), the wood splinters easily, but is very light and durable.

The stream is ideal for a swim on a hot day, and although the loop track is short, there are some rough and muddy patches.

13
short walks in
Taranaki

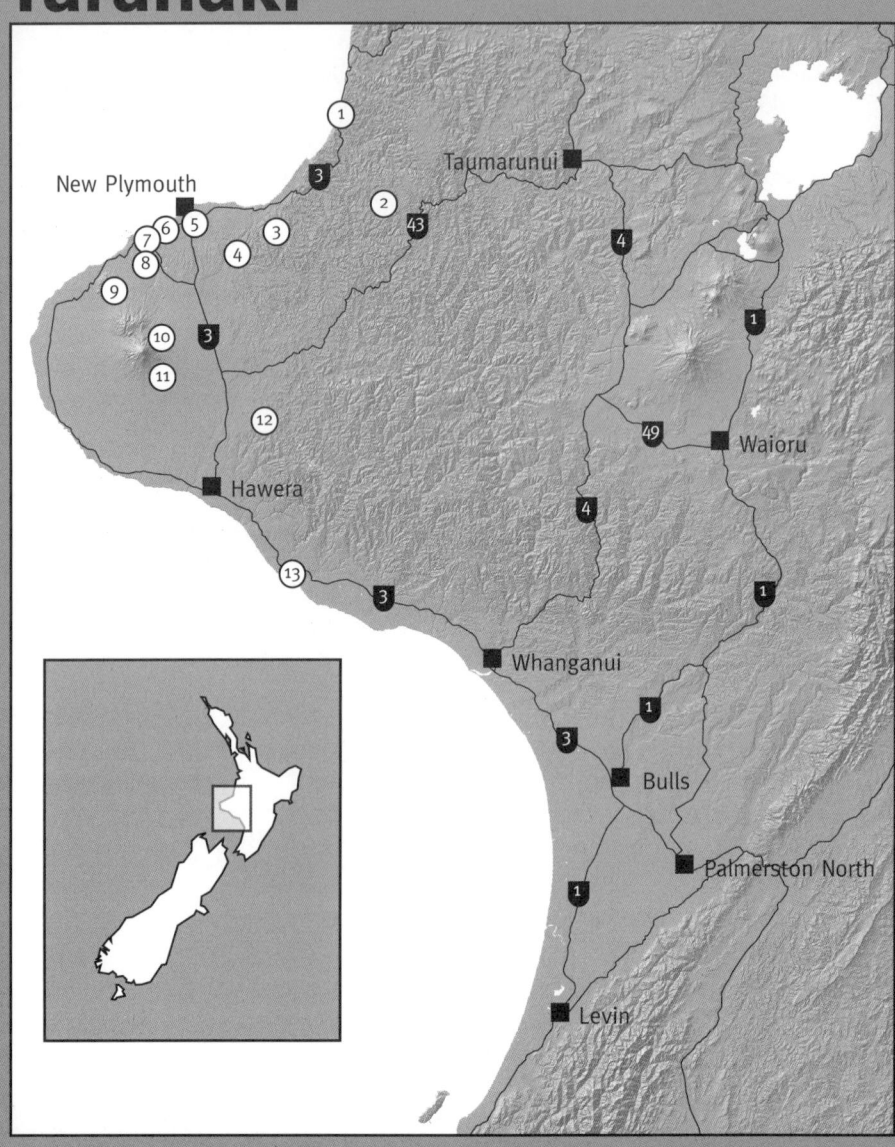

1 Three Sisters and an Elephant
Offshore rock stacks and dramatic coastal scenery.

Grade: Easy. **Time:** 30 minutes return.
How to get there: Clifton Road at the Tongaporutu River mouth, just south of Mokau.

Just offshore, near the mouth of the Tongaporutu River, are tall rock remnants known as the Three Sisters. Now nicknamed by locals as the 'two and a half sisters', two of the sisters are around 25 m, while the third is only a few metres high, worn away by the wind and tide. A century ago there was a fourth sister. Nearby is Elephant Rock, which – you guessed it – looks like an elephant. In addition to the sisters, there are several large caves and rock arches, one of which contains curious rock carvings of indeterminate origin.

The views along this rugged, wave-worn coast are dramatic, with Taranaki looming to the south, and offshore oil platforms just visible. However, the beach here is only accessible close to low tide (best on an outgoing tide) and even then you'll get your feet wet and your shoes very muddy.

2 Mount Damper Falls
The highest waterfall in the North Island.

Grade: Easy. **Time:** 45 minutes return.
How to get there: Moki Road, 16 km from the Whangamomona Road or from SH3 just south of Mokau.

At the Mt Damper Falls, a tributary of the Tongaporutu River plunges 74 m in a single fall over a sheer cliff into a pool below. The lookout point gives an excellent view high above the falls, but there is no access to the pool. A local story tells of the discovery of the falls by a local sheep farmer, who lost his prize sheepdog after it was dragged over the cliff by a wild boar.

Part of the track is through farmland, while closer to the falls the track enters pleasant bush. The track is rough and muddy, so make sure you wear old shoes.

3 Awatetake Pa

A bush-clad pa site overlooks the Waitara River.

Grade: Easy. **Time:** Allow 45 minutes return.

How to get there: From SH3 at Waitara take Princess Street, which eventually becomes Ngatimaru Road. The track begins on the corner where Ngatimaru Road meets Tikorangi Road West.

Located on a cliff high above the Waitara River, this pa is ringed on three sides by a single defensive ditch, one of the most impressive in the country. The description 'ditch' does these earthworks a great injustice, as even now they are very deep and broad, much more like a moat, and still difficult to scale. Once they would have been topped by a bank and palisading, making a very impressive and formidable sight. Rua or food pits are still visible throughout the pa, though today the site is covered in trees, including many old karaka and a particularly old totara, dating back to when the pa was occupied.

The track begins over a stile at the back of the gravel yard (and not down the farm track). From there it crosses farmland, marked by orange triangles, and is easy walking, but expect electric fences and gates.

4 Pukerangiora Pa

A key pa in the Taranaki War.

Grade: Easy. **Time:** 20 minutes return.

How to get there: From SH3 east of Waitara, turn into Waitara Road then continue for 7 km – the pa is on the left.

A major pa overlooking the Waitara River, Pukerangiora saw bitter fighting during the Musket Wars of the 1820s and 1830s. At one stage the pa fell to invaders, forcing many defenders, including women and children, to leap from the cliffs above the river.

During the New Zealand Wars of the 1860s, the pa was the centre of a campaign led by Major General Pratt, who adopted siege tactics, including a series of redoubts and a long sap, which are still clearly visible. Pratt's technique, described as 'a mile a month', drew criticism from the colonists; one report said, 'The war in Taranaki maintains its peaceful course.'

The British were not slow to adapt to Maori fighting techniques developed in response to the use of gun and cannon. Pa were built to withstand cannon fire and engineered to ensure that a full frontal assault was near suicidal. Moreover, Maori defenders would use a pa to slow down the attack and then quickly abandon the position to avoid heavy casualties in the face of an attacking force that had greater numbers and was better armed. In reality Major General Pratt knew that a drawn-out fight with careful advances was one tactic that would wear down his enemy, and when the sap eventually reached the palisading, a truce was agreed and the defenders abandoned the pa to Pratt.

The site is not well maintained and the signage is minimal and confusing, but don't be put off by that. The main car park is about 200 metres past the first sign and it is easy to miss. The military sap to the pa is behind the trees to the left of the first sign. The road from the turnoff is also signposted with the location of the redoubts built as part of the attack on the pa. From the point where the pa overlooks the river there are wide views back to the coast.

5 Te Henui Walkway, New Plymouth

A combination of mature native and exotic trees along a clear rocky stream.

Grade: Easy. **Time:** One and a half hours return to the Cumberland Bridge.

How to get there: With several entry points, the simplest is from the East End Reserve off the Coastal Walkway.

This deep, almost secret valley cuts across the city from the coast and is typical of the rocky streams cutting through this old volcanic landscape. The walk follows the stream though a mixture of mature native trees, formal landscaped gardens and exotic trees.

Two pa sites are located along Te Henui Stream and, typical of most pa in Taranaki, within 5 km of the sea. Walking upstream, the first – Pukewarangi – is on the hill to the left and recognisable by a group of tall pine trees crowning the summit. Parihamore is further upstream where the walkway finishes, at the end of Bell Street, behind the Polytechnic.

The valley shelters the track from the wind, the trees lending a cool atmosphere to an easy walk. When you reach the Cumberland Street Bridge you can either return the way you came or attempt the track on the south side of the stream, accessed immediately to the right of the bridge. This section of the walk is less developed and the signposting erratic, which can be very confusing for a visitor. It does, however, feature the historic Te Henui Cemetery with the graves of early settlers and soldiers, and the spectacular mosque-like Mohammed Islam Salaman tomb.

The Te Henui walkway is a good alternative if the weather is too rough for the waterfront walk.

6 New Plymouth Coastal Walkway
An excellent walkway along New Plymouth's waterfront.

Grade: Easy. **Time:** One and a half hours one way.
How to get there: Accessible at any point along the city's coastline.

New Plymouth has done a magnificent job of making its entire coastline accessible to the public, and this walkway is so popular that at times it has the feel of a pedestrian motorway. Walkers jostle with joggers, prams, skateboarders, roller-bladers and cyclists. Covering 12.5km from the port to Bell Block, the walk has coastal views, city beaches, boulder-strewn banks, sand dunes and in the north, the sheltered Lake Rotomanu. A highlight near the city centre is Len Lye's Wind Wand, 45 m high, made of fibreglass and designed to sway dramatically in the wind. In the north the stylish Te Rewa Rewa bridge, designed to reflect a breaking wave crosses the tidal Waiwhakaiho River.

The coastline is exposed to strong prevailing winds, but if the wind becomes too much, an alternative is to return via the more sheltered streets. Most people access the walkway from the city centre and parking here can be problematic, so as an alternative you can begin at one of the several access points north of the city with much easier (and free) parking.

7 Paritutu Rock
Dramatic coastal views.

Grade: Hard. **Time:** 30 minutes return.
How to get there: Centennial Drive, New Plymouth, near the port.

Paritutu and the seven small Sugarloaf Islands just offshore near New Plymouth's main port are the remains of old volcanic plugs, with the outer cone long since eroded. Undersea the terrain is just as interesting, with reefs, canyons and cliffs creating a unique marine habitat.

Established as a Marine Park in 1991, the islands are home to a wide range of seabirds and dolphins; whales frequent the area, with one of the islands once a whaling station.

Although the flat area at the top isn't very large, Paritutu was used as a pa by Te Atiawa right up into the 1830s, holding out against attack from Waikato in 1832, while other pa in the area fell. Nothing the Waikato warriors offered could induce the defenders to come down from their eyrie. Paritutu was well-stocked with food, though water was a problem with the only source halfway down the western face. This was solved by lowering someone down the cliff at night with calabashes, which were then hauled back to the summit. Any attempt to disrupt this by the enemy drew musket fire from the offshore island pa of Mataora and Motu o Tamatea and Paritutu survived the siege.

The climb to the top is steep and not for those afraid of heights, the rocky scramble made easier by steps and wire railings. The views are spectacular, south along the coast, southeast to the mountain and north over the port and city.

8 Ratapihipihi Reserve
Luxurious lowland bush on the outskirts of New Plymouth.

- **Grade:** Easy. **Time:** Two loops: one 20 minutes return; the other 30 minutes return.
- **How to get there:** At the end of Ratapihi Road off Cowling Road on the south side of New Plymouth.

Today the lowland forest of Taranaki is long gone, but this beautiful reserve is a rare view of what the bush was like before people arrived. The bush takes its name from a traditional method of hunting birds. By blowing through a leaf, a hunter perched high in a tree would attract birds such as kaka to come close enough to be killed by a blow from a short club.

There are two loop tracks on excellent paths and the walking is easy, with just some steps to climb.

9 Koru Pa, Oakura
An unusual stone pa.

Grade: Easy. **Time:** 30 minutes return.
How to get there: At Oakura turn left into Wairau Road and follow the signposts 4 km down this road.

Occupied from around 1000 AD to 1826, this is one of New Zealand's most ancient pa sites. Overlooking the Oakura River, Koru pa is unusual in the use of stone, which is very rare in New Zealand, where wood is more readily available. Occupied by Nga Mahanga a Tairi for many centuries, the pa fell to an overwhelming force of Te Atiawa in the early nineteenth century, and was finally abandoned in the 1820s, in the face of the Waikato invasion.

The site is well preserved with terraces, food pits and defensive ditches clearly outlined, with river stones used extensively on the outer facings of the ditches. The pa is bush-covered, which makes exploration more intriguing, though there is a good view of the river from a lookout point. The use of stone has been seen as evidence by some theorists that Aotearoa was inhabited by an ancient stone-using culture long before 1000 AD.

The walk to the pa is through a grassy open paddock and then through bush on the pa itself. Don't climb on the steep banks as the fragile stonework is easily damaged.

10 North Taranaki, Egmont National Park
Alpine vegetation and great views.

Grade: Mountain extremely challenging, walks medium.
Time: Veronica Loop Track – 2 hours, Holly Hut Track Lookout – 1 hour return.
How to get there: 12 km from New Plymouth, turn off SH3 at Egmont Village and follow Egmont Road to the North Egmont Visitor Centre.

No mountain in this country is more imposing or dramatic than Taranaki, standing alone and surrounded by some of the most fertile land in the country. The splendour of this peak wins the hearts of Maori and Pakeha alike; most New Zealanders know the story of the fight between Tongariro and Taranaki over the beautiful Pihanga, with the loser, Taranaki, heading off towards the setting sun.

Taranaki has a unique ecosystem, isolated from other mountainous areas of the North Island, the region has one of the highest rainfalls in New Zealand. The forest is goblin-like with every tree and rock festooned with lichens, mosses and ferns, all flourishing in the cool, very wet climate.

North Egmont is the most direct and popular starting point for climbing to the summit, a serious challenge which should only be undertaken with proper alpine gear and a good level of fitness even in summer. However, a number of good short walks start at the North Egmont Visitor Centre (altitude 936 m) and climb quickly through the forest to more sparse subalpine vegetation with hebes, tussocks and alpine plants, to lookout points with marvellous views over the coast. The centre itself has excellent displays of the natural and human history of Taranaki.

The Veronica Loop Track takes two hours return and is entirely within submontane forest with lower areas dense with ferns and mosses, while on the higher slopes of the track the vegetation is more open. The Holly Hut Track lookout (medium grade, one hour return) is found by following the Veronica Loop Track uphill to the junction with the Holly Hut Track. There are broad views over the Taranaki lowlands, while the mountain looms high above the track. Even within this short distance the vegetation changes markedly from alpine forest to more open subalpine shrubs and tussock. While this walk is all uphill, the track is well formed and the grade is more steady than steep.

11 Kapuni Loop Track, Dawson Falls
Virgin mountain forest frames an attractive waterfall.

- **Grade:** Medium. **Time:** One hour return.
- **How to get there:** Turn off from the centre of Stratford and follow the signs for 19 km.

A long drive through thick bush leads to the Dawson Falls Visitor Centre, the starting point for a number of tracks on the south side of Taranaki. The centre has up-to-date information on the tracks and weather and detailed displays on the unique flora and fauna. The falls were rediscovered in 1883 and named after the local postmaster at Manaia, Thomas Dawson, though they were already known to Maori as Te Rere o Noke after the prankster Noke, who hid behind the falls to escape his enemies when one of his practical jokes went too far. The Dawson Falls Hotel was built in 1895 and still offers accommodation.

The short track to the falls is well signposted and just below the car park. Leading through moss- and fern-encrusted forest, the track goes down steep steps, which are constantly wet and can be slippery.
The 18-m falls drop over an ancient lava flow, throwing up a continuous spray, adding to the high rainfall and keeping the vegetation wet throughout the year.

12 Lake Rotokare
A beautiful bush-fringed lake hidden in the Taranaki hills.

Grade: Easy. **Time:** One hour 30 minutes return.
How to get there: Turn into Anderson Road off SH3 just north of Eltham, turn left at Rawhitiroa Road and then right into Sangster Road.

Very little lowland forest has survived in Taranaki so this bush-fringed lake located in hill country east of Eltham comes as a surprise and unlike other Taranaki lakes, Rotokare is naturally formed and spring fed. Extensive beds of raupo ring this lake with its fiord-like arms, and the surrounding hills are densely covered by forest that includes mature kahikatea, maire and totara, even though the area was milled well into the middle of last century. A predator proof fence now surrounds the entire reserve which has huge enhanced the birdlife particularly kiwi and tieke and even the shy bittern despite the lake being popular with boaties and water skiers (though use is seasonally limited). There is an excellent information centre along with toilets and picnic tables by the lake. The walk around the lake starts from the carpark and is flat and easy.

13 Patea River
Views of an ancient pa and a derelict freezing works.

Grade: Easy. **Time:** 40 minutes return.
How to get there: The best point to start from is the car park at the river mouth, at the end of Beach Road.

Beginning from the old breakwater at the mouth of the river, this is a curious walk with the main highlights on the other side of the river, and best viewed from the walkway. The track meanders over sandy bluffs along the tidal Patea River.

The area was settled by the great Polynesian navigator Turi, who journeyed from Hawaiki and landed at Aotea Harbour, just north of Kawhia. From there Turi, his wife and a band of followers trekked overland through very rugged country and dense bush to make their home at the mouth of the Patea River. The famous monument to Turi and the waka *Aotea* is in the main street of Patea and is a rare example of New Zealand folk art.

Directly across the river is an impressive rocky bluff, the location of a formidable pa, one even the great warrior chief Te Rauparaha chose to bypass. The nineteenth-century watercolourist Charles Heaphy painted the fortified pa in 1839 and called it simply *Patea*. Later Edward Wakefield named the pa Haere Hau and noted that 'an assault would have been sheer madness'.

Further along the track is a view to the derelict Patea freezing works, once the economic mainstay of the town. The freezing works began life in 1883 as the West Coast Meat and Produce Company and at its height employed over 800 workers, before finally closing in 1982. The abandoned buildings slowly crumbled and collapsed, creating a scene of industrial decay not often seen in New Zealand, until fire swept through and destroyed the buildings in 2008.

Back at the breakwater is a small safe swimming beach and a very pleasant picnic area.

14
short walks in
Whanganui, Rangitikei, Manawatu, Horowhenua and Kapiti

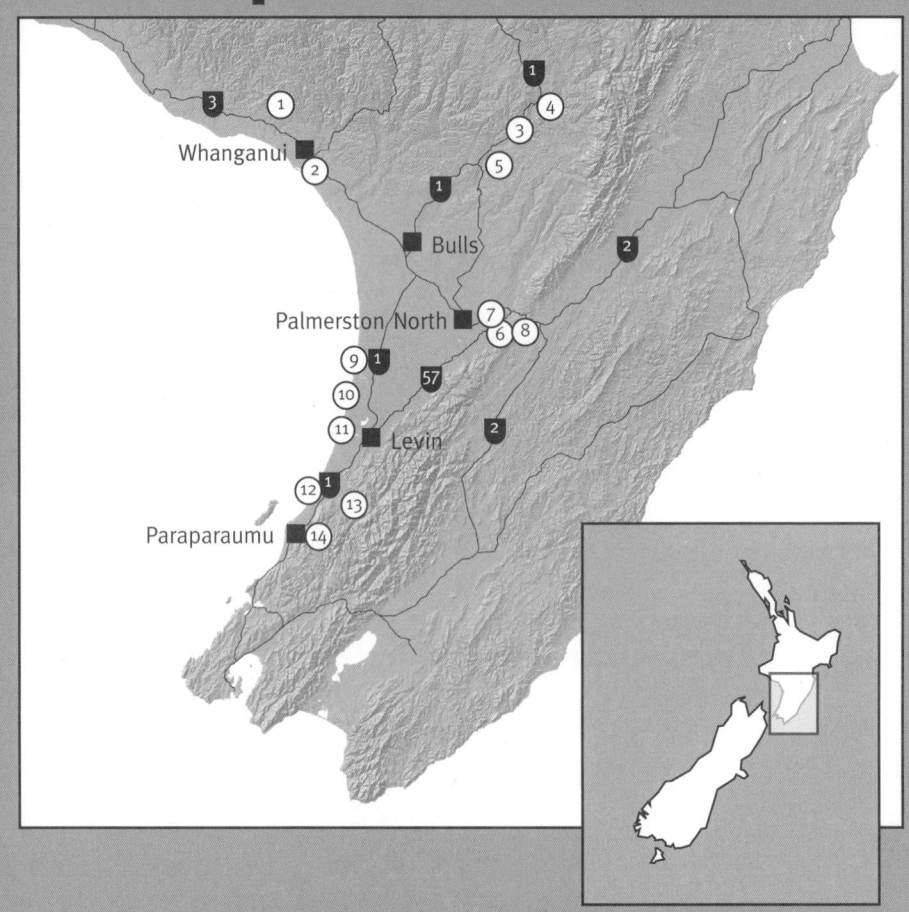

1 Bushy Park, Whanganui

A rare remnant of lowland rainforest, with an ancient rata.

- **Grade:** Easy. **Time:** Allow one hour.
- **How to get there:** Turn off SH3 at Kai Iwi, and follow Rangitatau East Road for 8 km to Bushy Park.

Owned and administered by the Forest and Bird Society, Bushy Park is a 90-hectare bush remnant and was bequeathed to the society in 1962 by Frank Moore, whose family had farmed the area since the 1860s. The heart of Bushy Park is a magnificent Victorian homestead complete with period furniture; outbuildings include stables and a small museum.

Visitors enter through double automated gates as the bush is now surrounded by a predator-proof fence built in 2004, in an effort to protect and restore native birdlife. The bush itself contains a network of tracks, all fairly easy to follow, with a host of informative labels and panels making this a great place to improve your knowledge of native trees and shrubs. A highlight among the many large trees is an old northern rata (possibly 1000 years old) said to be the largest surviving example of the northern species, with a height of 43 m and a girth of 12 m.

There is a small charge to enter, and Bushy Park offers light meals, accommodation and conference facilities.

2 Whanganui River Walk

A stroll along the banks of the Whanganui River.

- **Grade:** Easy. **Time:** Up to one and a half hours return.
- **How to get there:** Begin at the City Bridge at the end of Victoria Ave.

In legend the Whanganui River was created by Taranaki after his battle with Tongariro, when he headed south, carving out the river valley. He turned west at the coast, filling the valley behind him with tears. Kupe is said to have discovered the rivermouth, but the waka *Takitimu*, captained by Tamatea, first explored the river, closely followed by the *Aotea*, whose people later settled here.

In 1930 Whanganui was New Zealand's fifth largest city, but a lack of hinterland and the river's decline as an important accessway meant progress slowed, but left Whanganui with an outstanding collection of Victorian and Edwardian buildings.

In local Maori dialect the 'h' is silent, replaced by a short glottal stop. Ideally the word should be written 'W'anganui', but became *Wanganui*, reflecting local pronunciation. Following the wishes of local iwi, the New Zealand Geographic Board changed the river to *Whanganui*, but a referendum strongly favoured *Wanganui*.

Beginning at the City Bridge, follow the river upstream along Taupo Quay and into Somme Parade, past restored Victorian commercial buildings. This is the home of the *Waimarie*, lone survivor of a fleet of river paddlesteamers.

At the Dublin Street Bridge cross the river into Kowhai Park, a stretch of mature trees, plus a children's playground and excellent picnic spots. Exiting the park walk along Anzac Parade. Opposite the City Bridge is an historic elevator to the 33-m stone tower on Durie Hill, built in 1919, with great views over the city.

Return to Anzac Parade and cross the City Bridge back into the main street. The very impressive Post Office building (1902) on the corner of Victoria Ave and Ridgway Street, reflects the city's past. Further up the avenue is the National Bank, looking distinctly Victorian, with huge Ionic columns, though constructed in 1929.

Cross over and continue uphill to Queen's Park. Originally the site of Pukenamu pa, this hill was occupied by the Rutland Stockade during the New Zealand Wars. Now Whanganui's cultural heart, the hill is crowned by the Sarjeant Gallery. Constructed of Oamaru stone in 1919, it was purpose-built, designed to take maximum advantage of natural light. To one side of the park is the Whanganui Museum, housing a superb waka taua and a fine collection of Lindauer paintings. On the city side is the War Memorial Hall, winner of the New Zealand Institute of Architects Gold Medal.

Return to Victoria Ave and cross directly down Maria Place to St Hill Street. Directly ahead is Cooks Gardens Bell Tower, built on the site of the old York Stockade; the 1874 fire bell was used to ring the alarm for any fires in the city. In January 1962 Peter Snell ran New Zealand's first sub-four-minute-mile here.

At 69 St Hill Street is the elegant Whanganui Opera House. Built in 1899, this wooden building was the centre of entertainment in early Whanganui.

3 Mangaweka Scenic Reserve
Virgin bush above Mangaweka township.

- **Grade:** Medium. **Time:** 45 minutes return.
- **How to get there:** Just south of Mangaweka turn off SH1 into Te Kapua Road. The track begins about 1 km along this road but is not well marked, with a small sign reading 'DOC Walking Track'.

An old section of the Main Trunk railway line has been turned into a walkway. The track starts along a wide grassy track and the fragile nature of the papa rock is evident, with small rocks fallen from the crumbling banks littering the track. The track climbs steeply into the bush, levelling off as it winds its way among huge old rimu and totara trees. On the downhill section there are excellent views over Mangaweka township, the Rangitikei River and the dramatic papa cliffs so characteristic of the area.

4 Mangaweka Power Station
An old power station alongside the Rangitikei River.

- **Grade:** Easy. **Time:** 20 minutes return.
- **How to get there:** Just north of Mangaweka turn off SH1 into Ruahine Road, cross over the river and turn next left into Kawhatau Valley Road – the power station is on the left after 250 m.

Built in 1913 (primarily as a water reservoir; electricity was considered a minor byproduct), the power station in fact made Mangaweka one of the earliest towns in New Zealand to have a power supply. Little remains of the tiny power station, where a small building containing historic photographs shelters the site. The location is impressive. Across the river is the towering rail viaduct over the Rangitikei River, flanked by steep cliffs, and across the road is a short walk up to the weir along the Mangawharariki River. This beautiful small rocky gorge, scoured and shaped by eons of water action, leads to a concrete weir which is still intact. To the right of this is a small brick-lined tunnel. This was the original water intake for the power station, and a log which jammed the tunnel in 1937, causing the station to finally close, is still visible. Below the weir is a great swimming hole, though it's a bit of a tricky scramble to reach.

5 Pryce's Rahui Bush Reserve, Rangitikei
Huge native trees in rare lowland bush.

- **Grade:** Easy. **Time:** 30 minutes to one hour return.
- **How to get there:** At Rata turn off SH1 into Putorino Road – the reserve is 10 km down this road.

Though just a short distance off SH1, this magnificent small bush reserve doesn't attract many visitors and you are very likely to have the place to yourself. Located on an old river terrace of the Rangitikei River, Pryce's Rahui contains some huge trees, including kahikatea, matai, totara and kowhai. One kowhai stands over 10 m and certainly makes you reconsider the idea of a kowhai as a 'small' tree suitable for a courtyard garden.

There are a number of tracks marked in different colours, none of them particularly long (the kowhai is on the red track, and a giant matai on the yellow track). The red/blue combination will take around 30 minutes, while the yellow track takes around 60 minutes. Though it's a bit overgrown, the reserve is small.

6 Sledge Track, Kahuterawa Valley, Manawatu
A rocky stream cascades down a bush-clad valley.

- **Grade:** Easy. **Time:** One hour return to Argyle Rocks.
- **How to get there:** From Palmerston North head south towards Shannon, then turn left towards Woodville on SH57 – just past the junction turn immediately right into Kahuterawa Road. Continue down this road to the car park, 3.5 km past where the seal ends (the Kahuterawa Reserve is not the beginning of the track).

The Sledge Track begins to the left of the historic Black Bridge, built in 1900, and continues up the left-hand side of the stream along a steep bush-clad valley. Largely regenerated, the bush is attractive, with water dripping over moss-covered rocks, while below the stream tumbles over river boulders. Along the way there are a number of good swimming holes, including Argyle Rocks, a collection of large worn river boulders creating a pool in the river. Just beyond Argyle Rocks, Foulds Falls is a pretty waterfall on a side stream to the left of the track, although pine plantations on the other side of the valley detract a little from the experience. For the active the track continues on for another 2 km to a lookout point, and the return is by the same track.

7 Savage Crescent, Palmerston North
One of the best examples of unaltered early state housing.

- **Grade:** Easy. **Time:** One hour return.
- **How to get there:** Access off either College Street or Park Road between Botanical Road and Cook Street.

One of the Labour leader Michael Joseph Savage's key promises was to provide good housing for New Zealand's working population (as opposed to the poor), and the election of his government in 1935 heralded a boom in state housing, which lasted for decades. While state housing is ubiquitous throughout New Zealand, what makes Savage Crescent unique is that it is an early example of state domestic architecture, and has survived largely intact and unaltered. Developed between 1939 and 1946, the housing styles are varied, and contrast greatly with the more familiar 1950s weatherboard and tile houses. In addition, a park was developed in the heart of the Crescent to provide a recreation area for the neighbourhood. A leisurely walk around the Crescent will take an hour.

8 The Manawatu Gorge
An unusual river gorge.

- **Grade:** Medium. **Time:** Three hours one way.
- **How to get there:** SH 3 through the gorge has closed. From the Ashurst end take the Napier Road (old SH 3) and the parking area is 1 km from the bridge over the Manawatu River, east of Ashhurst. At the Woodville end the track begins on Balance Gorge Road just across the Balance Bridge.

Unlike most river gorges, created when a river cuts through hill country, the Manawatu Gorge was created in reverse – the river was there first. As the Ruahine Range rose along the Wellington fault line over the last million years, the river stayed put, creating the 6 km gorge.

As with many natural features, the creation of the Manawatu Gorge is steeped in mythology. On the heights of the Puketoi Range (east of Pahiatua) grew a giant totara with a deep passion to reach the sea. The mighty tree came down from the hills, at first turning northwest, gouging out the valley where the Mangatainoka River now runs. Its way to the east was blocked by the Tararua Range, but its desire to reach the sea was so great the tree smashed its way through, creating the Manawatu Gorge and the lower reaches of the river, finally reaching the coast at modern-day Foxton. The gorge was also known to Maori as Te Apiti, the narrow passage, and Te Au rere a te tonga, the rushing current of the south.

A track runs the length of the southern side of the gorge, though for the most part it doesn't follow the gorge, running slightly inland. With good views of the gorge, the grades are comfortable, though steep in places, and the track is excellent so it isn't a difficult walk, but you will need to organise return transport.

The road through the gorge permanently closed in 2017

9 Manawatu Estuary and Foxton Beach
A bird watching paradise by the beach.

Grade: Easy. **Time:** Estuary Walk – 45 minutes return. Dune Walk – 45 minutes return.

How to get there: Carpark at the end of Pinewood Road, off Holben Esplanade, Foxton Beach.

As the Manawatu River reaches the sea, it forms a broad and lazy S bend before meeting the Tasman Sea at Foxton Beach. This wide estuary of saltmarsh, tidal flats and sand dunes is the most important aquatic and wading bird habitat in the southern North Island and was declared a Wetland of International Importance in 2005. More bird species have been recorded here than anywhere else in New Zealand despite the river being among the top five most polluted rivers in New Zealand. Over 110 species have been spotted in the protected area which covers over 500 hectares on both banks of the river including 28 listed as national critical or nationally threatened. Godwit, wrybill, royal spoonbill, lesser knot, along with red-billed gulls, oyster catchers, pied stilts and black-backed gulls are all found here.

In recent years this area has been much improved and the path along the estuary has a bird hide, a lookout point at Dawick Ave and excellent information signage all along the river.

There are basically two choices of walk, both flat and easy. The first leads upriver along the estuary to the boat club and it is here that you will see the most birds. The second walk heads down to the sea and forms a loop through the partially protected dunes and along the river mouth. This route is also used by 4WD vehicles so take care.

10 Wreck of the *Hyderabad*, Waitarere Beach, Horowhenua
The remains of an old sailing ship.

Grade: Easy. **Time:** 30 minutes return.
How to get there: Off SH1 down Waitarere Beach Road 6.5 km north of Levin. At the beach turn left into Rua Avenue to Hyderabad Place.

Nothing beats the romance of a shipwreck, particularly the remains of an old sailing ship. But all that's left of the cotton trader *Hyderabad* are her rusting outlines after she was driven hard ashore in a storm in 1878, on a voyage from Lyttelton to Adelaide. No lives were lost, but the *Hyderabad* could not be refloated, though its cargo was quickly salvaged. Over the years the ship has been stripped of anything remotely valuable. Today only an outline of its ghostly shape remains, periodically covered and uncovered by the wind-driven sands.

From Hyderabad Place go on to the driftwood-littered beach and head south for about 10 to 15 minutes, where the outline of the wreck is clearly visible from a distance.

11 Lake Papaitonga
Dense virgin bush surrounds a small lake with two historic pa sites.

Grade: Easy. **Time:** 40 minutes return to the Otomuri lookout.
How to get there: 4 km south of Levin turn off SH1 into Hokio Beach Road and Lake Papaitonga is signposted to the left.

Papaitonga is a small lake in fine lowland bush, with titoki, kahikatea, nikau, karaka and kiekie. In 1897 noted naturalist Sir Walter Buller preserved this small piece of bush, and today the wetland is home to the elusive bittern and spotless crake. The walk begins through mature forest, crossing a small area of swampland before gently climbing to a lookout.

There are two small islands in the lake, Motukiwi and Motungarara. The smaller was artificially constructed, and both were occupied, protected by the lake.

In the early 1820s Ngati Toa chief Te Rauparaha visited with his family, hosted by Muaupoko at Te Wi near Papaitonga. Suspecting Te Rauparaha's real intentions, Muaupoko decided to kill the visitors. Te Rauparaha narrowly escaped, though his son and daughter and many of his relatives died. Biding his time, Te Rauparaha sought revenge.

In 1823 Te Rauparaha attacked the two pa, and one after the other they fell. Only a handful managed to escape the slaughter, but Te Rauparaha wasn't finished. After the 1823 attack, the few survivors returned and in 1827 they were again attacked by Ngati Toa. This time they were almost entirely annihilated, with just a few survivors fleeing into the mountains or finding refuge with other tribes. The lake pa were never reoccupied.

The track is in excellent condition, winding through fine lowland forest, with boardwalks through the swampy sections to two lookouts over the lake.

12 Waikanae River Estuary and Beach Walk
Picturesque views along the beach.

- **Grade:** Easy. **Time:** 50 minutes return.
- **How to get there:** Off SH1 at Otaihanga Road (the same access road as the Southward Car Museum). Otaihanga Road leads to Makora Road and the beginning of the walk at the Otaihanga Domain.

Although not marked, the walk begins over the swingbridge at the Otaihanga Domain, a popular family swimming spot in the stony waters of the Waikanae River. Turning left, the clear waters quickly give way to a tidal saltmarsh, with the small estuary prolific with aquatic and wading birds, despite the close proximity of housing. Eventually the track leads to a car park and from there it's a short walk to the beach.

With Kapiti Island just 5 km offshore, the area between the beach and the island is now the Kapiti Marine Reserve. The track is also used by cyclists, who are not always considerate of walkers.

13 Parata Track, Hemi Matenga Scenic Reserve, Waikanae
Stunning coastal bush and extensive vistas.

Grade: Medium/hard. **Time:** One and a half hours return.

How to get there: The main entrance up a narrow roadway off Tui Crescent, east of SH1 in Waikanae – parking is on Tui Crescent.

Put aside as a reserve in the early twentieth century by two brothers, Hemi Matenga and Wiremu Parata Waipunahau, this is one of the largest areas of lowland forest in the lower North Island. Comprised mainly of kohekohe, the addition of nikau palms gives this reserve a distinctive tropical look.

Beginning at the water reservoir, the track runs alongside a small stream and is overhung by large kohekohe trees. Initially the grade is gentle, then rises more sharply and becomes rougher and a bit muddy near the top. While it's an uphill climb, the grade is steady rather than steep. The outlook point is a grassy clearing with marvellous views over the narrow coastal plain, Kapiti Island, Cook Strait and in the distance, the Marlborough Sounds. Just beyond this lookout point is another viewing point looking over the Reikorangi Valley.

If the uphill track isn't for you, an easy, short 30-minute walk on an excellent track begins at the same point and exits 500 m south in Kakariki Grove.

14 Queen Elizabeth Park
A dune walk with views of Kapiti and good swimming.

Grade: Easy. **Time:** One hour 15 minutes.

How to get there: MacKays Crossing off SH1, just north of Paekakariki.

Queen Elizabeth Park protects a large area of coastal dunes, wetlands and farmland between Paekakariki and Raumati and can be accessed at several points, though the most popular entrance is at MacKays Crossing by the Wellington Tramway Museum.

The central car park at Wharetoa Beach is the starting point for two loop walks, one north towards Raumati, and the other south toward Paekakariki. Both have a seaward track following the dunes, with many excellent viewing points over the beach to Kapiti Island, south to Mana

Island, and across Cook Strait to the rugged hills of the Marlborough Sounds. Looping back on the inland track through farm and wetland, the going is more sheltered from prevailing westerlies. Depending on the tide and wind, another option is to walk part of the way along the beach. Both loop walks will take around one hour 15 minutes. Swimming on this section of coast is generally safe.

There is good access to the beach all along this coast, where the shy and secretive katipo, New Zealand's only poisonous spider, makes its home in the dunes and under driftwood.

The tramlines run from the main road to the beach on the weekend so you can park by the museum and catch the tram, a popular option if you have children.

24
short walks in
Wairarapa and Wellington

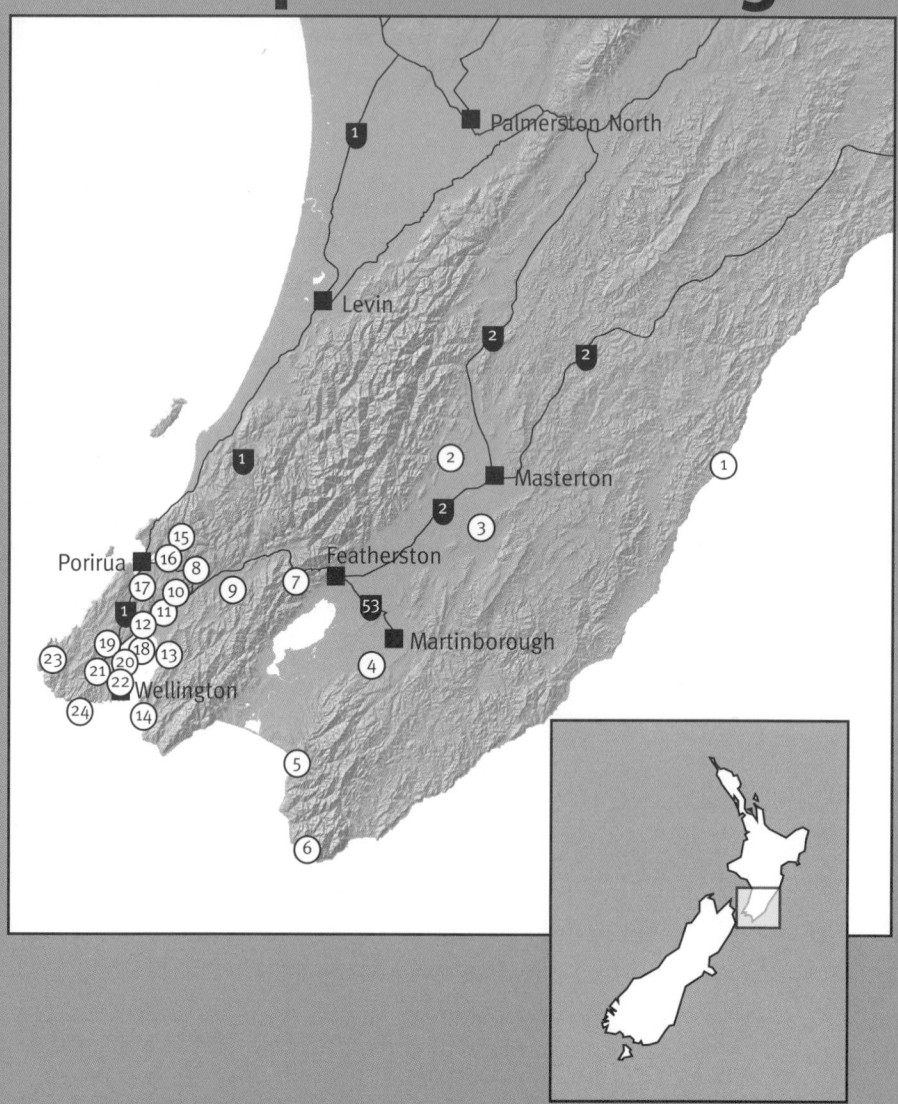

1 Castle Point
A classic lighthouse high above stunning coastal scenery.

Grade: Easy. **Time:** 40 minutes.
How to get there: 65 km northeast of Masterton.

The setting of Castle Point lighthouse is dramatic, on the raw face of Castle Point, overlooking a coastal settlement known for fishing and safe swimming. Huge waves from the Southern Ocean hammer the cliffs, thundering over the rocky reef protecting the lagoon. Built in 1912 and tapering from 5 m at its base to 3 m at the top, the lighthouse is one of New Zealand's most stylish.

This dramatic landscape was the location of one of Kupe's liveliest escapades. While sailing along this coast in the waka *Matahorua*, Kupe disturbed a giant octopus, living in a cave. The huge creature fled with Kupe in pursuit. The octopus turned to fight, wrapping its enormous tentacles around *Matahorua*. Kupe had to act fast – his waka was being pulled apart. He flung a gourd into the sea and the octopus, thinking a man had fallen overboard, released the waka and grabbed the gourd. Seizing his chance, Kupe killed the octopus with his adze.

The walk initially crosses the sandy spit between the beach and lagoon on a raised boardwalk, gradually climbing up to the lighthouse. From here the track drops to a lookout point, and you can clamber around the rocks to a point just above the boardwalk. If you climb up the rocks overlooking the reef and lagoon, take extra care, as this area has claimed several lives.

2 Mount Holdsworth Lookout
Beautiful bush lines an attractive valley stream.

Grade: Hard **Time:** One hour 15 minutes return.
How to get there: From Masterton take SH2 to 1 km south of the Waingawa River Bridge, turn right into Norfolk Road and travel a further 16 km to the parking area.

Holdsworth, tucked in foothills alongside the Atiwhakatu Stream, is one of the more accessible points in the Tararua Ranges. The walk starts just over the swingbridge, about 5 minutes from the car park. The camping area, set in a river glade, is particularly attractive.

The solid uphill trudge to Mt Holdsworth Lookout isn't up Mt Holdsworth, but leads to a lookout with a view of the mountain, across the valley. Beech is predominant, but keep an eye out for rare native mistletoe in wire cages, protected from browsing possums. Halfway up is a punganga pa, a last refuge in times of trouble. These were located in caves, on islands or in deep, inaccessible bush. Designed as temporary shelter, construction was rudimentary; all that remains here are basic earthworks, but they are not easily missed.

If this sounds demanding, Donnelly Flat Loop Walk is an easy alternative. Taking less than an hour, the track meanders through magnificent beech and rimu to a clearing on the Atiwhakatu Stream, in a bush-clad valley. Gold was discovered in 1873, and the flat is named after Tom Donnelly, a goldminer who died on Mt Holdsworth. The clearing is wide and grassy with access to the river, complete with barbecues and picnic tables. Beyond the flat, the walk swings away from the river and returns to the start point.

3 Carter Scenic Reserve, Carterton

The largest bush remnant on the Wairarapa Plain.

- **Grade:** Easy. **Time:** 20 minutes.
- **How to get there:** From SH2 in Carterton, take Park Road towards Gladstone (signposted from the shopping centre in the middle of Carterton) – turn into Gladstone Road and after 3 km the reserve is on the right.

Bequeathed by Charles Carter, an early Wairarapa pioneer, and for whom the nearby town of Carterton is named, this small 31-hectare reserve is all that remains of lowland forest in the Wairarapa.

Situated alongside the Ruamahanga River, the reserve is low-lying and swampy with kahikatea, flax and other water-loving plants dominating the vegetation. A boardwalk crosses the wettest parts.

4 Rapaki Hillside Walk, Martinborough
An open farmland track with surprising views of the Wairarapa.

Grade: Easy. **Time:** One hour return.
How to get there: From Martinborough head west on Jellicoe Street towards Lake Ferry – the walk is signposted to the left, 2 km from town.

A particularly pleasant walk on a warm summer's evening, this track is located on private land and leads gently uphill to a surprisingly broad view of the Wairarapa. Below is Martinborough surrounded by bright green vineyards and beyond, to the east, are the forested ridges of the Aorangi Range. North and west are the plains, bisected by the Ruamahanga River and bordered by Lake Ferry and the Tararua Range.

5 Putangirua Pinnacles
Dramatic hoodoos tower above a small stream.

Grade: Medium. **Time:** One and a half hours return.
How to get there: 12 km south on the Cape Palliser Road from the junction of Lake Ferry Road.

For thousands of years the Putangirua Stream has eroded the soft coastal soils to create an unusual 'badlands' landscape of deep gullies and tall pillar-like formations, known as 'hoodoos'. Hoodoos form when rock protects the soil from rain, preventing the soft gravels from eroding and creating high, fluted formations. While they are common along the coast, at Putangirua the concentration of hoodoos in one small valley is spectacular, made even more so by the way the walk takes you right into the heart of the valley.

The track follows the river up from the picnic area and camping ground. Subject to frequent seasonal flooding, there is no official track – just follow the riverbed up to the wide valley leading off to the left. With pretty rough going underfoot, both in the riverbed and the valley itself, you'll definitely need good footwear and be prepared for wet feet.

6 Cape Palliser Lighthouse
A picture-perfect lighthouse high above a wild coast.

Grade: Medium. **Time:** 20 minutes return.
How to get there: From Martinborough take the road south towards Lake Ferry, then turn to the left on the road to Ngawi – the lighthouse is 5 km past Ngawi.

From the lighthouse keeper's cottage, 258 steps lead straight up the rocky bluff to a fantastic view. Painted in red and white horizontal stripes in the traditional manner and perched 78 m above the sea, the 18-m lighthouse was built in 1897 to guide shipping around Cape Palliser. Here the perilous coastline combines rocky headlands and shoals with fierce weather blasting from the Southern Ocean. On the raw hillside, succulents and coprosma thrive in crevices.

Halfway between Ngawi and the lighthouse, keep an eye out for the seal colony on the rocks below. Take care if you plan a closer look – many seals rest beside the road and aren't easily spotted until you're almost on top of them.

7 Te Ara Tirohanga (Remutaka Trig Track)
Excellent views over the Tararua Range and the Wairarapa Plain.

Grade: Medium. **Time:** 45 minutes return.
How to get there: The track begins just below the west side of the Remutaka Summit on SH2.

The steep Remutaka Range between Wellington and the Wairarapa is a southern extension of the Tararua Range, which extends north to the Manawatu Gorge. Te Ara Tirohanga at 725 m is definitely subalpine, both in vegetation and climate. Even on a fine day it blows up here, and in very windy conditions think twice about climbing this track. On a good day, however, make the effort. It's a steady rather than steep 25-minute climb, with magnificent views from the top over the Wairarapa and the Remutaka Range.

If the wind on the summit gets a bit much, grab a respite in the tiny hollow just below the top. With a bit of shelter, this supports large shrubs, providing an effective windbreak.

8 Kaitoke Regional Park
Beautiful untouched forest.

Grade: Easy. **Time:** Allow one hour.
How to get there: The park is clearly signposted at Waterworks Road off SH2, 12 km north of Upper Hutt – the walks are from Pakuratahi, 1 km on from the main information board and ranger's office.

Covering 2860 ha, Kaitoke Regional Park has some of the finest untouched bush in the Wellington region, with magnificent stands of rimu, rata and beech. At its heart is the local water catchment area, purchased in 1939, with half of Wellington's water drawn from within the park.

A number of walks from Pukuratahi are easily combined, as some are very short. The main walk is a loop along the Hutt River, beginning over a long swingbridge from the car park. Immediately over the bridge is a short nature walk, with interpretive panels, taking around 15 minutes. The main track continues through magnificent forest to the Flume Bridge, with views down the Hutt River Gorge. Over the bridge is the Kaitoke Strainer House, an initial filter for the water system, with a fascinating map of Wellington's water system on the wall, and well worth a look. From here the track follows the sealed access road to the car park, but instead of walking along the road, take the short Terrace Track, which runs parallel, with fine bush and excellent tree identification signs. In addition to the walk, there are great picnic sites and swimming holes in the river.

9 Tane's Track, Tunnel Gully
An historic railway tunnel and magnificent beech forest.

Grade: Easy. **Time:** One hour.
How to get there: Turn right into Plateau Road off SH2 at the Te Marua store, just north of Upper Hutt.

Tane's Track leads from the car park, and it's easier to do this loop walk anticlockwise, as the signage in the first part is a bit unclear. The track leads to the right, and takes about five minutes to reach the Mangaroa Tunnel. Built in 1875, the 220-m tunnel is lined with a curiously inconsistent mixture of brick and stone. A torch is helpful, but not essential. After exploring the tunnel return to the large grassed area, and walk diagonally across, past the mountain-bike track to your right, and on to Tane's Track. At this point the track enters the bush, and loops through stunning beech forest with enormous trees, hundreds of years old. Near the end of the walk, near the car park, look out for an immensely tall rimu. Along the way there's also a small, picturesque waterfall trickling down mossy rocks. If you just want to go to the tunnel, a loop walk will take 20 minutes. The track and facilities are very well maintained.

10 Belmont Trig
Wide views of Wellington and Cook Strait.

- **Grade:** Hard. **Time:** Two hours return.
- **How to get there:** Follow Dowse Drive up from the Western Hutt motorway, just north of the Petone turnoff – turn left into Stratton Street and follow the signs to the car park on the right. The track starts just down the hill.

In 1981 local authorities purchased a sprawling area between the Hutt Valley and Porirua, creating Belmont Regional Park. The track is a solid uphill slog through farmland on a wide 4WD track, a steady climb but the views are worth it. At 457 m the trig is the highest point in the park and the views are endless, over Porirua, Hutt Valley, Wellington Harbour and city, and far across Cook Strait to the Marlborough Sounds and Kaikoura mountains. In the distance are the Rimutaka, Orongorongo and Tararua ranges. What's even better is that the view isn't revealed until the very top.

Just below the summit is a small patch of bush well worth exploring – while the trees are battered by the constant wind, the understorey is luxuriant, with delicate ferns and tender mosses.

11 Percy's Scenic Reserve
A hidden valley right by a busy motorway.

- **Grade:** Easy. **Time:** 40 minutes return.
- **How to get there:** Well signposted off Dowse Drive next to the Dowse interchange on the Hutt Motorway. The parking area is locked at dusk.

The land was originally purchased by the Percy family in the 1840s with the intention of building a watermill to process locally grown wheat but it wasn't until 1869 that the mill was finally built. In 1914, two of the Percy brothers began building an extraordinary garden which they continued to develop until they moved from the property in 1939. Highly unusual for the time, the brothers were very interested in native plants, in particular they were concerned that many plants were becoming extinct.

Today, not only does the reserve preserve a rare remnant of native coastal forest, but it is also is one of this country's most important native plant collections, many of which are rare and endangered.

The lower part of the garden is quite formal in layout, with lawns, paths and even a duck pond, though most of the plants are natives rather than traditional flower beds. The track to the waterfall quickly enters dense bush and it is hard to imagine that the busy noisy Hutt Motorway is just a short distance away. The valley tapers into a narrow rocky gorge with a board walk over the small stream. Just beyond is the waterfall tumbling 10 metres down rocks framed by mosses and ferns. While the water flow is not large the setting is very picturesque.

12 Korokoro Dam Walk
A deep, sheltered gully and an old reservoir.

Grade: Medium.   **Time:** 50 minutes.

How to get there: Follow Dowse Drive up from the Western Hutt motorway, just north of the Petone turnoff. From Dowse Drive follow the signs to Oakleigh Street car park.

Korokoro was New Zealand's first gravity-fed dam, built in 1903 to supply Petone with water. Set in verdant bush which has been protected since the dam was built, today the reserve contains mature nikau, rimu, rata, tawa and kohekohe. The name is closely related to the Maori name for the North Island, Te Ika a Maui – the Great Fish of Maui. In legend the whole island is the fish, Wellington Harbour is the mouth and Korokoro Valley is the throat – with this walk taking you into the very throat of Maui's great fish.

The loop walk drops down steeply to the Korokoro Stream at the bottom of the valley, for a good view of the multi-tiered dam. The return walk is longer, but on a much gentler grade.

13 Butterfly Creek, Eastbourne

A popular swimming and picnic spot in a deep valley.

- **Grade:** Medium. **Time:** One and a half hours from Kowhai Street and two hours from Muritai Park.
- **How to get there:** The two most common entry points are Kowhai Street and Muritai Park in Eastbourne.

The valley through which Butterfly Creek runs lies parallel to the coast, protected by a steep low ridge sheltering the valley from the worst of both southerly and northerly winds. Rata, beech and rimu dominate the forest.

The track has several entry points from Eastbourne. All involve a steady uphill climb over the ridge, but there is the compensation of fine views over the harbour, Matiu/Somes Island, Wellington City and the Hutt Valley.

The track is in excellent condition and leads to an attractive picnic spot in a glade of beech and there's a small swimming hole in the creek. Kowhai Street and Muritai Park are only 1 km apart so it's possible to create a loop walk, which will take a little over two hours.

14 Pencarrow Head and the Coastal Trail

Wild seascapes from a popular coastal walk.

- **Grade:** Easy. **Time:** To the lighthouse – three hours return.
- **How to get there:** From Eastbourne follow Muritai Road along the coast for 2.5 km to the end, also known as Burdans Gate.

Pencarrow Head at the entrance to Wellington Harbour has been created from gravel washed down to sea by the Orongorongo and Wainuiomata rivers, then heaped back on shore by strong southerly storms. Broad terraces along the coast present a graphic history of land creation – each represents the upward movement of the earth caused by successive earthquakes. Two small lakes just beyond the head were once tidal inlets; cut off from the sea by rising land, they are now freshwater lakes.

This coastal track, popular with walkers and cyclists, encompasses some of Wellington's wildest seascapes, wide open to the worst of the southerly weather – yet that very wildness is its greatest attraction. There are great views of the harbour and, on clear days, of the South Island and the Kaikoura mountains, snow-capped in winter – views enhanced by a short but steep climb to the old lighthouse. The entrance to Wellington

Harbour was even more treacherous in the days of sail, and the lighthouse, built in 1858, was New Zealand's first.

The track follows the coast from the road end right round to the mouth of the Wainuiomata River (three hours one way) – the walking is easy but the track is very exposed, for which you need to be prepared.

15 Battle Hill Farm Forest Park
Open farmland and a bush-clad battle site.

Grade: Medium. **Time:** One and a half hours.
How to get there: Battle Hill Farm Forest Park is on Paekakariki Hill Road, 6 km from the intersection with SH58 at Pauatahanui.

In 1846 this area was covered in bush; extremely difficult to travel through, in winter it was almost impossible.

After clashing with troops at Pauatahanui, Maori under Te Rangihaeata withdrew to a position in steep, rugged country. The British, heavily outnumbering them with 250 soldiers and 150 Maori allies, nevertheless realised a direct attack would be suicidal.

Action began on 6 August in bitterly cold weather, with heavy gunfire. After the deaths of three British soldiers, the attackers withdrew. Two days later mortars were hauled up the hillside, but the British withdrew on 10 August, leaving their Maori allies. The two sides skirmished inconclusively until Te Rangihaeata slipped away under cover of darkness.

Today Battle Hill is farmland, the bush mostly replaced by grazing sheep. The uphill walk is a solid climb – hauling heavy iron mortars under fire can only be imagined. Minor earthworks remain, but extensive panels make this a worthwhile excursion.

A number of tracks start by the farm buildings. The best is the Summit Loop Track (the first part is also Farm Loop Track). It follows a farm track uphill, and is steady rather than steep. At the top enjoy the atmosphere and the view before returning via the bush reserve. This starts with a very steep downhill walk, then follows the stream along a bushy valley. On a blustery day you'll be grateful to be out of the wind.

16 Pauatahanui Wildlife Reserve
A vast tidal marsh is home to numerous wading birds.

Grade: Easy. **Time:** 20 minutes to one hour.
How to get there: Off SH58 at Pauatahanui between Paremata and Haywards in the Hutt Valley.

The Pauatahanui Wildlife Reserve is a haven for wading and migratory birds and the largest unmodified estuarine saltmarsh in the southern half of the North Island. Five hides, all within easy walking distance, provide plenty of opportunity for birdwatchers to observe grey teal, shoveller, paradise ducks and pukeko, as well as Arctic visitors during the summer months, such as godwits and knots. The local Forest and Bird Protection Society has worked since 1984 to restore the wetland environment and provide access with paths, boardwalks and information boards.

17 Colonial Knob
A blustery hilltop with sweeping views.

Grade: Hard. **Time:** Two hours return.
How to get there: The main entrance is off Broken Hill Road, Porirua.

At 468 m, Colonial Knob is the highest point in the western Wellington hills, with sweeping views over Porirua Basin, Cook Strait and back across the hills to Wellington City.

There are two main tracks to the top. The track beginning off Broken Hill Road is shorter and steeper, while the Elsdon entrance leads to a longer but more even, gradual climb. Both start through fine bush reserves of mostly kohekohe and tawa, eventually emerging onto farmland scattered with gorse. The tracks through the bush reserves are excellent, while those on the higher ridges are rougher, but not difficult. The tops are very exposed and on a windy day the wind howls, in direct contrast to sheltered bush lower down.

If the weather is bad or the thought of a steep climb to the top is unappealing, the Elsdon Track through bush in the Porirua Scenic Reserve is worth visiting in its own right.

18 Matiu/Somes Island
An important nature sanctuary with a fascinating history.

⛰ **Grade:** Easy. 🕐 **Time:** Two hours.
🚢 **How to get there:** East by West stop at the island on their cross-harbour ferry route www.eastbywest.co.nz Ph 04 499 1282.

Around 1000 AD Kupe discovered Te Whanganui-a-Tara, Wellington Harbour, naming the two main islands after his daughters, Matiu (Somes) and Makaro (Ward). Maori never permanently occupied either, as they lacked a consistent water source.

Purchased by the New Zealand Company and renamed after Joseph Somes, the company's deputy governor, the island was used as a quarantine station from 1872, for both people and animals. During World War I detainees included Germans, a Turk, a Dutchman, a Swiss and a Mexican. During World War II members of Wellington's Italian, German and Austrian communities were detained, though many were refugees. Most of the buildings are from the animal quarantine period, though the barracks (1890) and hospital (1915) remain, along with World War II anti-aircraft gun emplacements (since removed, the guns were never fired).

The island is an important wildlife sanctuary, with extensive replanting by the Forest and Bird Protection Society. Otherwise rare kakariki are common here – like blackbirds they forage in leaf litter on the forest floor, as well as swooping and chattering overhead. With their boldness and ground-feeding habits, it's not surprising they're vulnerable to predators, and extinct on the mainland.

When you arrive, head to the visitor centre, then continue to the gun emplacements, which have a great view over the harbour. From here access the well-formed island circuit track, which is easy walking and, for the most part, high up with excellent views.

19 Te Ahumairangi/Tinakori Hill
A brisk uphill walk to a city lookout.

- **Grade:** Medium/hard. **Time:** 45 minutes return.
- **How to get there:** With numerous starting points, this one is from the top of St Mary's Street, off Glenmore Street, Thorndon.

Rising above Thorndon, Te Ahumairangi Hill (known locally as Tinakori Hill) is hard to miss. The steep hillside is laced with interconnecting tracks, with excellent signage. While the walk to the lookout is all uphill, most of the track is graded and relatively painless, easily within the capabilities of the moderately fit.

Known as the Northern Walkway, the first part is through low, regenerating bush, with great views. It was once dominated by huge pine trees, but in 2004 many were damaged in severe storms.

Higher up, the track narrows, entering more established native and exotic forest, emerging at the lookout. You are rewarded with great views, and excellent information boards detail the area's history.

Directly below, the Wellington fault line runs down the western side of the Hutt Valley, following the motorway along the harbour edge, along Tinakori Road and Glenmore Street, then through the Zealandia wildlife sanctuary.

At this point return the way you came or choose one of two loop tracks. The left loops downhill, rejoining the Northern Walkway about halfway down and back to St Mary's Street, taking less than an hour to return. The right continues along the ridge then winds down the hillside, emerging at Grant Road, from where it's an easy stroll up historic Tinakori Road to the start – around one and a half hours. This walk is easily accessible by foot from the central city. Parking in St Mary's Street is limited.

20 Wellington Waterfront
An historic wharf area packed with art, museums and restaurants.

- **Grade:** Easy. **Time:** One hour.
- **How to get there:** Start at any point; however, this walk is described from the Railway Station to Oriental Bay.

Successive councils and a vigilant and protective public have ensured Wellington's waterfront is one of this country's best public spaces. Once separated from the city by a busy roadway, today the waterfront is accessible and alive, with joggers, kayakers, ferry commuters and restaurant-goers, and packed with history, museums, art galleries and theatres.

Highlights, in order from the Railway Station include:
- Wellington Railway Station, built in 1937 in the Beaux Arts style.
- Shed 5 and Shed 3, built in 1887 and the oldest buildings on the waterfront; now restaurants.
- National Portrait Gallery housed in Shed 11 built in 1904-05.
- The New Zealand Academy of Fine Arts, established in 1892 and dedicated to exhibiting the best of New Zealand art.
- The Museum of Wellington City & Sea, located in the old Bond Store (built 1892).
- Frank Kitts Park, a children's playground centred on a lighthouse.
- Tanya Ashken's sculpture Albatross, made of white Ferro cement and unveiled in 1986.
- Paratene Matchitt's City to Sea Bridge, a fantasy link to the Civic Square, the old and new Town Halls, Wellington Art Galley and the Wellington Public Library designed by architect Ian Athfield and notable for its stylised nikau palms.
- The old Wellington Rowing Club boatsheds overlooking a small lagoon and now a restaurant. Built in 1874, the build has been moved several times before being shifted here in 1991 – the new rowing club buildings are next door.
- The dramatic statue of Kupe, discoverer of Aotearoa. Originally created in 1940 from Plaster of Paris, this bronze version was cast in 1999.
- Te Wharewaka o Poneke, housing three waka and a functions centre.
- Hikitia an historic steam-powered floating crane built in 1926 and still operational.
- Art Deco St John's Ambulance station now a bar.
- Lively Circa Theatre.
- Museum of New Zealand, Te Papa Tongarewa, looming large and grey, and packed full of national treasures and art.
- Waitangi Park with its intriguing saltmarsh gardens and playing fields.
- Chaffers Dock Apartments, striking Art Deco building constructed in 1939 as the Post and Telegraph Building.
- Blue and white boatsheds lining the small marina of pleasure craft at Clyde Quay.

- The Freyberg indoor swimming pool.
- The old ferryboat *Tapuhi II*, now a floating restaurant.
- Oriental Bay, a pleasant, sandy inner-city beach named after a 19th-century immigrant ship, centred on a fine old band rotunda and lined with stately Norfolk pines.

21 Otari–Wilton's Bush Native Botanic Garden and Forest Reserve
An outstanding collection of New Zealand flora in a bush reserve.

Grade: Easy. **Time:** Allow one hour.
How to get there: Wilton Road, Wilton.

Pioneer botanist Dr Leonard Cockayne, who was instrumental in collecting and classifying many native plants, established these gardens in 1926 as the Otari Open-Air Plant Museum, alongside a significant bush remnant next to the Kaiwharawhara Stream.

The reserve falls into two distinct parts. Beautifully laid out and close to the road, the formal gardens are easily accessible with the dramatic canopy walkway linking the two cultivated parts. To the left of the information centre are the older gardens, with impressive collections of hebe, flax, coprosma and threatened species (among others), while the fernery and alpine gardens in the themed area are equally worth visiting. New Zealand has over 600 native plants and a good percentage of these are represented here.

The original bush reserve is extensive and easy to explore. The nature walk loop, covering both gardens and an attractive section of bush between them, takes around 40 minutes though it does have a steep section with some steps. Beyond the Kaiwharawhara Stream are several loop walks through original bush areas that can take up to one hour, and it's worth taking the longer walk to view an impressive 600-year-old rimu.

22 Zealandia Ecosanctuary
Visit rare birds and animals in a Wellington bush reserve.

Grade: Easy **Time:** One and a half hours
How to get there: Waiapu Road, Karori.

Only 2 km from the city, this 250-hectare forest was originally Wellington city's water reservoir catchment area and was closed to the public for over

120 years. In the early 1990s Forest and Bird members developed a plan to create an urban sanctuary for native flora and fauna, and from this emerged a charitable trust, the Karori Sanctuary Trust.

A key element to the success of the sanctuary was the erection of 8.6 km of predator-proof fencing (a world first), followed by the eradication of predators within the fenced area. The park has been a resounding success and is now home to numerous native birds including saddleback, weka, brown teal, tomtit, kaka, whitehead and kiwi, as well as New Zealand's unique native reptile, the tuatara (best seen on a summer afternoon). The tracks and trails are easily accessible and suitable for all levels of fitness. You can even take a boat trip on the lower lake. For an additional fee, experienced guides take 2-hour tours, and for something different a night tour is also available. Evening hours are extended in summer, making the reserve accessible in the early evening when the birds are more active.

The reserve is open daily from 9 am to 5 pm (last entry 4 pm), For entry fees check the website. (www.visitzealandia.com).

23 Makara Walkway
Spectacular views over Cook Strait.

- **Grade:** Hard. **Time:** One and a half hours return to Fort Opau.
- **How to get there:** From the western end of Karori take the Makara Road to the beach.

Overlooking the wild waters of the Cook Strait and exposed to every wind, the sheer wildness of Makara is its essential appeal. This hasn't always been the case, as several Maori pa sites in the area testify to the rich resources of both sea and forest, with Captain Cook also remarking on the din of birdsong from the dawn chorus in the coastal forest, even though he was anchored almost a kilometre offshore.

Cook Strait (average depth 128 m) is in the westerly wind belt of the Roaring Forties, divides the two islands, and acts as a natural wind tunnel. Channelling northerly and southerly winds and creating a swift tidal flow, the strait is infamous for extreme weather, with fierce winds and huge swells. The southern coast around Wellington is particularly exposed to powerful storms that lash the coast with enormous waves and furious winds. Gusts of 248 kph were recorded at Hawkins Hill in Wellington in November 1959 and July 1962. Not surprisingly, two of New Zealand's worst maritime disasters occurred here – the sinking of the *Penguin* in

1909 off Cape Terawhiti with the loss of 75 lives, and of the ferry *Wahine* in 1968 with 52 lives lost.

Don't be put off by the wild weather, just make sure you come well wrapped-up and bring a sense of adventure. The walk begins at the southern end of the beach and traverses farmland as the track climbs solidly uphill, but the views along the way are magnificent, unfolding steadily as you climb. To the right, a narrow ridge crested by an equally narrow and rather rough track, leads to an ancient Ngati Ira pa. Higher still is Fort Opau, a World War II gun emplacement built to protect Cook Strait – the old concrete buildings will provide a welcome respite on a windy day. The strategic value of the site to both Maori and Pakeha is immediately obvious, with Mana and Kapiti islands to the north, the Marlborough Sounds to the west, and the Kaikoura mountains to the south. The fort was extensive, but now only the lookout posts and gun emplacements partially dug into the hillside remain.

If a climb up to the fort doesn't appeal, a return walk to the pa site takes around 50 minutes and a flat walk along the coast to the point below the pa about 25 minutes.

24 Red Rocks

An unusual outcrop of red rocks along Wellington's wild south coast.

Grade: Easy. **Time:** One and a half hours.

How to get there: At Owhiro Bay, follow the Owhiro Bay Parade west to the car park at the end.

Wellington's south coast faces directly into the Southern Ocean and with nothing between the city and Antarctica, the coastline takes the full force of wind and sea. In a storm huge seas pound the rocky coast, stripping it of substantial vegetation, with waves often coming over the road. Only the hardy coprosma survives in this harsh environment.

Red Rocks, a striking formation of red pillow lava, were formed underwater over 200 million years ago. Maori legend attributes the colour of the rocks to the explorer Kupe – while gathering paua, he gashed his hands on the rocks, which became stained with his blood.

A 4WD track follows the wild exposed coast, where bull kelp swirls in the brutal tides, oystercatchers scuttle along stony beaches and huge shingle fans sweep down the barren cliffs. On Sunday the track is closed to vehicles, but busy 4WD traffic can make this an unpleasant walk on a Saturday.

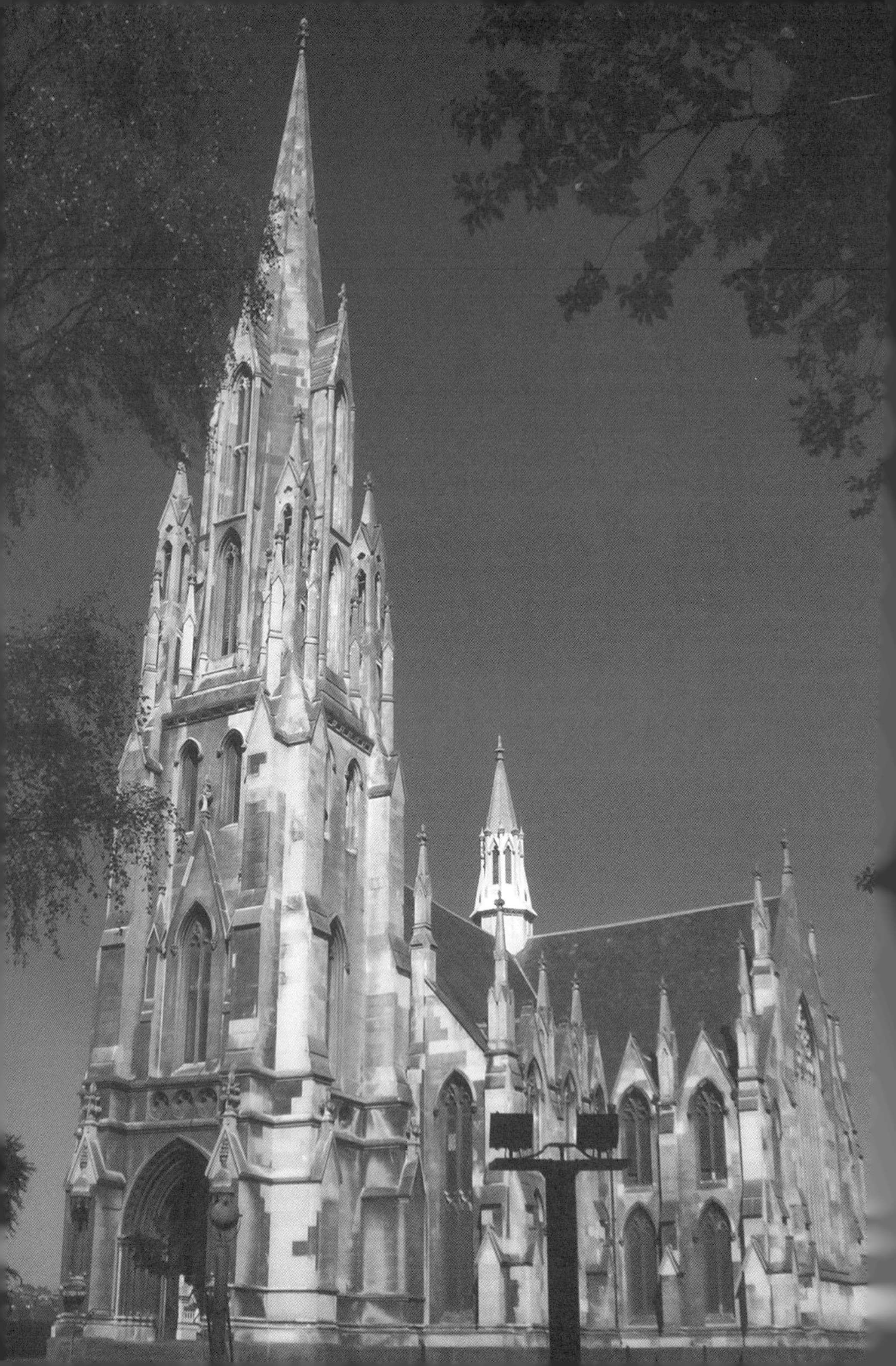

short walks in the
SOUTH ISLAND

12
short walks in
Marlborough and Kaikoura

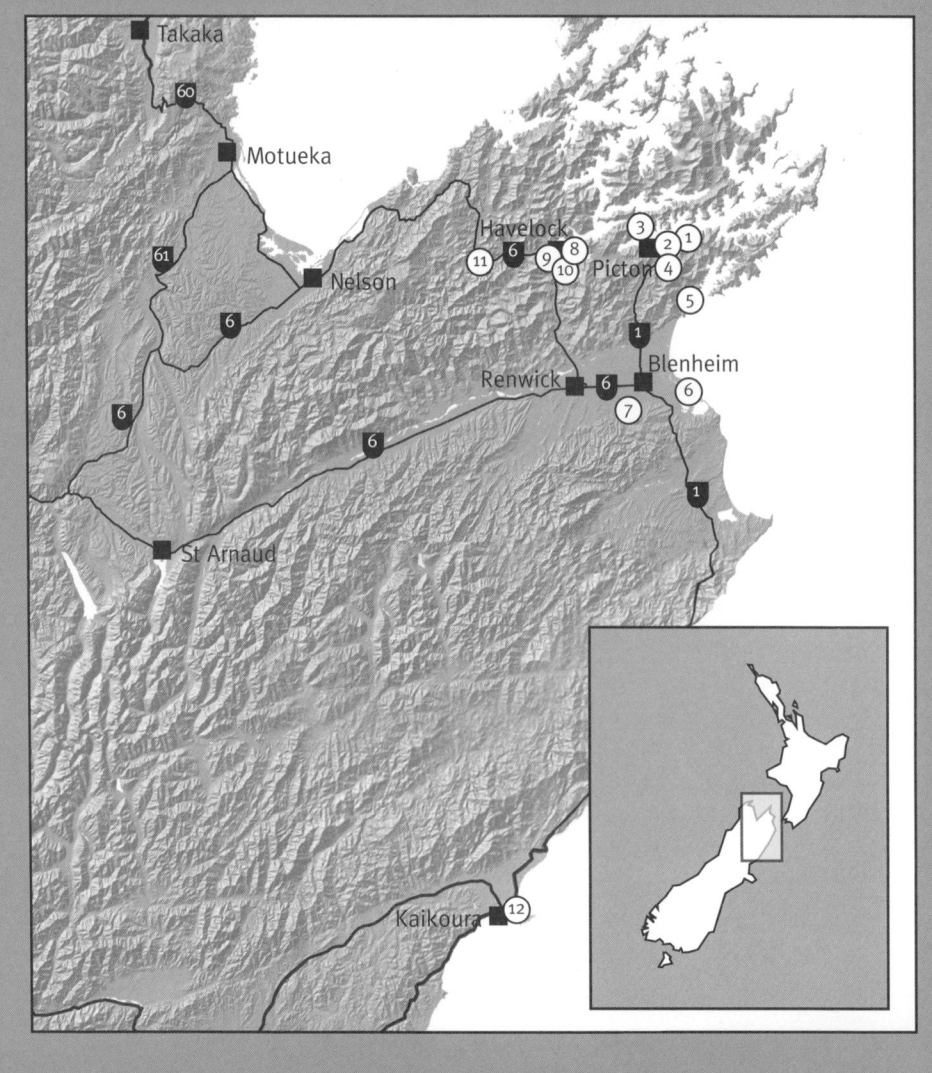

1 Karaka Point Track, Picton
Great views with a well-preserved pa site.

    Grade: Easy.   **Time:** 20 minutes return.
    How to get there: From Picton take the Waikawa Road to Waikawa Bay and continue along the narrow road towards Port Underwood – the walk is well marked on the left-hand side of the road.

Te Pae o Te Karaka pa was named after Ngati Mamoe chief Te Karaka, who settled here around 1700 and was killed in 1720 when Ngai Tahu captured the pa.

In the 1820s musket-wielding Te Atiawa invaded the Sounds and, after capturing several pa nearby, made their move on Te Karaka. The defenders believed they were safe in their strongly fortified pa. Approaching from the sea in waka, Te Atiawa launched an assault with heavy musket fire. Realising escape was the only option, the occupants fled through the land gates, straight into a trap. Te Atiawa warriors had hidden in the bush, and few escaped the deadly ambush. The pa was burnt, subsequently abandoned and never reoccupied.

In addition to great views over Queen Charlotte Sound, this pa is particularly well preserved with the clear outline of defensive ditches, house sites and kumara pits. Tracks from the pa lead down to two shingle beaches.

2 Queen Charlotte View and The Snout
A narrow peninsula juts far into Queen Charlotte Sound.

    Grade: Medium.   **Time:** One hour 20 minutes return to Queen Charlotte View; two hours 30 minutes return to The Snout.
    How to get there: From Picton take the Waikawa Road then turn left into Loop Drive, clearly marked and one-way. Continue along the drive to the car park just before the road turns sharply downhill to the right. The track begins from the northern side of this car park.

Marlborough is a region of two distinct halves, one of which is the water-bound Marlborough Sounds, an intricate and complex system of drowned valleys with fingers of bush-clad land and islands reaching into Cook Strait. The 4000 km of coastline is largely accessible only by boat and the myriad bays, beaches and coves are hardly touched by visitors, whose experience of the Sounds is mainly confined to the ferry trip through Queen Charlotte

Sound. Dolphins are common in the sheltered waters, and while the bush has mostly been cleared and milled, vast areas are now regenerating.

Today the end of the long peninsula is known to Pakeha as The Snout and to Maori as Ihu moeoni, the nose of the sand worm. The first section is a 10-minute walk along an unattractive access road flanked by gorse. The track narrows, entering regenerating bush with expansive views, which unfold the further you walk along the peninsula. Below, Queen Charlotte Sound is busy with small pleasure boats, and if you time it right a Cook Strait ferry glides past. From Queen Charlotte View there are excellent views to the north. On both sides of the peninsula numerous bays and bush-clad ridges line the Sound, and the town of Picton is behind you.

3 Bob's Bay Track, Picton
An attractive bay within easy reach of Picton.

- **Grade:** Easy. **Time:** One hour return.
- **How to get there:** Cross over the footbridge north of the town centre and walk along the shoreline past the marina to where the beginning of the walk is marked. If you drive to the track, watch where you park as certain areas are reserved for boat owners.

A popular walk and easily undertaken from Picton, the Lower Bob's Bay Track closely follows the coastline through regenerating bush to Bob's Bay. With clear water ideal for swimming, the beach is a mixture of sand and gravel, with a large and attractive grassy picnic area with toilet facilities.

Return the same way but this time turn left at the second 'Harbour View Terrace' sign, which leads to the higher track, referred to as the Upper Bob's Bay Track. When the marina comes into view take the right-hand track back down to the water's edge, where you started.

4 Humphries Dam Walk, Picton
A deep valley with mature trees and a reservoir.

- **Grade:** Easy. **Time:** One hour 20 minutes return.
- **How to get there:** From the south end of Nelson Square go up Devon St to Garden Terrace – where the track starts at the end, to the right.

The first section of the track starts out rather unpromisingly and follows a 4WD road through regenerating bush in a broad valley. The track soon narrows as does the valley and the bush here is in direct contrast to the scrubbier vegetation characteristic of the Marlborough Sounds. Mature beech trees dominate with the occasional large tawa and rimu, while the forest floor is lush with mosses and ferns flourishing in the deep, damp, cool shade.

The track meanders along a clear and rocky stream following the Picton water supply pipeline to a small concrete dam deep in bush, perfect for a swim on a hot day. If you're interested in extending the walk, a side track leads off to Barnes Dam, another reservoir.

There is also a large grassed picnic area and a good swimming hole just 200 m from the car park at the beginning of the track.

5 Black Jack Loop Walk, Whites Bay
A lovely sandy bay and a pleasant bush walk.

- **Grade:** Medium. **Time:** One hour 15 mintues.
- **How to get there:** From Blenheim take the road to Rarangi Beach and Port Underwood. Where the road starts climbing uphill at Rarangi, drive a further 4 km to Whites Bay.

Now best known as a wine label, Cloudy Bay is a broad bay at the mouth of the Wairau River. Tucked away on the road to Port Underwood are a number of pretty bays, including White's Bay, a sandy, bush-clad bay in direct contrast to the dry open country south of the Wairau River. Whites Bay takes its name from black American slave, Black Jack White, who jumped ship in 1828 in Port Underwood and settled in the area.

The first Cook Strait telegraph cable was hauled ashore in 1886, linking the South Island to Lyall Bay in Wellington. The telegraph building, prefabricated in Australia, housed staff from 1867 to 1873 and is still on site. While there are no large trees, the bush supports many native birds – fantails, kereru, tui and bellbirds – and there's a good camping site and safe swimming.

The track is in excellent condition, steady rather than steep, with an occasional glimpse through the trees over Cloudy Bay. The track follows a ridge to the lookout over Port Underwood and Cook Strait with the return walk beginning 100 m past the lookout and downhill all the way.

Pukatea Loop Walk is an easy 25-minute short walk that can be added, and follows a stream through the bush before emerging onto the road to Whites Bay.

6 Wairau Lagoon Walk, Blenheim
A walk through saltmarsh and shingle banks.

Grade: Easy. **Time:** Allow up to two hours.
How to get there: End of Hardings Road, 5.5 km south of Blenheim off SH1.

The Wairau Bar is one of New Zealand's most important archaeological sites, discovered in March 1942 when sixteen-year-old Jimmy Eyles was digging an air-raid shelter. Noticing unusual bones, shells and blackened stones, he kept digging.

He unearthed one of New Zealand's oldest occupied sites, dating back to the thirteenth century and initial settlement. Middens yielded evidence of early Maori diet – fish, seals, kiore, tuatara, porpoise, shellfish, kuri and birds, many of which are now extinct. Distinctive fishhooks, chisels, adzes, harpoon points and necklaces of cotton reel-shaped pieces held together by cord, in a style common in the Marquesas Islands, led archaeologists to surmise the legendary homeland, Hawaiki, was in Eastern Polynesia. In all, 50 burial sites have been excavated and 2000 personal items recovered.

The bar was Blenheim's main port until an earthquake in 1855 dropped the level of the Wairau Plain, deepening the Opawa River and allowing shipping access further inland.

Unfortunately this track begins in Blenheim's sewage treatment plant but quickly emerges onto a vast saltmarsh, home to unique salt-tolerant plants and alive with bird life. Generally well maintained, it's boggy and very wet in places, and you might consider gumboots.

Along the track is the wreck of the 125-ton steamer *Waverley*. Built in New Zealand in 1883, she was dismantled in Wellington in 1928 and sunk here as a breakwater.

7 Rotary Lookout/Quails Junction, Wither Hills Farm Park, Blenheim

Extensive views over the Wairau Plains, Richmond Range and Cook Strait.

- **Grade:** Medium. **Time:** Rotary Lookout, 45 minutes return; Quails Junction, one and a half hours return.
- **How to get there:** From Blenheim take Maxwell Road and turn into Taylor Pass Road – the track begins on your left, from the well-signposted car park.

The sparse Wither Hills are such an integral part of Marlborough it's difficult to believe they were once covered in dense forest. Early Maori destroyed much of this, either deliberately or accidentally, and what little was left was cleared by early European settlers. Once gone the bush never recovered and a recent fire in 2000 demonstrates the fragile nature of this landscape, in a climate of dry summers with strong warm winds.

The strikingly beautiful Wither Hills form a dramatic backdrop to Blenheim, and the great appeal of walking here is the constantly unfolding view. Tracks and access points provide walks of every type, with the Taylor Pass Road entrance both popular and accessible.

From the car park the Gentle Annie track to the left of the information board winds up through a gully to the Rotary Lookout, with seating and a shelter. The hills, tawny brown in summer, provide an impressive backdrop for views over the vine-covered Wairau Plains. To the northwest is the rugged Richmond Range, while to the east is Cloudy Bay, Cook Strait and the North Island. If you're feeling fit continue uphill to Quails Junction on the Twin Tracks Walk, to even more impressive views, then return down the Lower Quail Stream Walk. This walk is especially attractive in the mellow morning and evening light.

8 Cullen Point Lookout, Havelock

An easy walk to a viewpoint over the Mahau Sound.

- **Grade:** Easy. **Time:** Lookout, 20 minutes return, 45 minutes return including the base walk
- **How to get there:** Queen Charlotte Drive, 3 km from Havelock.

This short walk through bush (with some steps) leads to a lookout high above the Mahau Sound with expansive views on one side, and the town of Havelock, famous for mussels farmed in the rich waters, on the other. Another track off to the left drops down to a small tidal beach and then encircles the base of the point. Attracting far fewer visitors than lookout, this is a very pleasant quiet stroll through bush and along the water.

Just near the start of the Lookout track, a rougher path drops down to the right and this walk, circling the base of the promontory, attracts far fewer visitors

9 Motuweka Pathway, Havelock
An easy stroll along a river estuary and harbour mole.

- **Grade:** Easy. **Time:** 40 minutes return.
- **How to get there:** The track begins in Havelock cemetery, at the end of Slogan Street which runs off Outram Street, off SH6.

Walk through Havelock's historic cemetery, which is situated on a low bluff overlooking the Waituna River estuary. From the cemetery the track drops down to a wide saltmarsh of multi-hued sedges, grasses and rushes and continues round to the estuary and onto the mole enclosing the Havelock Marina. Native trees and shrubs have been recently planted and now flaxes and elegant native toetoe arch over the pathway.

Birdlife is prolific in the tidal reaches of the river and the low mole is a perfect spot for bird watching. Just offshore, tiny Motu Paemanu (Bird Perching Island) is true to its name. As well as native and introduced birds such as stilts, shags, oystercatchers, gulls, dotterels and ducks, the rich feeding ground also attracts migratory birds including godwits and royal spoonbills. Take time to sit at the very end of the mole and watch the boats coming and going.

10 Waterfall Track, Havelock
A hidden gem in the middle of Havelock.

- **Grade:** Easy. **Time:** One hour return.
- **How to get there:** This track begins at the end of Inglis Street, just off SH6 in the middle of Havelock township.

While the waterfall is modest, it is very pretty and the walk is through attractive native bush containing some large trees, including an enormous kahikatea and several large tawa. At night glow-worms can be seen on the damp banks. The pool below the waterfall is large enough to cool off on a hot summer's day.

The track is an easy uphill slope to the falls and about halfway up is a stunning moss 'waterfall' created by water dripping steadily down a 4-m bank, resulting in layers of delicate moss cascading down the slope in a sparkling fall. The walk back is for the most part a 4WD track and not nearly as picturesque, ending at the top of Lawrence Street, which leads back to SH6, a short distance away from the start.

11 Pelorus Bridge Walks
Short walks through untouched forest and along the river bank.

Grade: Easy. **Time:** One hour return.
How to get there: SH6, 18 km west of Havelock.

Walks around Pelorus Bridge access some of the best mature lowland forest in Marlborough. In addition to black, red, hard and silver beech are miro, tawa, totara and kahikatea, with some trees, such as miro, not found further south. Prolific birdlife includes bellbirds, tui, kereru, kaka and kakariki. This is also the home of the long-tailed bat, which can be seen flitting over the river on summer evenings.

The junction of the Pelorus/Te Hoiere and Rai rivers was part of a Maori trail passing over the Maungatapu Saddle, linking Tasman Bay to the Sounds, and location of a small kainga called Titi Raukawa, though bitter fighting during the Musket Wars saw the village abandoned. By the time Europeans arrived the area was largely uninhabited.

The bridge was first built in 1859, and it was in this area that the notorious Burgess Gang murdered four miners, though they were soon captured and brought to justice.

The Circle Walk starts across the road bridge and begins immediately to the right, continuing to the substantial suspension bridge over the Rai River, where it joins the Pelorus River. Beyond the bridge the track forms a loop, part of which follows the high bank of the Pelorus River with views over the water and Totara Flat.

The Totara Walk starts on the car park side of the bridge and leads through beech and totara, with parts of the forest floor a solid carpet of fern. There is one particularly impressive large totara, and two short side tracks lead to excellent swimming holes.

Across the road by the café, the Tawa Walk is a flat easy loop through a particularly fine stand of virgin tawa and kahikatea, offering a strong contrast with the drier, more open Totara Walk. Here the giant trees have a very dense subtropical understorey of shrubs, ferns and mosses.

12 Kaikoura Walkway and Seal Colony
Coastal and mountain views from a peninsula steeped in history.

> **Grade:** Easy. **Time:** Lookout Point – 10 minutes return; Whalers Bay Lookout – 45 minutes return; South Bay Lookout – 1¼ hours return, South Bay – 1¾ hours return.
>
> **How to get there:** All walks begin at Point Kean at the end of Fyffe Quay.

The Kaikoura mountains are two separate ranges, and between them runs the Clarence River. The highest point of the Seaward Kaikoura Range is Mt Manukau at 2610 m, while inland the peak of Tapuae o Uenuku 'the footprint of the rainbow god' reaches 2885 m. A northern extension of the Southern Alps, the Kaikoura Ranges formed along New Zealand's Alpine Fault and initially rose out of the sea 30 million years ago. More recent mountain-building activity in the past 200,000 years has seen these mountains rise sharply, a process that is ongoing.

Once hunted to near extinction, whales are protected in New Zealand waters and have transformed Kaikoura from a sleepy seaside town into a bustling tourism centre. Giant sperm whales live in coastal waters all year round, while pilot, blue, southern right and humpback whales migrate through Cook Strait.

The Kaikoura Peninsula is where Maui braced his foot in his struggle to haul up Te Ika a Maui (the North Island), while Kaikoura is a shortened version of Te Ahi Kaikoura o Tama ki Te Raki, 'the fire that cooked the crayfish of Tama ki Te Raki'.

First occupied by Waitaha, then Ngati Mamoe and later Ngati Kuri, the peninsula had at least eleven pa. In 1828 Te Rauparaha attacked to avenge an insult by the Kaikoura chief Rerewhaka. Luck favoured the invaders, as the locals were expecting relatives. Seeing waka offshore, the unarmed defenders left their pa to greet them, gifting Te Rauparaha an easy victory. As many as 1000 died or were taken as slaves, with the rest fleeing south. Many years later, Ngai Tahu drove the invaders back.

The Kaikoura Walkway has walk options for every level of fitness. All begin at Point Kean at the eastern end of the peninsula.

Most people go to the first lookout (with an excellent view of a stepped pa), but continue along the cliff for views of the mountains, with seals, seabirds and an attractive shoreline. The complete Kaikoura Walkway is a bit of slog, with the most interesting section at the very end. While it is possible, returning along the shore below the cliffs can be tricky at high tide. If this appeals, start your walk around the rocks by the car park, the section most affected by the tide. If the tide isn't right and you need to turn back, you only have to retrace your steps a few hundred metres. A further option is to be dropped off at Point Kean and walk the whole track via South Bay back to town, taking two and a half hours.

The entire coastline of the peninsula was affected by the 2016 earthquake where the land rose over one metre and around the carpark, the effects are highly visible. Once the sea came right up to the parking area at high tide and seals frequently hauled themselves up on the rocks and occasionally into the car park. Today the area around the carpark is a broad rocky shelf quite a distance from the sea.

18
short walks in
Nelson and Golden Bay

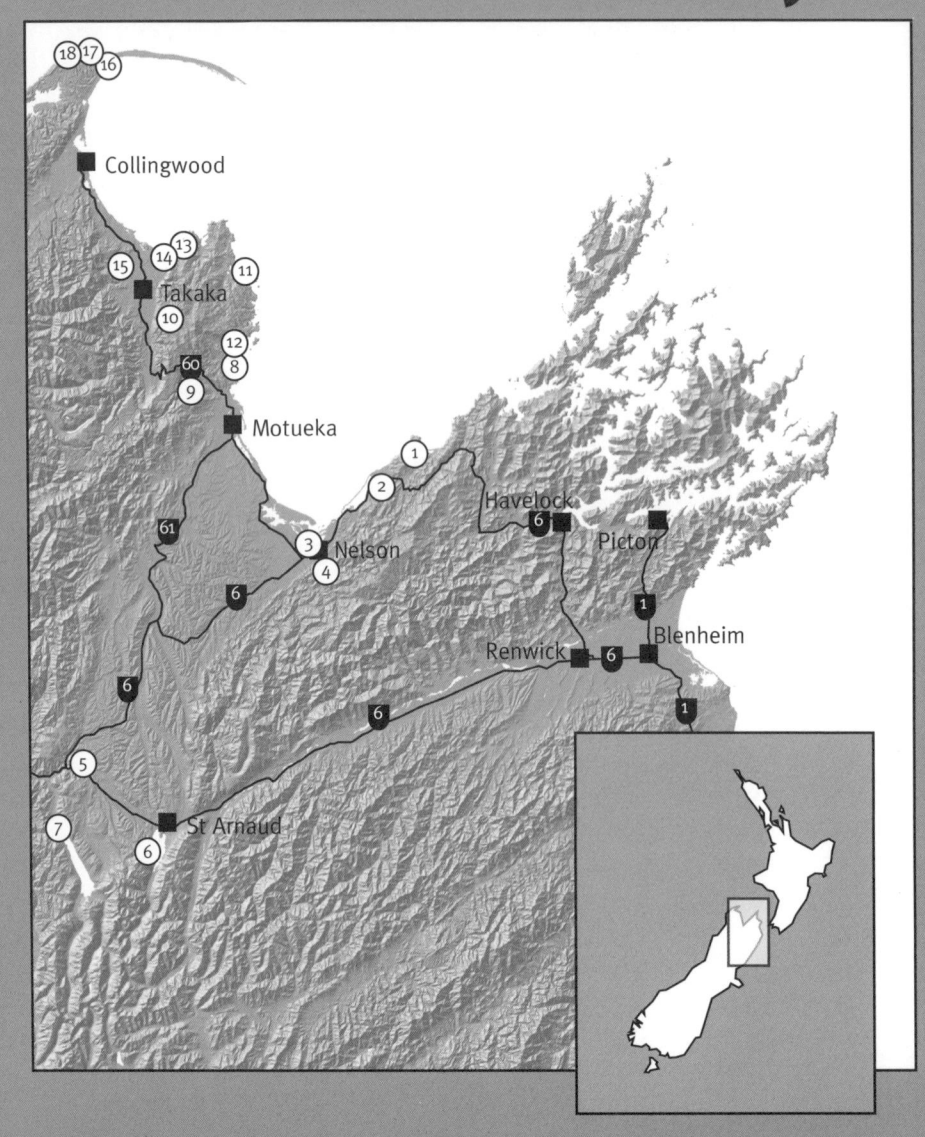

1 Cable Bay Walkway
Great views west over Tasman Bay to the mountains beyond.

Grade: Hard. **Time:** 50 minutes return.
How to get there: From Nelson take SH6 towards Picton and after 12 km turn left into Cable Bay Road, continuing another 8 km to the beach – the track starts to the left.

Known to Maori as Rotokura, the bay was renamed to honour the first international telegraph cable from New Zealand to Sydney laid in 1876, which came ashore here. A short climb from Cable Bay leads to an excellent information board.

The walkway runs from the left of Cable Bay beach and up through farmland, bush remnants and pine forest to the Glen; the entire walk is two and a half hours one way. While both ends have short walks to lookouts with great views, the Cable Bay end is the more attractive walk, but a solid uphill slog. Watch out for the electric fence near the top, which runs close to the track. The loop walk from the Glen is more a steady uphill walk, though the track is rough and the landscape less attractive. There are terrific views over Tasman Bay, the Boulder Bank and the northwest Nelson mountains.

2 The Boulder Bank, Nelson
A rare natural phenomenon.

Grade: Easy/medium. **Time:** 30 minutes or all day – you choose.
How to get there: Access is off Boulder Bank Drive off SH6, 7 km north of Nelson.

The Boulder Bank is so fascinating it's hard to believe it is entirely natural. Over 13 km long, the bank is formed of large granodiorite boulders from Mackay Bluff, moved southwest during northerly storms. That these large stones have been moved by waves, wind and tide to form a precise line for such a distance is extraordinary and it isn't surprising to learn this is one of the few such examples in the world.

Known to Maori as Te Taero o Kereopa, the bank has a close connection with Kupe. When two of his men, Kereopa and Pani, decided to settle rather than continue voyaging, they deserted in two waka and headed towards Waimea (Tasman Bay). Kupe set off in hot pursuit in his waka *Matahourua*. With a powerful karakia, Kereopa called on the gods to create a barrier between them. The gods answered. Boulders from Horoirangi (Mackay Bluff) collapsed into the sea, forming a long line, with Kereopa on the inside. Now able to keep ahead of Kupe, Kereopa made it to shore and disappeared into the deep bush.

At first glance the Boulder Bank looks tempting for a long walk, but in reality it is made of loose stones and boulders, with walking surprisingly hard work. However, a short section at the beginning is a smooth, level path and an easy stroll. How far you go after that is up to you.

3 Botanic Reserve and the Centre of New Zealand
The birthplace of New Zealand rugby and a lookout over Nelson City.

- **Grade:** Medium. **Time:** 30 minutes return.
- **How to get there:** The Botanic Reserve is across the footbridge over the Maitai River at the end of Hardy Street, and the track to the Centre of New Zealand begins on the far side of the reserve.

The Centre of New Zealand Walk begins from the Botanic Reserve and leads up a short but steep hill to a great viewpoint over the city. Contrary to popular local belief, it isn't the geographical centre of New Zealand, but a convenient hill used by an early surveyor, John Browning, charged by the government to link earlier surveys.

The first game of rugby in New Zealand was played on the Botanic Reserve between Nelson Football Club (Town) and Nelson College on 14 May 1870. The Nelson Football Club originally played an odd mix of soccer and Victorian (Australian) rules football, but in 1870 changed its name to the Nelson Rugby Club, becoming the country's first rugby club. At that stage rugby was played by teams of 20 and points were scored by kicking goals. To be able to kick a goal the ball had to first be touched down, which gave the team the right to 'try' for a goal. For the record, Town beat College two goals to nil.

To extend your walk, return via the Maitai Valley.

4 The Grampians
Excellent views over Nelson City and Tasman Bay.

Grade: Medium. **Time:** Lookout – one hour 30 minutes return.
How to get there: The walk begins from the corner of Trafalgar Street South and Van Diemen Street, behind historic Fairfield House.

Lying directly south of Nelson City, the Grampians are easily recognised by the tall communications towers on the top. While there are several entrances, most are badly marked so if you're a visitor either start at Fairfield House, or in the city, at the end of Collingwood Street. The walk begins with a solid uphill climb on a zigzag path to the trig, which has good views over the city. If you find this section a physical challenge, be aware there are several similar steep climbs to the top lookout, so you might like to stop here. The lookout is just to the right of the last uphill section to the transmitter. The views are fantastic over the Waimea Plain, the mountains to the west and Tasman Bay to the north, with the city below. There's no point trudging up to the transmitter, as this area is overgrown with no views.

5 Kawatiri Railway Walkway
A pleasant river and bush walk with an historic railway bridge and tunnel.

Grade: Easy. **Time:** 30 minutes return.
How to get there: The walk begins at the junction SH6 and SH63.

In 1929 the Nelson/Inangahua railway reached Gowan Bridge, just south of Kawatiri Junction, with the long-term intention of linking Nelson to the West Coast. Despite strong public pressure, the line was never completed and the entire link closed in 1955.

From the car park the track follows the old railway embankment to the remains of a railway bridge over the Hope River, now topped by a footbridge. Over the bridge the track leads to the Pikomanu Tunnel, with the 1923 date of construction proudly proclaimed above the entrance. While a torch isn't necessary, it is wet and uneven underfoot. Just beyond the tunnel are the concrete foundations of yet another bridge. The loop walk continues to the left up a short flight of steps through beech forest, passing by a shallow cave, once an explosives store.

At the car park there are excellent photos and information about the railway line as well as the remains of the original road bridge.

6 Lake Rotoiti
A lake and forest walk, part of a 'mainland island'.

- **Grade:** Bellbird and Honey Dew easy; Loop Walk medium.
- **Time:** Bellbird Walk – 10 minutes; Honey Dew Walk – 30 minutes; Loop Walk – one hour 30 minutes.
- **How to get there:** The walks start from Kerr Bay in St Arnaud township on SH63 between Blenheim and Murchison.

The mountains of the Nelson Lakes National Park are part of the Alpine Fault running the length of the South Island, with Lake Rotoiti and Lake Rotoroa the result of glacial action. The dense forest here is mainly red and silver beech with mountain beech at higher altitudes. The birdlife is prolific and includes bellbirds, robins and kaka.

While Lake Rotoroa is larger and deeper, Lake Rotoiti, source of the Buller River, is more accessible with a wider range of facilities. Water taxis operate on both lakes, with a lake cruise on Lake Rotoiti.

The early explorer Rakaihautu landed near Nelson and decided to journey into the interior. As he worked his way inland, he dug deep trenches with a gigantic ko or digging stick. The trenches filled with water and became Lake Rotoiti (small lake) and Lake Rotoroa (long lake), while the soil became mountains.

The walks begin from the eastern side of Kerr Bay and are essentially loop walks, each progressively larger. The forest is part of a 'mainland island' so keep an eye out for a glimpse of rare kaka and kakariki.

The Bellbird Walk is an easy stroll along the lake and through a short section of forest, while the Honey Dew Walk continues further with a slight uphill section before looping back through bush. The Loop Walk follows the shoreline past several small beaches, then climbs steadily uphill as it follows a ridge. This track can be rough and muddy in parts – the open beech forest means regularly checking you're still following the orange triangles.

7 Lake Rotoroa Nature Walk
Magnificent beech forest on the edge of Lake Rotoroa.

- **Grade:** Easy.   **Time:** 25 minutes return.
- **How to get there:** Turn off SH6 12 km north of Gowan Bridge or 6 km south of Kawatiri Junction.

While it's larger than Rotoiti, Lake Rotoroa attracts fewer visitors. This short walk starts from the car park by the boat ramp. The loop track begins to the left of the car park and continues along the lake edge with views deep into the lake. Old kowhai trees overhang the placid water and huge beech trees soar into the sky, while a solid carpet of crown ferns cover the forest floor. A short 10-minute return walk on the Flower Brothers Track starts in the opposite direction, leadibng through a stand of kahikatea to where the lake outlet forms the Gowan River.

8 Split Apple Rock
An intriguing split rock.

- **Grade:** Easy.   **Time:** 30 minutes return.
- **How to get there:** From Kaiteriteri Beach take the Sandy Bay Road north for 4 km, then turn into Tokongawa Drive – after 2 km turn right into Moonraker Way and park.

This curious split rock sits just off a narrow beach in Towers Bay, north of Kaiteriteri. In Maori tokongawa means 'burst open rock' and refers to a legend where two brothers (or two chiefs, depending on the story) fought over this particular rock and, rather than continue the argument, decided to cut the rock in halves. The reason for the fight has long been forgotten.

A short walk down steps and through regenerating bush leads to a long beach of golden sand. The rock sits just off the beach.

9 Riwaka Resurgence
The Riwaka Stream emerges from the base of Takaka Hill.

- **Grade:** Easy.   **Time:** 5 minutes return.
- **How to get there:** The Resurgence is on Riwaka Valley Road, clearly marked to the left at the very base of Takaka Hill on the Motueka side – the track begins at the end of this road.

Takaka Hill, between Tasman and Golden bays, has both spectacular views and fascinating geology. Famous for its distinctive marble, its stone was quarried to build Nelson Cathedral, the old Parliament Buildings and the Beehive. While the Riwaka Resurgence is not quite as dramatic as it sounds, it is a picturesque spot nonetheless.

A short bush walk through mature beech leads to the base of a cliff where the crystal-clear waters of the Riwaka Stream emerge from under Takaka Hill, after flowing underground for 4 km. The cave is popular with divers, who can follow the stream underground for up to 800 m, reaching a giant chamber with limestone formations. There is a pleasant picnic spot by the car park.

10 Harwoods Hole and Gorge Creek Lookout
The deepest vertical cave in New Zealand.

Grade: Easy. **Time:** One hour 30 minutes.
How to get there: From the Takaka Hill road, 21 km from Motueka, turn right into Canaan Road and follow the unsealed, rough narrow road for 10 km to the car park at the end.

Harwoods Hole is a dramatic tomo over 170 m deep, and the deepest vertical cave shaft in the country. The hole wasn't explored until December 1958, with the Starlight Cave, which leads from the bottom, discovered the following month.

The track is easy walking through beech forest, though near the hole it becomes a bit of a rocky scramble, while the edge is a jumble of boulders which require a reasonable degree of fitness to negotiate. It's hard to see into the hole, but soaring cliffs on all sides give a very good idea of the extent. With no barriers, take care close to the edge. Cavers regularly use the hole, so don't be tempted to throw rocks into the shaft.

A short side track leads up to Gorge Creek Lookout on top of a sheer escarpment with views over Gorge Creek and back towards the hole, giving a much better idea of the size of this giant tomo. In the bush keep an eye out for tomtits, kakariki and robins.

11 Abel Tasman National Park
Small but perfectly formed.

- **Grade:** Medium/easy. **Time:** You choose.
- **How to get there:** 30 km east of Takaka, unsealed, narrow and winding beyond Wainui Inlet.

Abel Tasman National Park is New Zealand's smallest, at just over 22,000 ha, and has the reputation of being one of the most crowded, especially December to February. Named after Dutch explorer Abel Janszoon Tasman, the combination of lush bush, spectacular coastline, clear water and stunning beaches make this park hard to resist. 'Golden' descriptions of the beaches don't do the colour justice, though Golden Bay takes its name from gold strikes, not sand. In 1993 an area around Tonga Island was made a marine reserve.

The DOC Great Walk is a 51-km coastal track of mainly easy walking, linking a series of stunningly beautiful beaches with some of this country's best coastal scenery. Unfortunately it's also one of the most popular. If crowds bother you, plan a trip outside the mid-December to mid-March period, though even then you're unlikely to have the track to yourself. The two main access points are at Marahau at the southern end, and Totaranui (via Takaka) in the heart of the park. However, all the track is accessible by water taxi so you can create your own short walk at any point. Most water taxis are based at Marahau and Kaiteriteri near Motueka, so this is a good option if you don't want to drive to Totaranui – and you see some magnificent coastal scenery on the way.

Two short walks lead from Totaranui – Anapai Bay to the north and Waiharakeke to the south (with shorter walk options). Totaranui Beach is a very beautiful beach in its own right with a huge camping ground, an information centre and a boat ramp at the northern end of the beach.

Anapai Bay is a beautiful untouched beach with dark golden sand and stunningly clear water ideal for swimming. The walk begins on the flat, skirting the estuary and an open grass area with an old homestead, testament to a time when the area around Totaranui was once farmed. The track then climbs a short uphill section over a headland, beyond which it follows a gully thick with native bush including rimu, rata and beech. The walk will take around one hour 40 minutes return.

To reach Waiharakeke Bay head to the southern end of Totaranui, where a good track follows the coast to Skinners Point (30 minutes return) with a fine lookout spot over Totaranui Beach to the north and Goat Bay to the south. Goat Bay (40 minutes return) is a small sandy beach backed by native bush and perfect for swimming. Further on, Waiharakeke Bay is a much longer beach with deep golden sand and the lush subtropical bush for which this area is justifiably famous.

12 Coquille Bay
An accessible and attractive beach.

- **Grade:** Easy. **Time:** Two hours return.
- **How to get there:** The walk begins at the car park by the café at the northern end of Marahau township, 17 km north of Motueka.

If time is short and the long drive to Totaranui not an option, this walk at the southern entrance to Abel Tasman National Park is a good alternative. The track begins at the wide Marahau River estuary. The estuary is very tidal, as is the first beach, Tinline Bay, attracting a good number of wading birds. From Tinline the track crosses a low ridge and then drops to Coquille Bay, a sheltered sandy beach backed by dense native bush and ideal for swimming. The bay is named after the ship the *Coquille* commanded by the French navigator, Jules Dumont d'Urville, who arrived in the northern part of the South Island in early 1828.

13 Wainui Falls Track
A beautiful bush walk to a thundering 20-m waterfall.

- **Grade:** Easy. **Time:** One hour return.
- **How to get there:** From Takaka take the road to Totaranui – at the Wainui Inlet a clearly marked road sign to the right leads to the falls.

While thousands flock to Totaranui, this beautiful waterfall is largely ignored and you are very likely to have this track to yourself. Beginning through farmland with a couple of shallow stream crossings requiring a bit of rock hopping, the track enters lush bush as the valley narrows, following the stream. This part of the track is within Abel Tasman National Park, and the mature native bush is a fine mix of beech, rata and nikau. The boulder-strewn stream is impressive, with huge water-worn rocks the size of small trucks. The falls thunder over a 20-m drop into a deep shady pool, keeping the rocks around the pool wet and consequently slippery, so take care. The track is in good condition, though the wire suspension bridge might be a bit challenging for those unsteady on their feet.

14 Grove Scenic Reserve
Lush bush entwined with limestone boulders.

- **Grade:** Easy. **Time:** 30 minutes return.
- **How to get there:** On the road from Takaka to Pohara Beach, the reserve is signposted from Clifton.

Although this reserve is very small, it is a marvellous combination of huge weathered limestone rocks, twisted rata trees and secret pathways. The track wanders through huge boulders entwined with rata roots and dense with nikau palms. Best of all is a narrow cleft through towering rocks, which leads to a lookout high above Golden Bay.

15 Te Waikoropupu (Pupu) Springs
A huge natural spring with the world's clearest water.

- **Grade:** Easy. **Time:** 25 minutes return to the springs, 40 minutes for the loop walk.
- **How to get there:** Take SH60 4 km west of Takaka – after crossing the Takaka River turn left and continue for a further 2.5 km.

Claimed to produce the clearest springwater in the world, the springs are a series of eight interconnected vents, discharging up to 14,000 litres per second at a constant temperature of 11.7°C. The water is a mixture of salt and fresh water, with the huge underground water system extending under the sea.

The springs are home to Huriawa, one of the most important taniwha in Aotearoa. Known as a kaitiaki (guardian) taniwha, Huriawa uses this spring as a resting place when not clearing waterways both above and below ground, especially after flooding. Underground caves and rock formations are all the work of Huriawa, who travels throughout the North Island and as far south as Lake Pukaki. Once an important ceremonial site for Maori, the waters of the springs were used for healing; today the area is a wahi tapu.

The walk is on an excellent track through bush which includes fine old totara and rimu trees, the remains of gold diggings from the late nineteenth century and a surprising number of native birds. The loop walk is only a few minutes extra and where you are most likely to see them.

16 Farewell Spit Beaches
A loop walk including both 'inside' and 'outside' beaches.

Grade: Easy. **Time:** One and a half hours return.
How to get there: At Puponga turn right, following the road to the beach just beyond the information centre, or park and take the short walk to the beach.

Over 30 km long, Farewell Spit is one of the world's longest recurved sand spits. The delicate ecosystem is home to a rich variety of birdlife (over 90 species recorded) including migratory birds such as godwits and red knots, which arrive in their tens of thousands in the spring to feed in the shallow waters. The very shallow water is also a death trap for whales, with regular strandings, mainly of pilot whales. Whale strandings along the eastern shore are a common occurrence, with a surprising Maori legend as to why. Kuku (mussels) and pipi fought for supremacy of the sandy beach. The pipi won, driving the mussels to the rocks. The noisy fight drew the attention of Takaako (a shark) and Te Pu (a whale) – while the fight held no interest, the victorious pipi with their large tasty tongues were excellent food. Te Pu and Takaako rushed the pipi, which quickly pulled their heads into the sand and the great sea-creatures ended up stranded with their mouths full of sand.

At the end of the spit are an old lighthouse and a significant gannet colony. Only 2.5 km of the spit is open to the public – access to the entire spit is limited to the tour operator, Farewell Spit Eco Tours (www.farewellspit.com).

Farewell Spit Beach walk is within Puponga Farm Park, a working farm at the base of the spit, in an area of outstanding beauty. This loop walk follows the 'inside' beach (Golden Bay) and the 'outside' beach (Tasman Sea).

From the car park, walk north along the inside beach to the end of the row of pine trees. At the end of the pine trees, turn left and cut across the spit through farmland and swamp to the outside beach. In sharp contrast, the outside beach is a huge stretch of white sand pummelled by relentless surf. Turn left and walk down the shoreline until a red disc marks the return to the car park via a narrow gully of nikau palms and across farmland. If you have time, continue further down the outside beach to the rocky cliffs – Fossil Point – where fossils are visible in the mudstone. Blue penguins and fur seals are also a common sight.

17 Pillar Point Lighthouse
Magnificent views of Farewell Spit and as far north as Taranaki.

- **Grade:** Medium.   **Time:** One hour return.
- **How to get there:** Signposted off the road to Wharariki Beach.

Following a 4WD track of loose stones and rock through wind-stunted manuka, this track is a steady uphill walk to a modern lighthouse. Just below the lighthouse are concrete foundations, all that remains of a World War II radar station. While the Pillar Point Lighthouse is rather ordinary, the views are fantastic and give the best overview of the region. To the west is Cape Farewell, directly north Farewell Spit curves far out into the sea, while to the east lie Golden and Tasman Bays. On a very clear day, Taranaki is just visible.

It's also worth taking the short walk to Cape Farewell, on the same road. This easy 15-minute return walk up a farm track leads to a coastal lookout point atop cliffs with a huge rock arch and giant caves, pounded by waves far below. At 40 degrees 30 minutes south, this is the most northerly part of the South Island and lies directly east of the Manawatu in the North Island.

18 Wharariki Beach
Wind- and sea-sculpted rock formations and seals.

- **Grade:** One hour return.   **Time:** Easy.
- **How to get there:** At Puponga where the road turns left from the sea continue straight ahead (the road to the spit is to the right) and continue 5 km to the car park at the end.

Facing the turbulent Tasman Sea, Wharariki Beach stands in direct contrast to sheltered Golden Bay to the east. This beautiful wide sandy beach is flanked by dramatic rock formations blasted into shape by waves, driven by fierce, relentless westerlies.

The walk to Wharariki Beach is mainly through farmland, with a small remnant of coastal bush near the beach, which unfortunately is not safe for swimming. Keep an eye out for fur seals, which like to roll in the sand, making them very difficult to see.

19
short walks on the West Coast

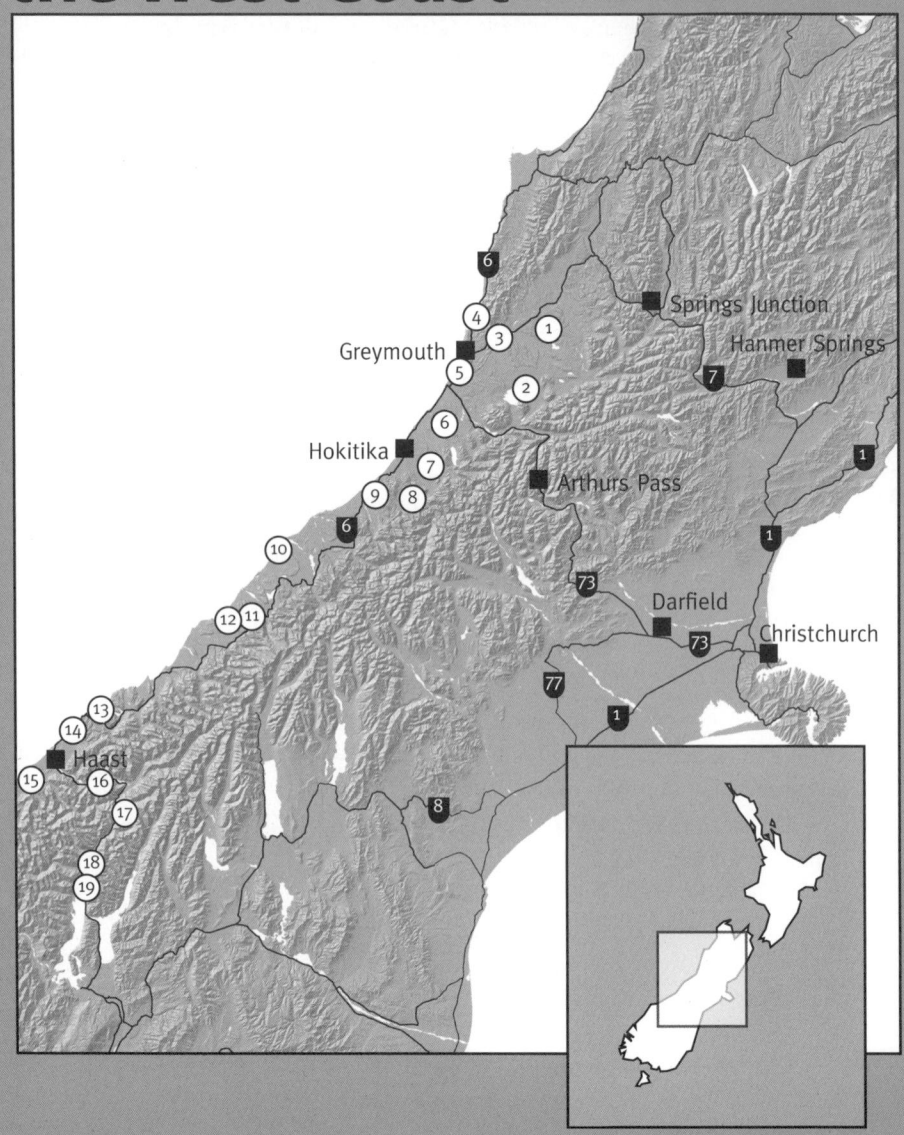

1 Nelson Creek
Remains of the gold-rush days.

Grade: Easy. **Time:** Colls Dam, 30 minutes return; Tailrace Walk, 20 minutes return.
How to get there: From SH7 north of Greymouth turn off at Ngahere – Nelson Creek is 7 km from the turnoff.

When gold was discovered here in 1865, the following boom was short-lived and the bush quickly returned, leaving old tunnels and deep-water races. Two easy walks begin over the river, which is accessed first through a hand-made miner's tunnel topped by an old beech tree, then over a suspension bridge. By the car park there is a large pleasant picnic area, good camping facilities and a swimming hole in the river.

The Colls Dam loop walk through mature beech forest crosses a number of narrow but very deep water-races and tunnels. These took the water from Colls Dam to the river, scouring out the soft alluvial gold-bearing soils, which were sifted in search of a fortune. While the walk includes Colls Dam itself, what appears to be a track around the dam is a dead end.

The Tailrace Walk goes in the opposite direction (to the left over the suspension bridge) and follows the track up a wide gully formed by sluicing, then through a forest of red and silver beech. The loop walk leads back to the river, past deep-water races and an old tunnel, which can be explored. Back at the river there is a small side creek where you can legally fossick for gold and keep what you find. This track is rough in places.

2 Rangitane Walk, Lake Brunner
A river and lakeside walk through mature forest.

Grade: Easy. **Time:** 30 minutes return.
How to get there: At Moana turn right into Ahau Street, following the road to the car park by the lake edge.

Lake Brunner covers an area of 40 sq km and is 100 m deep. While partially cleared of forest along much of the shoreline, the lake has some very attractive bays. At Moana the banks of the Arnold River, the lake's outflow, are lined with very handsome forest, with several huge trees.

The walk begins across an attractive suspension bridge. Turning right over the bridge, the track leads through a grove of kamahi, a small tree with beautiful mottled white, grey and brown bark, the colours blending tastefully with green mosses. The mixed podocarp forest also has kahikatea, rimu and beech, with a ground cover of Prince of Wales fern, with its dark and delicate feathery fronds. Kereru flop noisily about the treetops. The walk forms a loop with views over the river. Back at the bridge a short side track continues to the western shores, with views across to the mountains.

3 Brunner Mine Industrial Site
Scene of this country's worst mining disaster.

Grade: Easy. **Time:** Allow 45 minutes.
How to get there: 12 km north of Greymouth on SH7 towards Reefton.

Thomas Brunner first discovered coal in the area in the 1840s, though mining didn't begin until 1864. At the height of production eight mines were working near the Grey River and in 1876 a suspension bridge was built, linking mines on the north bank with transport on the south. The Brunner Mine is now remembered as New Zealand's worst mining disaster. On 26 March 1896, at 9.30 am, an explosion deep underground killed 65 miners; their memorial is on the north side of the river. The mines eventually closed in 1942.

The remains are extensive on both sides of the river, including the impressive Tyneside Chimney and beehive coke ovens. Good information boards with historic photographs make this a very worthwhile stop.

4 Point Elizabeth Lookout
Nikau palms and a great coastal lookout.

Grade: Easy. **Time:** One and a half hours one way or one hour 15 minutes return to the lookout.
How to get there: For the south entrance, from Greymouth take the road north to Westport over the Grey River Bridge. Immediately over the bridge turn left and follow the road along the coast 6 km to the very end. The northern end is 11 km north of Greymouth on SH6.

Point Elizabeth is a high bluff just north of Greymouth and a major obstacle for gold miners, who used the beach as a highway to travel north and south. In 1865 this track was constructed to improve access. Gold was also mined on the point and part of the track follows the line of the old water-races.

From the beach the track climbs a short distance before levelling off; from here the track is mostly flat all the way to the lookout, with the constant boom of the sea along almost the entire walk. Passing through dense groves of kiekie and nikau, the track traverses an area of pure flax just before the lookout. Nikau at Point Elizabeth is at its most southerly growing limit on the West Coast.

The views from the lookout are far to the north along this wild coast: to the south the breakwater at Greymouth is just visible; offshore two small rocky islands are home to numerous seabirds.

5 Coal River Heritage Park Walk
Historic reminders of gold and coal.

- **Grade:** Easy.
- **Time:** 20 minutes return.
- **How to get there:** Mawhera Quay, Greymouth.

In Maori legend, the Mawhera Gap where the river breaks through the low coastal range was one side of a great canoe gradually filling with water, threatening to inundate the entire South Island. Tu Te Rakiwhanoa, a powerful ancestor, smashed through the canoe and saved the island. The principal pa (also called Mawhera, 'widespread river mouth') was on the hill just above the centre of Greymouth, the focal point of the pounamu trade with Ngai Tahu at Kaiapoi in Canterbury.

From the early gold boom days in the 1860s, through coal, timber, fishing and back again to coal, Greymouth has long been a busy port. The Heritage Park runs along the Grey River stopbank from the railway station (1897) to the port loading area, and includes the restored Harbour Board building (1884), signal station (one of only two left in New Zealand), the dredge buckets from the *Mawhera* (built in Scotland in 1908), and old railway carriages and stock. Interpretive panels with historical photos make this an interesting short walk.

6 Roadside Tunnel Loop Walk
A tunnel and a walk through old gold workings.

Grade: Easy. **Time:** 20 minutes return.

How to get there: From Hokitika head north for 10 km on SH6 and turn right into the Stafford/Dillmanstown Road – the car park is on the left 6 km down this road and the walk starts on the opposite side of the road.

The tunnels on this walk were originally constructed to carry water to the gold diggings. The beginning of the walk is through a short tunnel in a fern-lined bank opposite the car park. Emerging under a boulder cliff into regenerating bush of rimu and kamahi, the track then drops down to a creek, which disappears into another dark tunnel. Everywhere there are piles of rocks left over from mining activities, with the track lined, and in some places constructed, with these boulders. Eventually the track loops back through a third tunnel to emerge a short distance from the car park.

7 Lake Kaniere
A deep lake surrounded by mature forest.

Grade: Easy. **Time:** Kahikatea Forest Walk – 10 minutes return; Canoe Cove Walk – 20 minutes return.

How to get there: From Hokitika turn off SH6 into Stafford Street and then into Lake Kaniere Road – continue on for 18 km. Turn right into Sunny Bright Road and drive to the picnic area for the Kahikatea Forest Walk. For the Canoe Cove Walk, the track begins 1 km north of the Sunny Bright Road turnoff, to the left opposite Milltown Road.

Lying to the east of Hokitika in the foothills of the Southern Alps, Lake Kaniere is a deep lake (194 m), surrounded by mature forest, overlooked by two mountains, Mt Graham (828 m) and Tuhua (1124 m). A 7000-ha reserve protects the bush adjoining the lake, including fine stands of mature kahikatea growing right to the edge. The views across the lake are superb, but the sandflies can be fierce. Late autumn/early winter is a good time to visit Westland; most of the tourists have gone, the weather is settled with calm clear skies, and early snow on the mountains makes the views even more dramatic.

The Kahikatea Forest Walk begins over a boardwalk through flax, then moves into dense native bush thick with mosses and ferns and dominated by spectacularly tall kahikatea. The track follows a pretty bush stream back to the car park. Fringed by flax and large trees and with views right down the lake to the mountains, the picnic area is very attractive in its own right, but don't forget the insect repellent.

In stark contrast, on the Canoe Cove Walk rimu dominates the forest, which is also much more open and lighter in character. The track leads down to a small beach and a quiet tree-lined backwater with peaceful views across the lake.

8 Hokitika Gorge Walks
Turquoise waters swirl through a narrow limestone gorge.

- **Grade:** Easy. **Time:** 15 minutes to the river, 45 minutes for the loop walk
- **How to get there:** From SH6, take the road out towards Kokatahi, and then follow the signs to the gorge via Kowhitirangi and Whitcombe Roads. A total distance of 33 km

Finally bursting out of the mountains, the Hokitika River is forced through a narrow rocky gorge and while this is appealing in itself, it is the vivid turquoise water that really steals the show. Arising high in the mountains, fine mineral particles are suspended in the river water, giving it a startling opaque blue-green colouring. There is an easy walk for everyone, from a very short stroll to a lookout, through to a longer loop walk through mature podocarp forest.

9 Ross Water Race Walkway
Old gold workings and historic buildings.

- **Grade:** Easy. **Time:** One hour.
- **How to get there:** The walk begins from the Ross Visitor Centre – while you can drive past the centre, the road is very narrow, parking is limited and turning is extremely difficult.

Gold mining has continued in Ross ever since gold was discovered in 1864, with new mining operations opening up closer to the sea. In 1909, the largest gold nugget ever found in New Zealand was discovered in Jones Creek, just behind the town. Weighing 3 kg, the huge lump of gold was named the Honourable Roddy, after the then Minister of Mines, the Honourable Roderick McKenzie.

From the car park follow the roadway up Mt Greenland Road (not steep despite the name), and follow Jones Creek to the end of the road. The Honourable Roddy was found here in this stream, where you can try your hand at gold panning. Pans are available for hire from the friendly visitor centre and panning is best just after heavy rain. At the end of the road the track leads to the right up through regenerating bush via old tunnels, a miner's cottage and the historic Ross Cemetery, with views over Ross and to the north.

Back at the visitor centre, take time to view the old cottage, the Ross jail, a reconstructed water wheel and an old sluicing gun.

10 Okarito Trig Walk
Superb views to the mountains.

Grade: Medium. **Time:** One hour 15 minutes return.

How to get there: From SH6 turn off to Okarito and drive 13 km to the coast. At Okarito turn left (there is only one road) and the walk begins at the end.

The views from the Okarito trig sum up everything you come to the West Coast to see. Initially the walk begins through bush, with nearby surf sounding like the continuous roar of a jet engine. The uphill stretch is a solid climb but not too steep, with your reward at the top, where pristine forest stretches endlessly north and south. Directly to the east is Mt Elie de Beaumont; to the southeast are Aoraki Mt Cook and Mt Tasman, with the Franz Josef Glacier tucked below. Immediately to the north the myriad arms of the Okarito Lagoon slide gently into dark forest, while just to the south Three Mile Lagoon is visible, with the coastline disappearing into the horizon.

11 Fox and Franz Josef Glaciers
Glaciers within 20 km of the sea.

Grade: Easy. **Time:** Franz Josef – one hour return; Fox – one hour return.
How to get there: Franz Josef Glacier is signposted off SH6 just south of Franz Josef township – the walks begin at the terminal car park. Fox Glacier is well signposted off SH6 just south of Fox Glacier village.

New Zealand is one of the few places in the world where glaciers reach such low levels, with Fox set in a dramatic steep-sided glacial valley, while Franz Josef is surrounded by bush. Once stretching far out to sea, after thousands of years of warming weather, both are now confined to the mountains. From a distance they appear grubby and disappointing; at the glacier face, the creaking and groaning of slowly grinding blue-green ice is awe-inspiring.

The Maori name for Franz Josef is Ka Roimata o Hine Hukatere – the Tears of Hine Hukatere. According to legend, when Hine Hukatere's lover, Tuawe, was swept away by an avalanche her tears froze. Fox Glacier is Te Moeka o Tuawe, the final resting place (moeka) of Tuawe.

Short walks lead to both terminals and guided walks are available on the glaciers themselves. The length of each walk varies – floods frequently wash away the walkways, which are reconstructed to suit the new conditions. While there are cafés at Fox and Franz Josef, accommodation is at a premium in summer.

Named by explorer Julius von Haast in 1865 after Franz Josef, Emperor of Austria, this glacier is steeper, faster moving and more easily photographed. The walk starts through forest then follows the riverbed to a lookout near the terminal. Sentinel Rock is a short side track climbing up to a lookout with great views and particularly good for taking photographs.

In contrast, Fox lies in a shattered valley, with cliffs shorn clean by moving ice. The walk to the terminal is worthwhile just to appreciate the sheer power and force of this glacier, but it's dangerous to walk on the ice or directly up to the terminal without a guide. The ice is very unstable and recent fatalities occurred when people went beyond the barriers.

12 Lake Matheson

A small lake perfectly reflects nearby mountains.

Grade: Easy. **Time:** One hour 30 minutes.
How to get there: 5 km west of Fox Glacier township.

Possibly the most photographed lake in New Zealand, Lake Matheson is famous for the mirror image of Aoraki Mt Cook, Mts Tasman and La Perouse reflected in the still waters. The best time for photographing the reflection is early morning before the wind ruffles the surface.

Known as a 'kettle lake', Lake Matheson was formed by a large section of ice left behind when Fox Glacier retreated from its last advance around 14,000 years ago and the depression created by the melting ice filled with water. Even if you're not a morning person, the loop walk is an attractive stroll around the lake, fringed by kahikatea and rimu forest with snow-topped mountains in the distance.

13 Munro Beach Walk

A wild beach is home to the Fiordland crested penguin.

Grade: Easy. **Time:** One and a half hours return.
How to get there: Off SH6, 30 km north of Haast at the southern end of Lake Moeraki.

Flanked by rocky headlands and pounded by wild weather straight off the Tasman Sea, the small sandy cove of Munro Beach is home to fur seals and the very rare Fiordland crested penguin/tawaki. Fewer than 3000 pairs remain. The birds are very striking with white on the front, blackish-blue colouring on the back and white stripes about the face. In addition, a thin band of yellow runs over the eye and down the back of the neck, culminating in a tuft of feathers.

One of the three penguin species to breed on the mainland (the other two are the blue and yellow-eyed penguin), the best time to see them is early morning or late afternoon, from July through to November. Like most penguins, they are somewhat timid, so it's best to sit still rather than wander over the beach.

The track to the sea is flat, easy walking and meanders through very handsome mature native bush with towering rimu trees.

14 Ship Creek Walkway
Two unmissable coastal walks.

Grade: Easy. Time: 50 minutes.
How to get there: On SH6, 15 km north of Haast.

Kahikatea Swamp Walk begins from the car park, crosses back under the highway and follows Ship Creek through thick forest to the small loop through a kahikatea swamp. Mainly on raised boardwalks, on this section of the 20-minute walk huge and ancient trees, heavy with mosses, creepers and lichens, rise straight out of the murky, dark waters, heavily stained with plant tannin. These are kahikatea at their most impressive.

Dune Lake Walk takes 30 minutes and is much more open. It starts out along the beach, leading to a lookout tower atop a dune. From the lookout the view is south along the beach, and stretches all the way to Jackson Head, 50 km to the south, while inland the view is over dune country backed by the splendid mountains of the Southern Alps.

From the lookout, the track skirts a small lake fringed by reeds then finally loops back through rimu forest to the starting point. Considering its proximity to the sea, the bush is amazingly lush. It's also worth spending some time on the beach, with water-worn driftwood lining the sand and wild surf creating air heavy with salt spray.

15 Hapuka Estuary Walk
Three distinct ecosystems in one short loop walk.

Grade: Easy. Time: 20 minutes return.
How to get there: From Haast head south along the coast towards Jackson Bay for 15 km. The walk begins on the left, 2 km after crossing the bridge over the Okuru River.

This short flat walk encompasses three interlinked ecosystems – forest, wetlands and estuary. Starting through bush dominated by rimu and kahikatea, the first section is dense, with the semi-climbing kiekie giving the bushscape a distinctly subtropical feel. Some of the rimu here are estimated to be between 500 and 800 years old. Emerging from the shade, a raised boardwalk traverses a wetland thick with flax and manuka before the track follows the riverbank back to the car park. The dark tea-coloured water is overhung with old kowhai trees, and whitebait are prolific during the season.

The young of various species of the galaxiidae family, whitebait come to the rivers around the New Zealand coast between mid-August and mid-November. After the adult lays its eggs on vegetation along the banks of a river in autumn, the newly hatched larvae are swept out to sea, from where they return the following spring as whitebait. The fish then live out their adult lives in freshwater streams and rivers. The Craypot Café on the beach at Jackson Bay is famous for its whitebait fritters.

16 Roaring Billy
Roaring Billy rushes down a series of cascades.

Grade: Easy. **Time:** 25 minutes return.
How to get there: On SH6, 27 km from Haast.

This is the wettest part of the road with rain falling on an average of 180 days a year and with an annual fall of over 5500 mm. Roaring Billy Stream is a tributary of the Haast River and at this point crashes down a series of boulder-strewn cascades. A level walk through beautiful beech forest dense with mosses and ferns takes you to the edge of the Haast River, at this point a wide gravel riverbed.

17 Haast Pass Lookout
A tough but short walk to a lookout in both directions.

Grade: Hard. **Time:** 40 minutes return.
How to get there: On SH6, 61 km from Haast.

Zigzagging up through beech forest which gradually thins as you climb, this track finally reaches a lookout over the pass. The view is down the bush-lined pass both east and west with snow-capped mountains in every direction. It's a bit of slog but the track is well formed, so take your time – the views are worth it.

18 Blue Pools
Trout swim lazily in deep clear pools.

Grade: Easy. **Time:** 30 minutes return.
How to get there: On SH6, 72 km from Haast.

This easy walk on a good track is through handsome virgin beech forest to a series of deep clear-water pools on the confluence of the Blue and Makarora rivers. The pools, overhung by ancient beech trees, vary in colour between blue and green but regardless of colour, the water is very cold at any time of the year. Keep an eye out for enormous brown and rainbow trout both at the pools and in the river by the swingbridge. The trout are more common in winter when they come upstream to spawn.

19 Makarora
A primeval forest of mature native trees.

Grade: Easy. **Time:** 15 minutes return.
How to get there: 80 km east of Haast and 65 km west of Wanaka on SH6.

A mixture of beech, matai, kahikatea and miro, the dense forest around Makarora contrasts dramatically with the dry landscape only a few kilometres to the east. Despite its small size the forest still supports a good number of native birds, including kaka, the elusive bush parrot. The South Island kaka, *Nestor meridionalis meridionalis* differs from its North Island counterpart in that it is a heavier bird, has much brighter plumage, especially the crimson feathers under the wings, and a distinctive white crown. Once common throughout the South Island, the kaka is particularly vulnerable to predators as a fledgling, as it leaves the nest before being able to fly.

The township of Makarora grew as a milling centre supplying the Otago goldfields with much-needed timber. The short flat walk passes through a small remnant of this great forest and includes an old pit for handsawing, the log still complete with saw.

14
short walks in
Buller and Lewis Pass

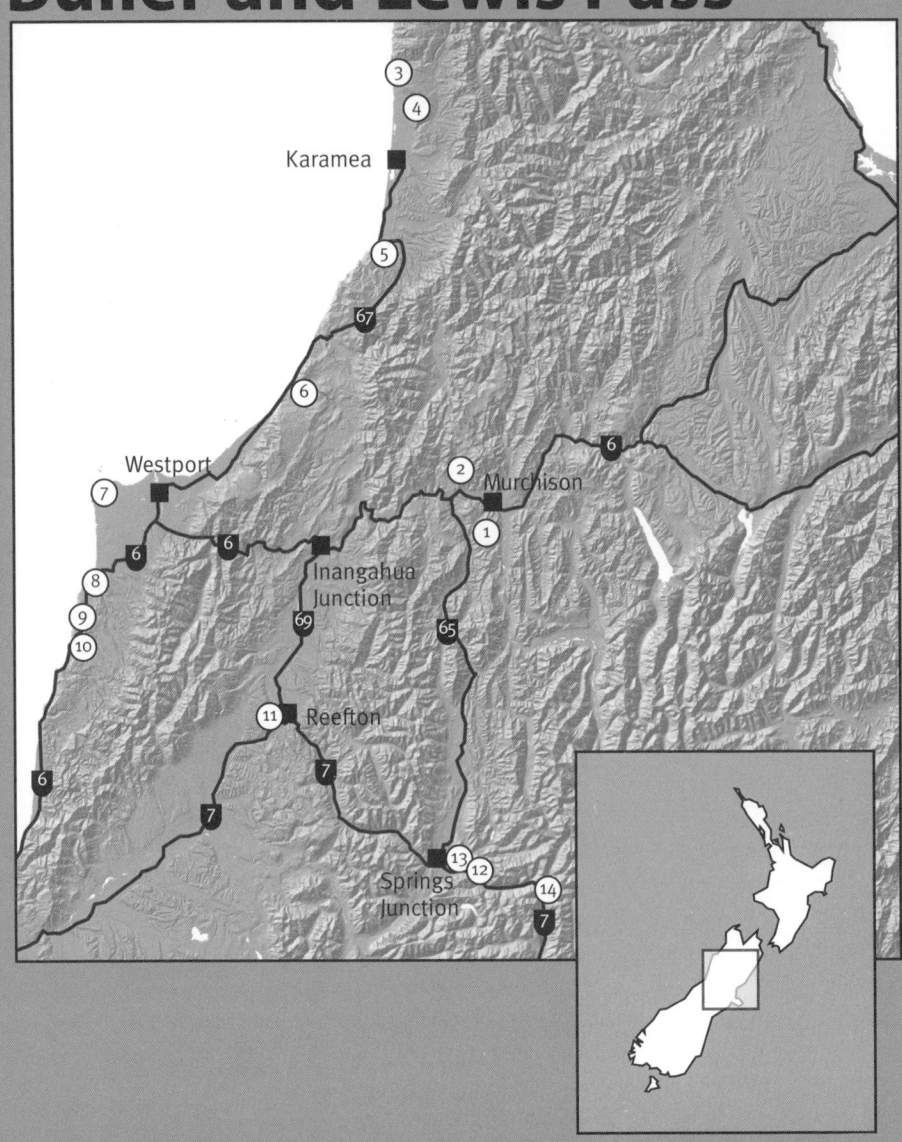

1 Six Mile Walk

New Zealand's oldest hydro power station.

> **Grade:** Easy. **Time:** One hour 15 minutes return.
> **How to get there:** Turn off SH60 into Fairfax St (where the museum is) and continue down the Matakitaki Valley for 10 km. The walk begins to the left of the tiny powerhouse.

Commissioned in 1922 and closed in 1975, Six Mile is New Zealand's oldest hydro power station. What makes this walk unique is that most of the infrastructure is still in place, including the well-preserved but tiny powerhouse. Located at the beginning of the walk, the equipment here appears in such good working order, it looks as if it would start with the push of a button.

From the powerhouse the walk follows the intake pipe up a short hill to the water race. An unmarked short loop to the left through the blackberry leads to the holding pond at the end of the water race. Here the walk enters beech forest thick with moss, continuing on to the water race intake by a small weir on the Matakitaki River. The return loop track parallels the main track, follow the water race high above the river and back to the beginning.

2 Croesus Battery, Lyell Walkway

A forest walk through the remains of a gold-mining settlement.

> **Grade:** Easy. **Time:** Croesus Battery and the Old Dray Road – one hour 30 minutes.
> **How to get there:** In the upper Buller Gorge, 16 km north of Inangahua on SH7.

In 1862 when gold was discovered in Lyell Creek a township quickly sprang up and by 1873 included a school, post office, church and six hotels. While other gold towns have disappeared under gorse and blackberry, here the bush looks pristine and untouched, the creek runs swift and clear – yet this valley was once home to thousands and alive with feverish activity. Excellent information boards in the car park feature numerous historic photographs showing the flourishing town in the late nineteenth century.

It's a short walk (15 minutes return) to the old cemetery, from where the track continues through the beech forest to Croesus Battery. The old stamper and other machinery still remain on the creek bank. Returning from the battery, take the Old Dray Road track to the right, which continues downstream, emerging just below the car park. While most of the track is in excellent condition, there are some rough patches here due to slips in this steep and wet country.

By the car park is a large grassed area, ideal for picnics and camping, though the usual warning about sandflies applies.

3 Scotts Beach, Kahurangi National Park
A bush walk leads to a wild beach.

Grade: Easy. **Time:** Two hours return.
How to get there: From Karamea township head north along the coast for 15 km to the southern end of the Heaphy Track at the Kohaihai River.

Occupying the northwest corner of the South Island, Kahurangi National Park covers over 450,000 ha, New Zealand's second largest after Fiordland. With some of New Zealand's most ancient rocks, our oldest fossils (sponges, trilobites and molluscs dating back 508 million years) were found here. The park is also famous for dramatic limestone landscapes, with cave systems around Mt Arthur and Mt Owen New Zealand's longest and deepest. Flora is diverse, from temperate coastal forest with palms and ferns, to extensive beech forests in the east, with the higher areas home to 80 percent of New Zealand's alpine plants and 20 species of carnivorous land snail, rarely seen. Despite its size, the park isn't very accessible – tracks crossing the park require stamina and time.

This well-maintained section of the Heaphy Track to Scotts Beach is so beautifully graded you'll hardly raise a sweat on the initial uphill section to Scotts Lookout, though the views are modest. After the downhill stretch, Scotts Beach is stunning – white sand backed with luxuriant bush, but too dangerous for swimming. There is a sheltered grassy picnic area with toilets and fireplaces, where you can also camp.

The easy Nikau Walk (10 to 40 minutes return) branches off the beginning of the Heaphy Track right after crossing the swingbridge over the Kohaihai River. The track loops through swathes of nikau palm, with a massive southern rata tree. Ngaio and karaka are present, with jet-black fantails common.

For the very fit, the Zigzag Track branches off to the right at the beginning of the Heaphy Track, a short (25 minutes return) but relentless uphill climb to a lookout above the coast. Open vegetation reveals continuous views, which helps alleviate the uphill grind. From the top there are excellent views of the Kohaihai River and beach.

4 Oparara Basin Walks
Magnificent limestone arches and caves.

Grade: Oparara Arch – easy; Moria Gate – easy; Crazy Paving Cave and Box Canyon Cave – easy. **Time:** Oparara Arch – 40 minutes return; Moria Gate – one hour return; Crazy Paving Cave and Box Canyon Cave – 20 minutes return.

How to get there: From Karamea drive north for 10 km, then turn right into McCallums Mill Road, following the unsealed, narrow road for another 15 km.

The Oparara Basin lies within the Kahurangi National Park, an area of exceptional natural beauty. The birdlife is prolific, and there's a good chance of spotting the rare blue duck, which makes its home on the boulder-strewn Oparara River.

The car park is the starting point for three shorter walks in the magnificent virgin bush and fascinating limestone landscapes of the Oparara River Valley. The road into the basin is a challenge: narrow, winding and unsealed with stretches where it's difficult to pass. A DOC sign at the beginning advises the road is unsuitable for caravans and campervans, though shorter-wheel-based campervans will manage. Weka are common in the car park so keep a close eye on your belongings as they're cheeky enough to jump in if you leave the door open.

The Oparara Arch is reputed to be the largest natural arch in New Zealand. There are two arches over the Oparara River, enclosed by huge limestone cliffs. The main arch is over 200 m long, through which the river flows. Although you're unable to walk through, a viewpoint allows a peek to the other side. The second arch is gigantic and towers far above the river. It is massive, yet appears so fragile it feels uncomfortable to stand beneath. This easy flat walk to the arches is through virgin beech forest and along a beautiful stony river, home of the rare blue duck.

Moria Gate is lower and even more delicate. The walk proceeds through mature beech forest dripping with moss, with access through a small side cave which is a bit of a scramble, though chain ropes help. You emerge onto a sandy ledge inside the arch itself, with both ends visible. The rocks within the cave have a dimpled pattern from the action of water over the years, and if the water is low you can wade upstream for a view of the arch from outside. If you're in the mood for a longer walk, the track continues on to Mirror Tarn, then joins the road for a short stretch back to the car park.

The short walk to the Crazy Paving Cave and Box Canyon Cave is through beautiful beech forest – the car park is 2 km beyond the Oparara Arches car park. Torches are necessary. The name of the first cave comes from the patterns on its floor, formed by mud drying and shrinking over time, and cracking into patterns. A little further along, and accessed by steps, is Box Canyon Cave, a large roomy cave deep in the limestone hill.

The caves are home to New Zealand's only cave spider, *Spelungula cavernicola*, and while the elusive arachnid isn't easily visible, the delicate egg sacs hang from the roof. Discovered in 1957, the spiders occupy the area near the cave mouth and feed primarily on cave weta and flying insects.

5 Lake Hanlon
A quick walk to a small, bush-fringed lake.

Grade: Easy. **Time:** 30 minutes return.
How to get there: 20 km south of Karamea, on SH 67.

Towards Little Wanganui River, and just below the Karamea Bluffs (rising to 400 m), is tiny Lake Hanlon. Formed by the 1929 Murchison earthquake, this pretty lake is fringed with beech and rata, a particularly attractive sight in summer.

Weka are members of the rail family, common around Lake Hanlon and throughout northern Westland. Endemic to New Zealand, four subspecies of this flightless bird were once widespread throughout the country, but today it's seen more commonly on offshore islands and in the northern part of the South Island. Initially relatively unaffected by the arrival of people, the weka population drastically declined in the first half of the twentieth century. However, around the Gisborne area the population remained strong, but in the 1980s mysteriously collapsed from 90,000 birds to fewer than 2000 within 20 years. No one is quite sure why.

6 Charming Creek Walkway

An old railway line to the Mangatini Falls.

Grade: Easy. **Time:** One hour 45 minutes return.
How to get there: At Ngakawau on SH67 turn into Tylers Road, just before the bridge over the Ngakawau River.

The Charming Creek Walkway follows the line of an old private railway along the Ngakawau River and through a deep gorge. The railway was opened in 1914 to bring coal down from the Charming Creek Coal Mine, but was also used to extract timber. Finally closed in 1958, most of the line is still intact, as are the three tunnels. The old bridge foundations remain as the foundations of the 'bins' (an area used for sorting coal). More recent slips and rockfalls demonstrate what a daunting task it must have been to both build and maintain the line. The bush along the way is luxurious and glow-worms can be found in the tunnels and some of the railway cuttings.

The Mangatini Falls tumble down a side stream into the Ngakawau River. At the base of the falls is the rare daisy *Celmisia morganii*, found only in the Ngakawau Gorge (most Celmisia are alpine plants).

As the walkway follows the railway line it is for most part flat and if you intend to do the whole walk it will take three hours one way.

7 Cape Foulwind Walkway

Grade: Easy. **Time:** One hour one way.
How to get there: From Westport head south, and just over the Buller River turn right into Cape Foulwind Road. It is 12 km to the lighthouse and a further 5 km to Tauranga Bay. If heading south take Watsons Lead Road which joins SH6, 16 km north of Charleston.

To Maori, Cape Foulwind was known as Tauranga, 'sheltering anchorage', breaking the worst of the southerly winds. This protected fishing waka and sheltered the small plain around the mouth of the Kawatiri (Buller) River.

This easy walk follows the clifftops from the lighthouse to Tauranga, with marvellous views to the north and dramatic coastal vistas along the way. A heavy swell makes this walk even more dramatic. The seal colony is a great spot to watch fur seals, with lookout points directly above. The number of seals varies with the season, though the best time to see seal pups is between December and March. However, keep a sharp eye out as seals are hard to see and not confined to the colony: there may be more seals here than you first think.

Punakaiki Coast

A stunning combination of sea, beautiful bush, and dramatic rock formations, Punakaiki is more than just the pancake rocks and blowhole. There are a number of excellent short walks, good accommodation and cafes, and the road along the coast is spectacular in its own right.

8 Truman Track
From forest to a dramatic rocky coast.

Grade: Easy. **Time:** 30 minutes return.
How to get there: On SH6, 2 km north of Pancake Rocks.

The Truman Track is well worth combining with a visit to Pancake Rocks. An easy flat path winds through a mature forest of matai, rimu and rata, to a short coastal strip of flax and finally down to a small sandy cove (not safe for swimming). There are dramatic views along this rugged mountainous coastline and at low tide it's possible to explore the sea caves and the rocky shore. Blue penguins nest here from August to February, with the best viewing times around dawn and dusk.

9 Pororari Gorge Lookout Walk
Dense rainforest along a deep limestone river gorge.

Grade: Easy. **Time:** 40 minutes return to the lookout.
How to get there: 1.5 km north of Punakaiki on SH6.

The track alongside the Pororari River is just 1.5 km north of the Pancake Rocks and twists its way to the sea through a deep gorge with towering limestone bluffs. Lush bush thick with ferns, kiekie and nikau palms overhangs the track, giving it a distinctly tropical feel. The track begins under the Pororari River Bridge and is flat all the way to the lookout, which has views deep into the limestone hills. The track continues further upstream, so if you feel like walking more keep on going until you've had enough.

10 Pancake Rocks and Blowhole
Spectacular blowholes, sea caves and arches.

〽️ **Grade:** Easy. 🕐 **Time:** 30 minutes return.
🚶 **How to get there:** On SH6 at Punakaiki.

The Pancake Rocks, featured on a thousand calendars, attract a huge number of visitors and can be very crowded, but when a heavy swell is running this place is so spectacular, the stop is worth it despite the crowds. The unusual rock formations began forming 30 million years ago when limestone was overlaid with softer mudstone in a succession of layers. Over the years sea and wind have eroded the softer mudstone layers, creating a stacked pancake effect. An excellent well-formed path wends through lush coastal bush to dramatic bluffs, sea caves, arches and surge pools. Numerous narrow fissures in the rocky seascape act as blowholes, which are best at high tide or in rough weather. The largest blowhole, Putai, can be seen and heard from quite a distance when a huge sea is running.

11 Victoria Conservation Park, Progress Water Race
A riverside walk through beech forest.

〽️ **Grade:** Easy. 🕐 **Time:** Two hours return.
🚶 **How to get there:** 4 km east of Reefton on SH 7.

To the west of Lewis Pass is the Victoria Conservation Park, the largest conservation park in New Zealand, encompassing the Victoria and Brunner ranges and the headwaters of the Grey, Inangahua and Maruia rivers. Covering a huge area of over 206,000 ha, the landscape is very mixed, from pristine landscapes to areas once the site of feverish mining activity for gold and coal.

The subalpine vegetation is predominantly beech – and the only area of the country where all five types of beech tree grow together.

Beginning from the swingbridge picnic area, a footbridge crosses the river to a good track meandering through dense beech forest following the bank of the dark, tea-coloured Inangahua River to Deep Creek.

12 Lake Daniells Walk
An alpine lake walk.

Grade: Easy. **Time:** 3 hours return.
How to get there: 5 km from Springs Junction.

Lake Daniells is a small, pretty alpine lake at the head of the Alfred River, a tributary of the Maruia River. This easy walk is through dense beech forest along the Alfred River and Fraser Stream. Another track circumnavigates the lake, with a large camping area at the beginning. Near the entrance, by the road, is an intriguing fence – not to keep in stock, but to monitor any movement in the Alpine Fault. If time is tight then the short walk to the Sluice Box takes only 15 minutes return. Here the wide Maruia River runs deep and clear as it's forced through a narrow gorge of marble rock.

13 Waterfall Track
An elegant waterfall.

Grade: Easy. **Time:** 20 minutes return.
How to get there: On SH7, 9 km east of Springs Junction.

An elegant, slender waterfall dropping 40 m is the highlight of this bush walk through massive ancient beech trees. Just below the top of the falls the water strikes a rocky ledge and dissipates into a fine spray, reforming into a more substantial flow lower down.

14 Tarn Walk
A mountain tarn and thick beech forest.

Grade: Easy. **Time:** 20 minutes return.
How to get there: On SH7, 23 km east of Springs Junction

Located just below the highest point in the Lewis Pass, and well worth stopping for, this is a well-formed track with boardwalks for protecting the delicate flora. Not only is this part of the pass the watershed for the major rivers flowing east and west, it also marks the dramatic climatic differences found on either side of the Main Divide. West of the Lewis Pass the forest flourishes in the wet climate, in direct contrast to the dry, open and sparse vegetation of the east, on the Canterbury side.

The track skirts a small mountain tarn by the car park, and on a still day, it is a great place to take a photo of the mountains reflected in the water. From here the walk loops through stunted alpine beech forest hung with fine mosses reflecting the harsh alpine climate. There are views deep into the snow-capped mountains to the north, including Gloriana Peak. Amateur botanists will welcome the excellent labels to assist with the identification of alpine plants along the track.

10
short walks in Canterbury and Arthur's Pass

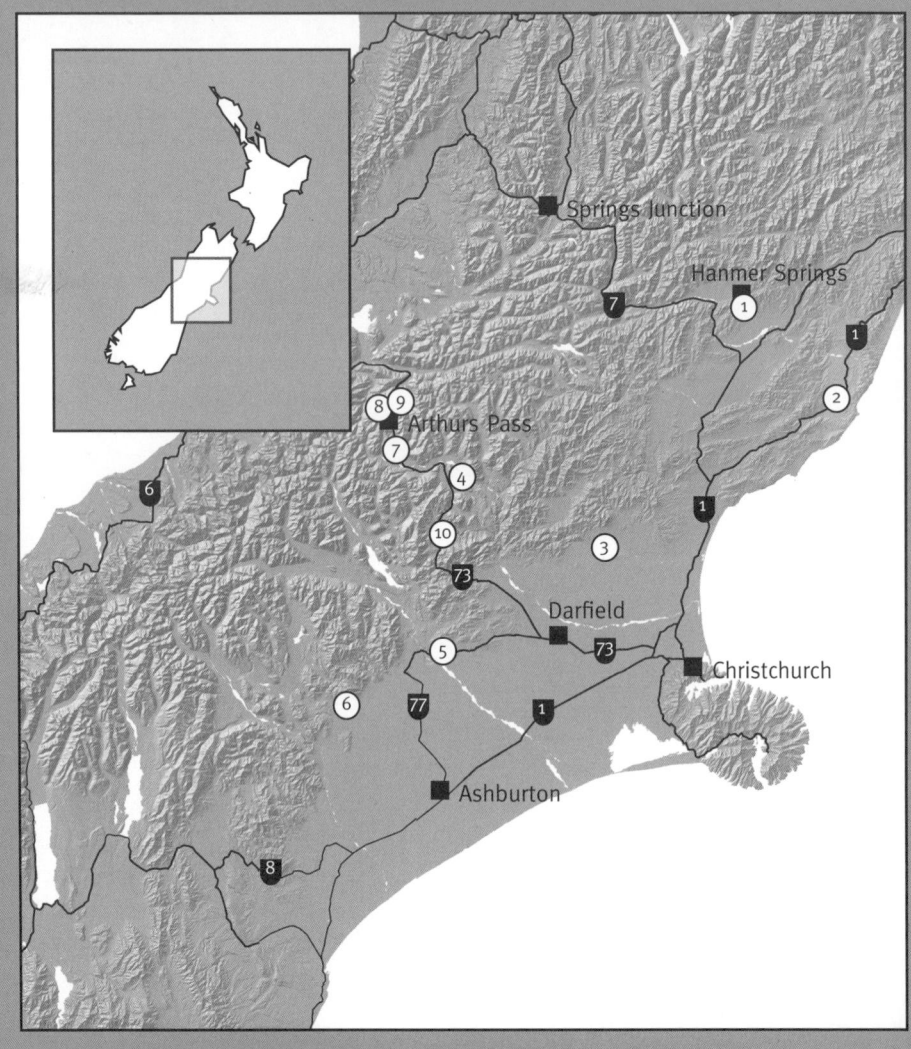

1 Conical Hill and Woodland Walk, Hanmer Springs

A fascinating walk through exotic forest.

Grade: Easy/medium. **Time:** One and a half hours.
How to get there: The walk begins at the north end of Conical Hill Road, Hanmer's main street.

The area around Hanmer is a mixture of exotic and native forest, but here imported trees grab all the attention. In 1903, prison labour planted extensive areas of Douglas fir and *Pinus radiata* for timber production. At the same time other species were planted for beautification or to test their suitability for timber. The forest area is close to the village and especially attractive in autumn, when the deciduous trees change colour in the cool mountain climate. This combination of two short walks can be done together or separately. A very popular walk on an excellent track, the trek up Conical Hill is a steady climb through mainly conifers, including pine, fir, larch and cypress. From the lookout at the top of the hill (550 m) there are great views over the township and surrounding mountains.

Return the same way. About halfway down take the Majuba Track, leading off to the left. This track joins the Woodland loop track by the wetland. Appropriately named, the Woodland Walk meanders through an extensive collection of northern hemisphere deciduous and evergreen trees. The track exits on to Jollies Pass Road, 1 km from the main street.

2 St Annes Lagoon

A pretty lakeside walk brimming with birdlife.

Grade: Easy. **Time:** 30 minutes.
How to get there: On SH1, 3 km north of Cheviot.

A pleasant short walk, this small lake is packed with birdlife attracted by water in the usually dry North Canterbury region. Known to Maori as Mata Kopae, the lake was a valuable seasonal hunting ground and a welcome stopping point for those travelling between Kaikoura and the main Ngai Tahu settlement at Kaiapoi. Planted with lovely deciduous trees, the walk is particularly pretty in autumn when the trees are changing colour. This is a good spot to take a break and stretch your legs on the road between Christchurch and Picton, or for a shady picnic on a warm day.

3 Wooded Gully/Red Pine Track, Mount Thomas
Deep lush forest alive with bellbirds.

- **Grade:** Medium. **Time:** Two hours return.
- **How to get there:** From Rangiora, take the Lowburn–Glentui Road, with Mt Thomas clearly signposted to the right – the car park is 3 km down the end of this road.

A series of low peaks lie northwest of Christchurch above the Waimakariri River – Mt Thomas, Mt Richardson, Mt Oxford and Mt Grey. Sandwiched between open plain and rugged mountains to the west, this area of deep wooded gullies and magnificent beech is home to numerous native birds. Exposed to fierce northwest winds which frequently reach gale force, the peaks are a mixture of open tussock land and sparse beech trees. Mt Thomas (1034 m) is the most accessible and while the top is open and often snow-covered in winter, the lower slopes are characterised by fine beech forest and lush valleys. The tramp to the top will take around five hours return. The walk is through handsome beech forest with the occasional glimpse of the plains to the east. In addition to bellbirds, keep an eye out for kakariki, the rare native parrot. Start at the main noticeboard and follow the Wooded Gully track signs uphill. Continue past the junction with the Kereru Track, after which the path becomes steeper and narrower. Eventually you reach the junction with the Red Pine Track – turn left and head back downhill until you rejoin the Kereru Track back to the car park.

The Kereru Track is a shorter option, the loop walk taking less than an hour. There is an excellent camping ground and picnic area at the beginning of the tracks, with great views.

4 Kowai Bush Walk, Springfield
A rare surviving patch of foothills beech forest

- **Grade:** Easy. **Time:** Bush Loop Walk: 20 minutes
- **How to get there:** Just 750 metres west of Springfield on SH 73 (to Arthur's Pass) turn right into Pococks Road and 1 km on, over the railway line, turn left into Kowai Road. The reserve is on the right, 3km down Kowai Road.

Open to the public, this small privately-owned reserve is a rare survivor of

Above: The Boulder Bank at Nelson is an extraordinary natural phenomenon created by wind and tide.
Left: At Cape Farewell dramatic sea cliffs mark the northernmost point of the South Island.
Below: Lake Rotoiti is one of two glacier lakes in the heart of Nelson Lakes National Park.

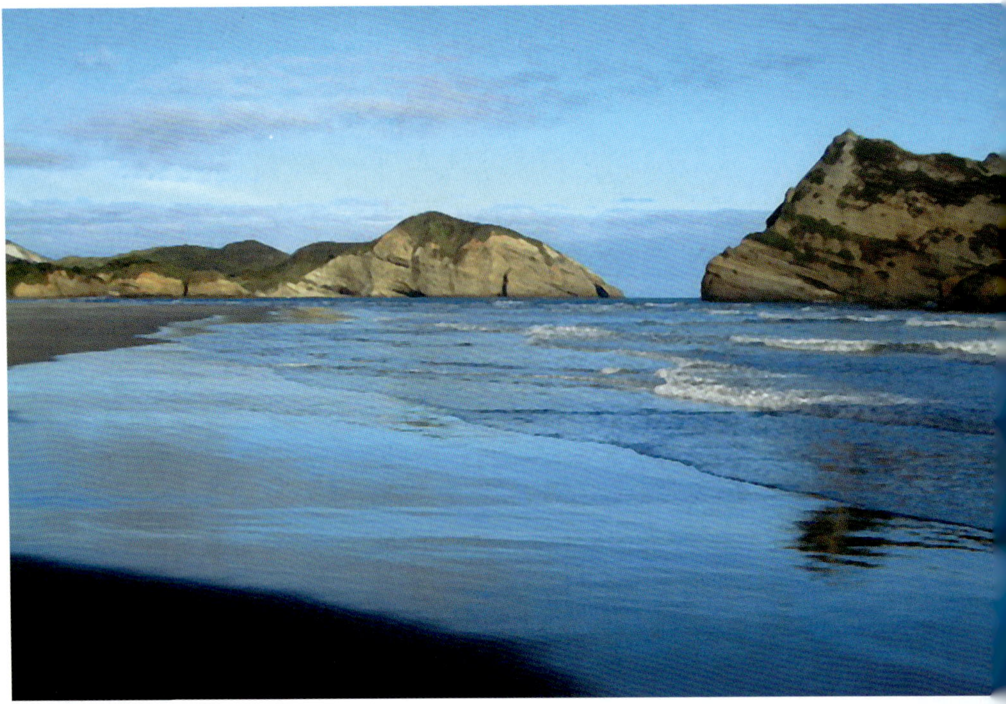

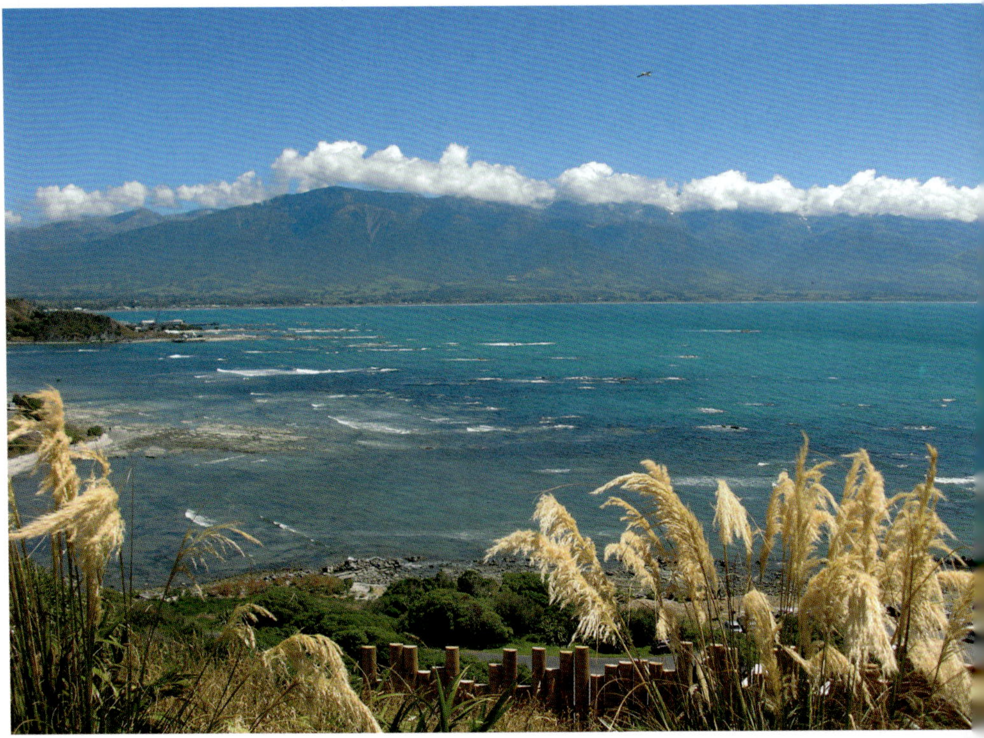

Opposite above: There are fantastic views on the walk from Wharariki Beach to Pillar Point Lighthouse at the top of the South Island.

Opposite below: Towering mountain ranges rise out of the sea at Kaikoura.

Right: Several walks through fine lowland bush start at the Pelorus Bridge, west of Havelock.

Below: Wither Hills behind Blenheim were once covered in dense native bush.

Left: The Mangatini Falls are a highlight of the Charming Creek Walkway along an abandoned railway line in the northern Buller region.
Above: Highly unusual rock formations at Punakaiki take the full force of the west coast surf.
Below: Scott's Beach at the beginning of the Heaphy Track is reached by an easy walk.

Above: Spectacular views are the reward for a short but steep climb at Haast Pass.
Below left: Fox Glacier terminates just 10km from the sea on the West Coast.
Below right: Stunning native forest fringes the placid waters of Lake Brunner, south east of Greymouth.

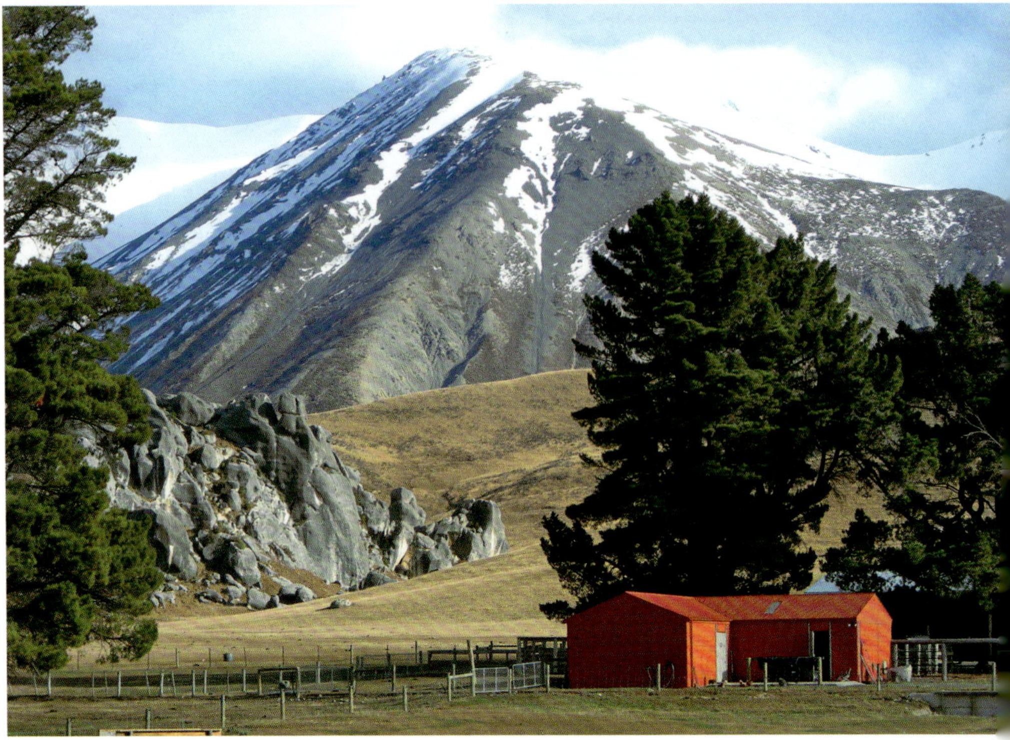

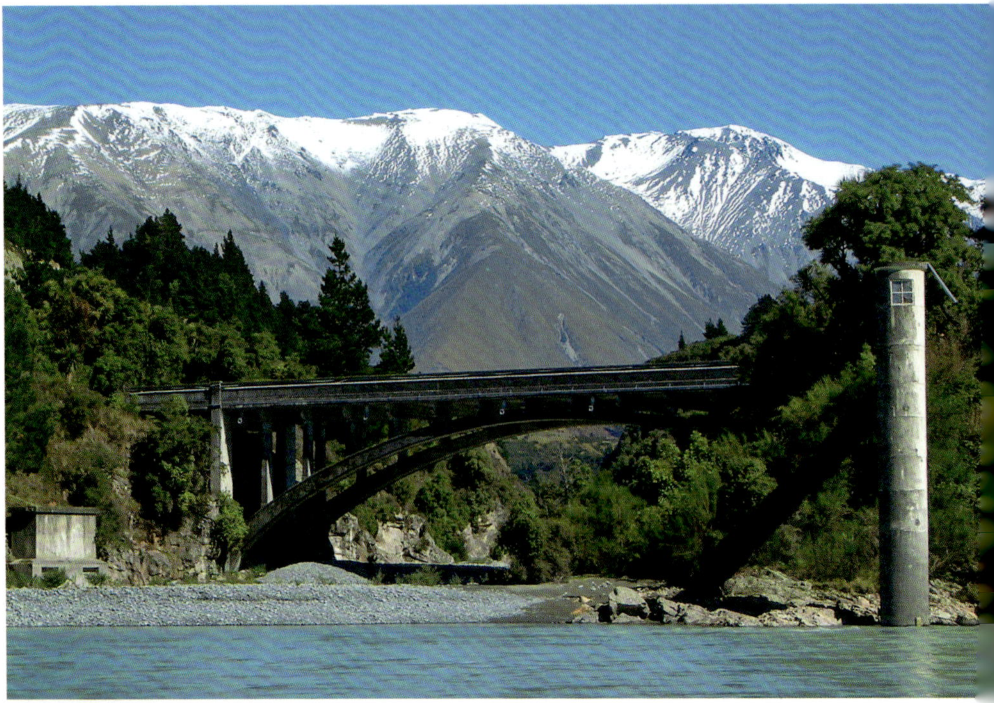

Opposite above: Weathered limestone rock formations lie off the road at Castle Rock on the way to Arthur's Pass.
Opposite below: An historic bridge marks the beginning of a walk along the Rakaia Gorge.
Above: Numerous walks along the old crater rim offer grand views of Lyttelton Harbour.
Right: A long empty expanse of beach is part of the walkway at Brooklands Lagoon north of Christchurch.

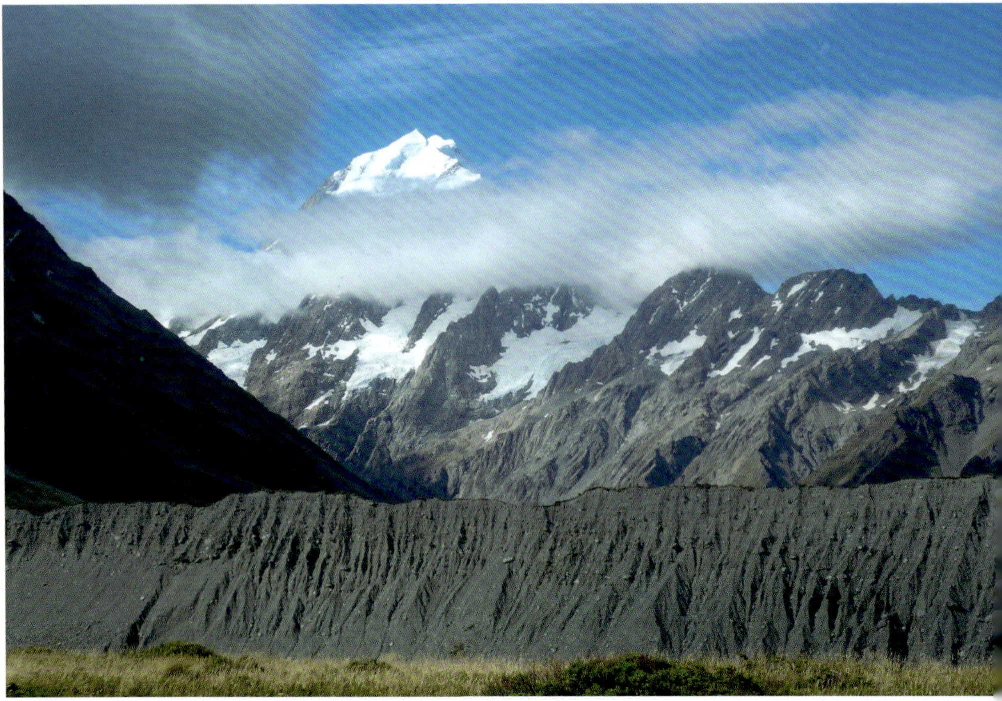

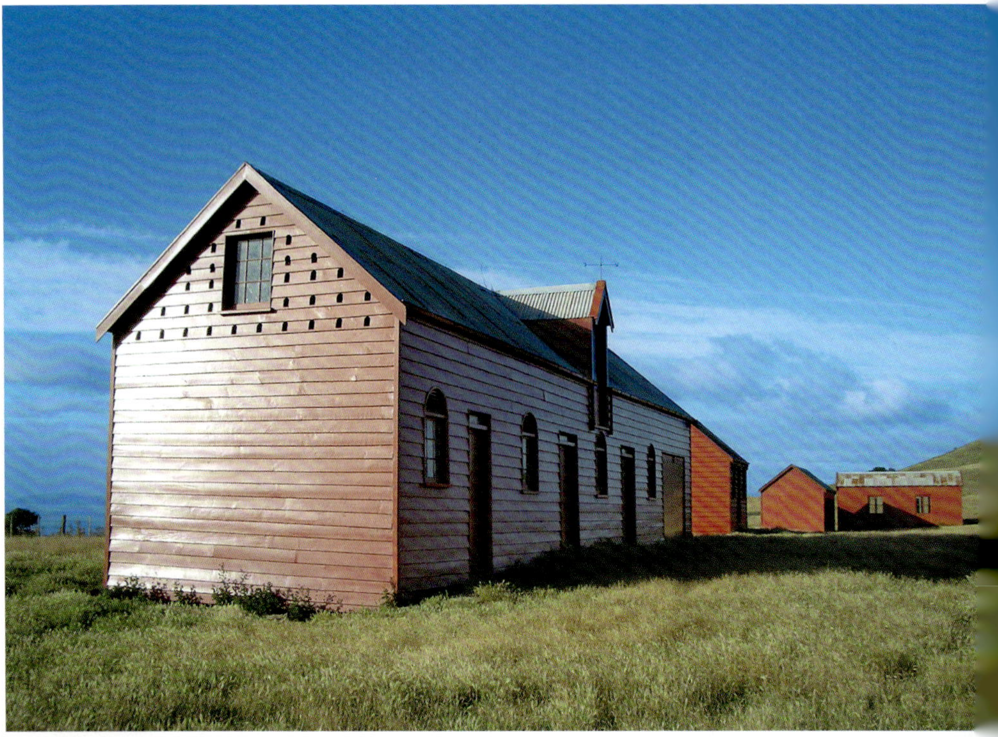

Opposite above: Spectacular views of Aoraki/Mt Cook from Kea Point overlooking the Mueller Glacier.
Opposite below: Beautifully preserved farm buildings are the highlight of this walk at Matanaka, north of Dunedin.
Above: The Criterion Hotel is just one of Oamaru's fine Victorian limestone buildings.
Right: An historic wooden lighthouse marks the start of a coastal walk at Katiki Point, on the Moeraki Peninsula.
Below: Ancient fossils are exposed in the limestone formations at Elephant Rocks in the Waitaki Valley.

Above: Historic limestone kilns feature on the track along Bob's Cove, near Queenstown.
Right: Rock formations known as 'tors' are common at Flat Top Hill near Alexandra.
Below: Rustic stone miners' cottages sit among the tussock at Bendigo.

Above: The Basket of Dreams sculpture is the highlight of the Time Walk up Queenstown Hill.
Right: Stroll along the Routeburn River on the way to the Double Barrel Falls, near Glenorchy.
Below: The Waterfall Creek track follows the shores of Lake Wanaka.

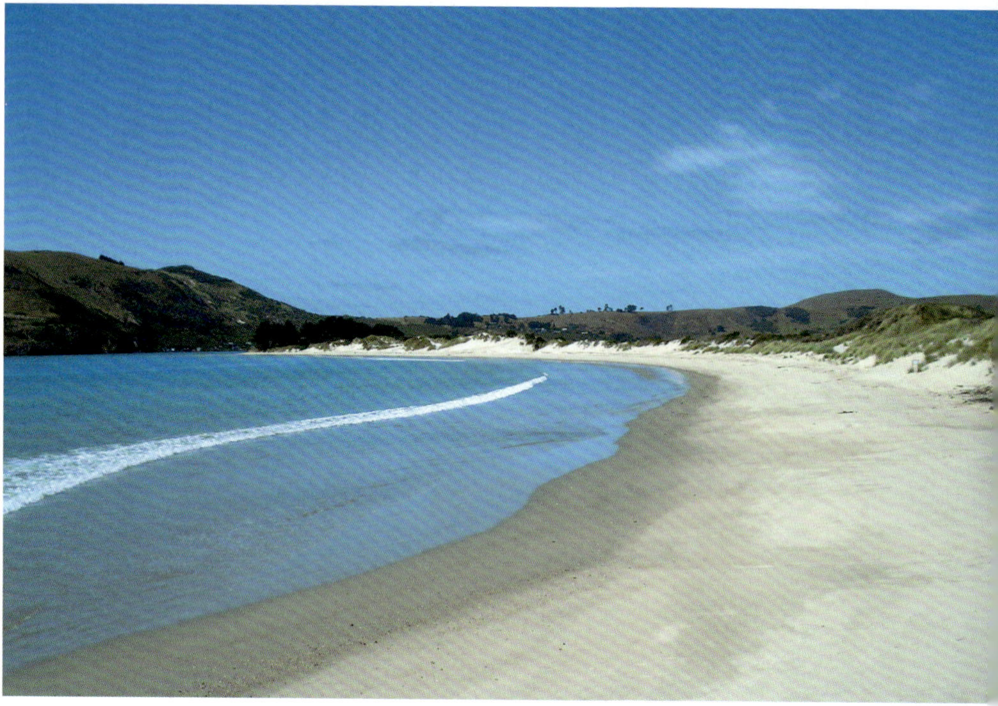

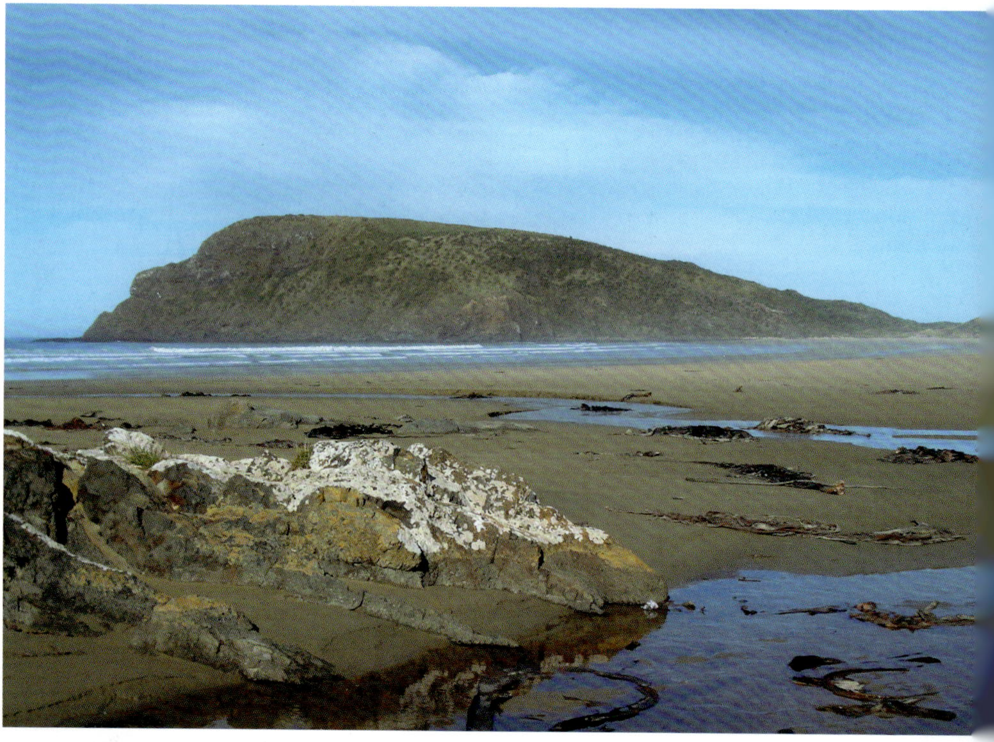

Opposite above: The crisp white sands at Aramoana are home to seabirds, penguins and seals.

Opposite below: Cannibal Bay is but one of the numerous unspoilt beaches found on the Catlins coast.

Right: First Church makes an elegant focal point on a walk around historic Dunedin.

Below right: Dramatic coastal views looking south from Nugget Point.

Below: Two small hills, known as The Pyramids, are found on the walk to Victory Beach.

Bottom left: Nugget Point in South Otago is named after these rocky islets.

Left: Multi-hued mosses and delicate ferns cover every surface in the Fiordland forest.
Below: A short walk from the busy Milford Road leads to tranquil Lake Gunn.
Opposite above: Wild, isolated and rarely visited, Lake Hauroko is worth the trip to southern Fiordland.
Opposite below: On the road to Milford Sound, a walk to The Key is well rewarded with spectacular alpine views.

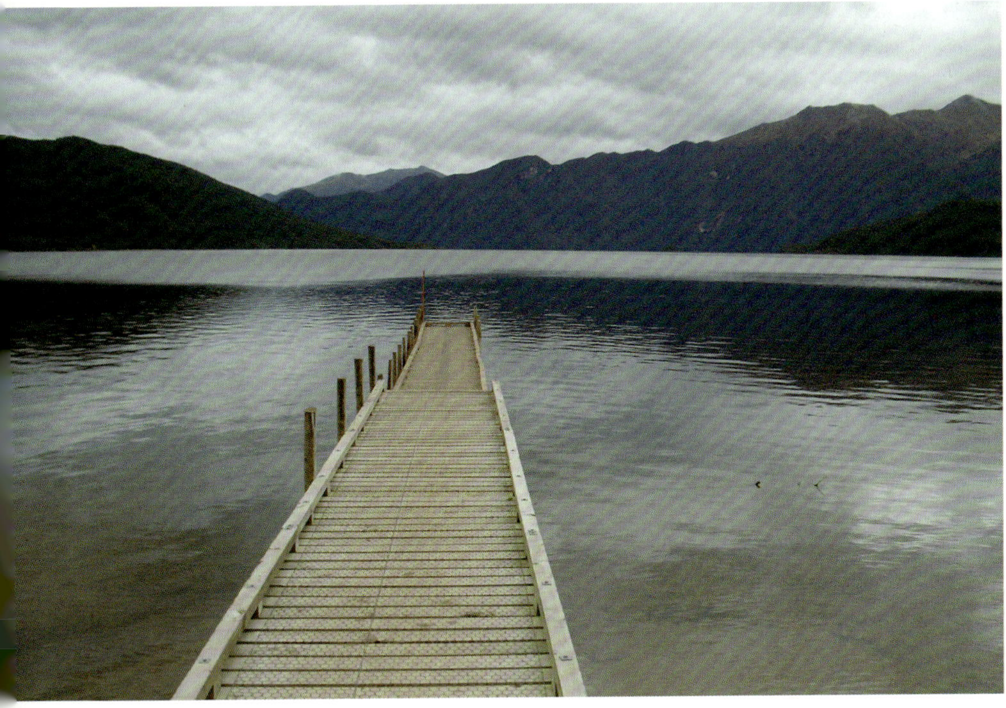

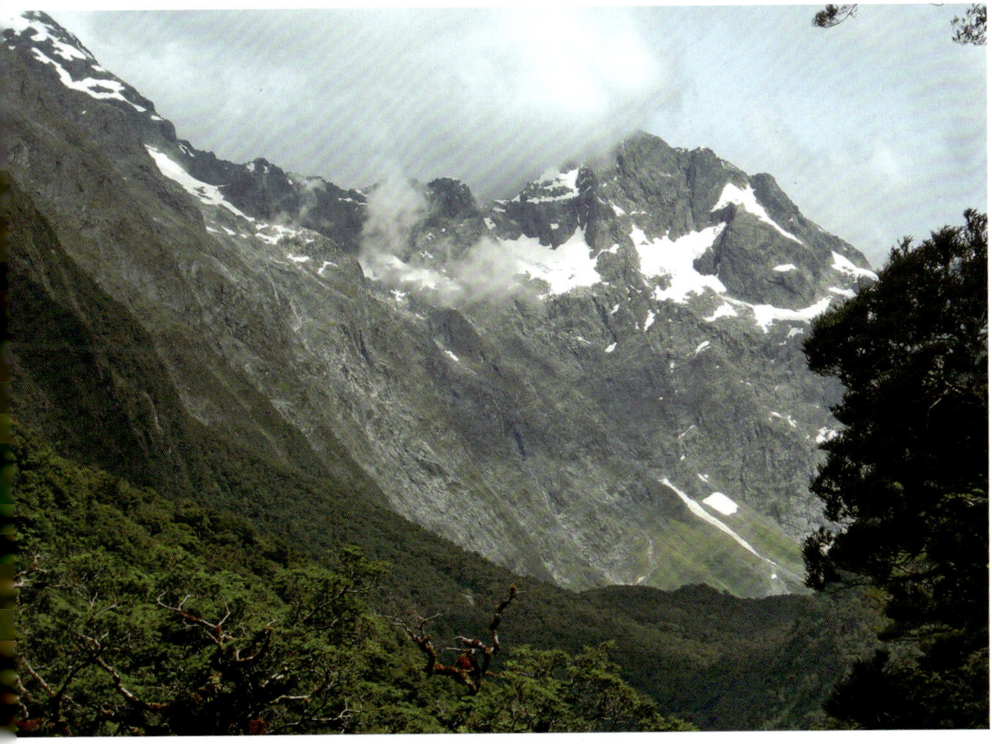

Above: Expansive views of the Southland plain from Tussock Creek Reserve near Winton.
Right: Brightly coloured lupins can be found all along the Eglinton Valley, north of Te Anau during the spring.
Below: Dense forest is a feature of Croydon Bush in the Hokonui Hills, Southland.

the vast beech forests which once covered these foothills and today is home to a surprising range of native birds. A series of very short, interconnected tracks lace the reserve and although the tracks are frequently very narrow with little signage, they are not hard to follow. Besides the reserve is tiny and it would be impossible to get lost. There are some signs to help with plant identification and active predator trapping ensure the birds remain safe. A longer loop track skirts through farmland around the outside of the reserve.

5 Rakaia River Gorge Bridge Walk
The wide Rakaia River is forced through a narrow gorge.

Grade: Medium. **Time:** One hour return.
How to get there: The walk begins at the car park below the bridge on the north bank of the Rakaia River on SH77.

The bridge over the Rakaia River is the starting point of a great walk along part of an impressive gorge. A ferry service operated here until 1884, when two bridges linked both banks and Goat Island. Part of a much longer track on the north bank of the river, this walk is a significantly shorter option with attractive views of the gorge and bridge. The path is undulating and, for the most part, high above the swirling turquoise river as it narrows through the rocky gorge.

Although the vegetation is sparse, many fine old kowhai trees overhang the water. Eventually the track zigzags up a steep bluff to a wide grassy terrace with an excellent view downriver and over the bridges to the plain beyond. In strong nor'westers, large dust storms are created along the broad riverbed.

6 Mt Somer Blackburn Coal Mine Walk
A coal mine, beech forest and great views of Mt Somers and the Canterbury Plains.

Grade: Medium/Hard. **Time:** One hour 15 minutes.
How to get there: From Take the Ashburton Gorge Road for 14km, turn right into Jig Road (gravel) and drive 4km to the carpark at the end.

The cool beech forest of the Canterbury foothills around Mt Somers and Staveley are in direct contrast to the open plains below and the dry tussock mountain country inland.

The walk to the Blackburn Coal Mine follows the line of the old railway line along Woolshed Creek and then climbs up the Miners Track to the old mine.

Coal was mined in the area though without a lot of success. A short-lived operation began in 1864 and after a long series of openings and closures, mining operations ceased for good in 1968. Two inclines transported coal down the steep hillside from the mines above and the remains of these can be seen along the first and easy part of the walk. The track then climbs steeply uphill with lots of steps to a large open area complete with slag heap, rusting machinery and a 'mine entrance'. From here there are fantastic views over the rocky heights of Mt Somers and the Canterbury Plains beyond.

7 Devil's Punchbowl Falls
A dramatic 131-m waterfall.

Grade: Easy. **Time:** 50 minutes return (add 10 minutes if walking from the information centre).
How to get there: The track begins on Punchbowl Road off SH73, 600 m west of the information centre.

The weather here is notoriously changeable so check at the excellent DOC information centre if you have any concerns. Just a short distance from Arthur's Pass township is the impressive Devil's Punchbowl Falls, which drops 131 m down a sheer cliff. The popular walk along an excellent track begins by crossing the footbridge over the Bealey River and climbs steadily uphill through mountain beech, culminating in a flight of wooden steps to the lookout.

8 Bealey Valley Walk
An alpine walk to a tussock clearing.

Grade: Easy. **Time:** The Chasm – 20 minutes return; Tussock Clearing – 30 minutes return.
How to get there: Off SH73, 3 km north of the information centre.

The Chasm is a narrow rocky passage on the Bealey River and beyond is a very pleasant short walk, wandering through moss-carpeted beech forest to a wide clearing with red tussock. From the clearing there are wide views down through the pass and across to Temple Basin.

9 Dobson Nature Walk
Fascinating alpine vegetation.

- **Grade:** Easy.   **Time:** 45 minutes return.
- **How to get there:** Begins off SH73, 3.7 km north of the information centre, at either the Temple Basin ski area car park or opposite the Arthur Dobson Memorial at the top of the pass.

Located at the very top of the pass (923 m), this is the most accessible alpine walk on the pass road. From a distance the alpine vegetation looks uniformly dull and uninteresting, but close-up the variety and diversity of the plants is astounding. Mountain flax, tussock, turpentine bush, hebe and Mt Cook lily are among the plants growing here in profusion. Particularly common is the giant Mt Cook lily, which is in fact not a lily, but the world's largest buttercup. Easily recognised by its large round fleshy leaves, it seems far too delicate for this harsh mountain climate. The peak period to see alpine flowers in bloom is from November to February.

From the car park the well-formed track is an easy uphill climb, which then loops down to a small wetland alongside Lake Misery and back to the road.

10 Castle Hill/Kura Tawhiti Walk
Weathered limestone rock formations in open grass country.

- **Grade:** Easy.   **Time:** Allow one hour.
- **How to get there:** On SH73, 3 km east of Castle Hill, 55 km east of Arthur's Pass.

The Castle Hill rocks are limestone, weathered by years of wear by water and wind, and contrast with the greywacke rocks of the surrounding mountain ranges. The rocks are a 10-minute walk from the road, and well worth it because they are much more impressive close-up than from a distance. Once you reach the rocks there is no set track as such, so you can take as long as you like to stroll around.

The Canterbury earthquakes in 2011 and 2012 did considerable damage to this region's tracks. While many tracks have reopened, some are only partially opened, and others remain closed. Unstable rocks pose the greatest problem so some tracks may never reopen and others may vary somewhat from the old paths.

18
short walks in
Christchurch and Banks Peninsula

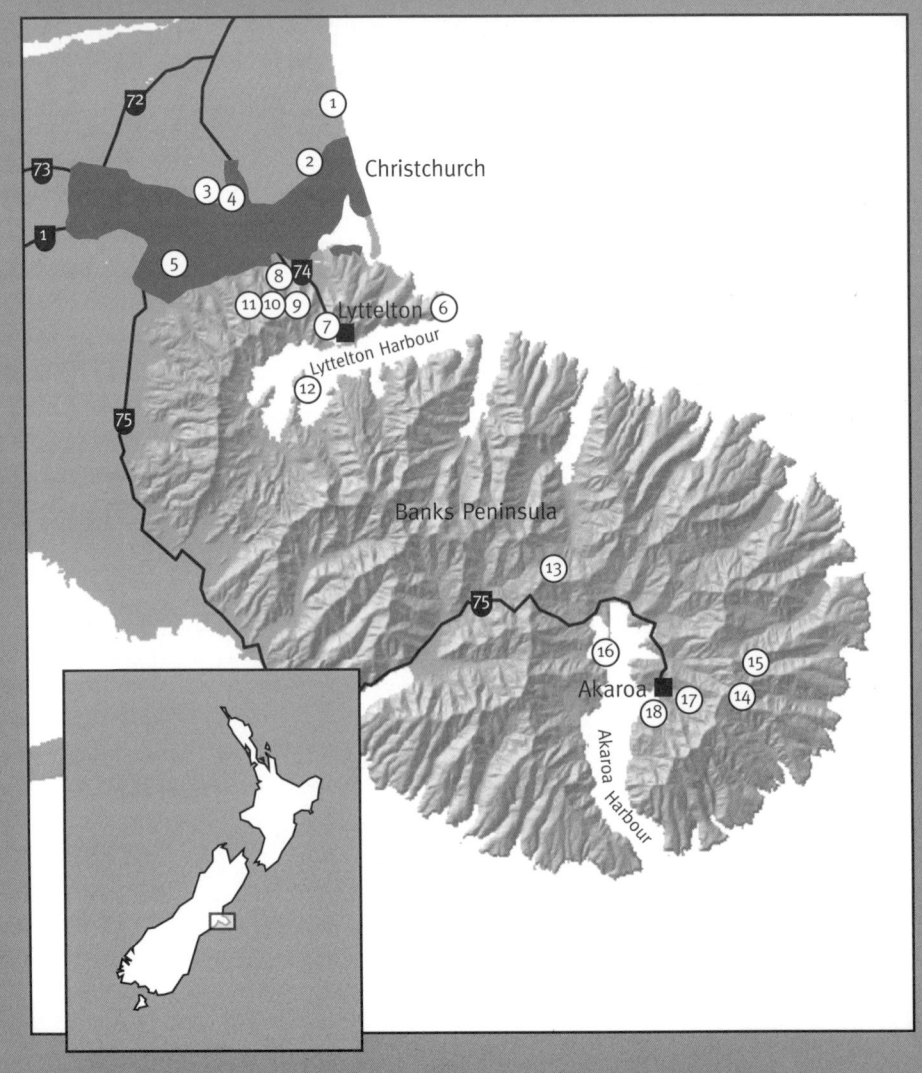

1 Waimakariri River Mouth and Brooklands Lagoon
A beach, dune and lagoon combination.

Grade: Easy. **Time:** Brooklands Lagoon – 30 minutes return; Waimakariri River Mouth – one hour return.

How to get there: Spencer Park is located on Heyders Road, off Lower Styx Road, northeast of the city.

Situated just south of the mouth of the Waimakariri River, Brooklands Lagoon is a 270-ha tidal wetland with a wide range of shorebirds. Over 70 species have been recorded here, including oystercatchers, red-billed gulls, spotted shags, white-faced herons, Caspian terns, banded dotterels and stilts. Fringed by a shallow saltmarsh and hardy native trees, including resilient ngaio, high dunes protect the lagoon from the sea and relentless easterly breezes. Accessible on both sides, the Brooklands Lagoon has a number of easy tracks, all beginning from the information board at the entrance to Spencer Park. The short, sandy loop track has a raised viewing platform giving a good outlook over the tidal flats and a bird hide on top of a small dune.

The longer Waimakariri Walkway to the river mouth runs parallel to the beach along the eastern side of the lagoon (the track begins at the car park by the beach) and even on a hot day the vast beach is largely empty. Start this walk by strolling north along the beach towards the mouth of the Waimakariri River. When you've had enough of the beach (and the wind), find a path through the dune to the track running along the eastern side of the Brooklands Lagoon, from the car park to the river mouth.

2 Travis Wetland Perimeter Walkway
Prolific birdlife in a unique wetland.

Grade: Easy. **Time:** Loop walk – one hour 30 minutes return.
How to get there: Located in Burwood, for visitors the best place to start is at the Beach Road entrance, which has information, parking, toilets and is close to the bird hide.

Considerably modified by human activity over the past 700 years and now encircled by houses, this wetland is home to a surprising number of native and introduced birds. Over 50 species visit, including black swans, shovelers, pukeko, grey ducks, mallards, Canada geese and scaup, with five species of native duck breeding here. In addition to native fauna, the wetland is home to 60 native plant species. For birdwatchers, hides overlook the deep ponds which form the heart of this large reserve, now undergoing considerable restoration with an energetic planting and weed-removal programme.

The Canterbury earthquakes have resulted in this area becoming even wetter, though liquefaction has made the waterways shallower than in the past. From the car park there is a short walk to an excellent bird hide overlooking a deep pond thronged with birds. Another 20 minutes further on is a tall viewing tower with a wide perspective of the wetland. The track skirts around the edge of the wetland and back to the car park. Be aware cyclists also use the track.

3 Riccarton Bush, Riccarton House and Deans Cottage
A bush remnant and two historic houses.

Grade: Easy. **Time:** 20 minutes return.
How to get there: Kahu Road, Riccarton.

Riccarton Bush is a small remnant of the kahikatea forests once common on the swampy plain around Christchurch. Maori settlers reduced the forest by burning, and European settlers by felling, reducing vast forests to mere fragments. Now protected by a predator-free fence, the reserve is too small to sustain much native birdlife, though the vegetation is surprisingly diverse – kahikatea, totara, rimu, beech, matai and kowhai, with some trees over 600 years old.

With great foresight, the Dean family preserved the bush, and their cottage is the oldest surviving building on the plain. Built in 1843 to house newly arrived settlers William and John Dean, timber for the cottage came from the nearby bush. Originally closer to the road, the cottage has been moved to its present site.

Riccarton House is a large and grand Victorian affair, and like many colonial houses, built in stages over many years, as money became available. The first part was completed in 1856, and the last stage, which gives the house its present character, in 1900. Riccarton House was substantially damaged by the recent earthquakes and is due to reopen in 2014. The bush and cottage are open.

4 Christchurch Botanic Gardens

A marvellous large park of mature trees, sports fields and home to the Botanic Gardens.

Grade: Easy. **Time:** 1 Hagley Park circuit: 1¾ hours, North Hagley Park circuit: 1 hour, Christchurch Botanic Gardens: 45 minutes.
How to get there: Rolleston Avenue, Christchurch.

In 1850, surveyors included in the plan of early Christchurch a park of approximately 202 hectares, and although since reduced in size to 161 hectares, the park today is a mixture of gardens, woodland and sports fields (including the Hagley Golf Club established in 1904). The park is essentially divided in two by Riccarton Avenue, with the southern end being mainly sports fields. In spring the daffodils, bluebells and blossoming cherry trees along Harper Avenue are particularly spectacular. Inside the park, the Christchurch Botanic Gardens nestle within a loop of the Avon River, and the formerly swampy area north of the river has been transformed into two small lakes, Victoria and Albert. The complete circuit of the park is 6 km and is popular with joggers.

Covering an area of 30 hectares, the long established botanic gardens are reputed to contain more than 10,000 plants. An oak tree planted in July 1863 commemorating the marriage of Prince Albert of Great Britain to Princess Alexandra of Denmark is regarded as the first official planting. Particularly impressive in summer are the fine herbaceous borders well suited to the southern climate, while grouped in the centre of the gardens are the tropical, cactus and orchid houses and a ponga-lined fern house. The elaborate Peacock Fountain, originally erected in 1911 and for many years dismantled and stored due to maintenance problems, was finally restored in 1996. Ornately Edwardian in style and made of cast iron, the fountain was made in the Coalbrookdale foundry in Shropshire, England.

5 Halswell Quarry Park
An old stone quarry, wetlands and themed gardens.

- **Grade:** Easy. **Time:** Quarry Rim Walk 30 minutes, conservation area 10 minutes, Sister City Gardens 30 minutes
- **How to get there:** The main entrance is off Kennedy Bush Road, Halswell.

Halswell was once the site of an extensive quarry, providing stone for many of Christchurch's best-known buildings. Opened in the late 1850s and known as Rock Hill, the quarry finally closed in 1990. Today the 60-hectare site is gradually being transformed into extensive gardens, though the quarry itself remains largely untouched. By the entrance a small conservation area centred on a wetland has several deep ponds surrounded by native plants that appreciate wet feet. Surrounding the quarry are six themed gardens featuring the plants and gardening styles of Christchurch's six sister cities in England, USA, South Korea, China, Australia and Japan.

Near the main carpark is an old stone building known as 'The Whare'. Constructed in 1922 of locally quarried stone (naturally) to replace a wooden building that burnt down, this small low building was the single men's quarters and provided accommodation for up to 12 quarrymen at any one time. While The Whare is simple and sturdy, it was not exactly homely, with the men sharing two large bedrooms and a single living area.

The Quarry Rim walk is superb and as the name suggests the path circumnavigates the bare face of the workings. Excellent informative panels detailing the geology and history of the quarry and numerous lookout points make this a very enjoyable excursion for all ages. It is a modest climb up to the top, but the track is well formed and not difficult.

Both the conservation area and the Sister City gardens are flat easy walking and in amongst all this are numerous places for picnics with large grass areas for that game of touch or cricket.

6 Godley Head Walkway
Sea views in every direction.

Grade: Medium. **Time:** Godley Head – three hours return, Taylors Mistake to Boulder Bay – one hour 45 minutes return.

How to get there: The usual starting point is from the car park at Taylors Mistake, but the track is also accessible from the car park at the end of Summit Road.

It's not hard to see why this is one of the region's most popular walks. An excellent track winds along the coast through open grass and tussock, passing the Boulder Bay cribs, with sea views all the way. The track gradually rises from the rocky shore to Godley Head. While the dense native forest has long gone, small patches of native vegetation cling to the rocky bluffs and steep gullies, including sedge, kawakawa and star lily.

Reintroduced to the area around Boulder Bay is the white-flippered penguin/korora, considered to be either a morph of the blue penguin or a distinct species, Eudyptula minor albosignata. One of the smallest penguins (35 cm tall), the white-flippered penguin is bluish grey with a distinct narrow band of white around the edge of the flippers. This endangered bird is native to Canterbury and nests only on Banks Peninsula and Motunau Island.

The views from the 120-m headland are superb, to the north over Pegasus Bay and south over the entrance to Lyttelton Harbour. A lighthouse was built here as early as 1865, and in 1939 a substantial coastal battery protected the harbour. At one point 400 men and women were stationed here and three gun emplacements and several other military buildings still remain.

Numerous tracks wind down through the open hillside back to Taylors Mistake, but be aware mountain bikers also use these tracks and can take them very fast, especially downhill.

7 Bridle Path Walkway

The original track from Lyttelton to Heathcote.

Grade: One-way to Lyttelton – hard; Heathcote to the Summit – hard; but Summit to Heathcote, medium. **Time:** One-way to Lyttelton – one hour 30 minutes; Heathcote to the Summit – two hours return; but Summit to Heathcote – 40 minutes.

How to get there: The Christchurch end of the track begins at Bridle Path Road, Heathcote.

When Christchurch was first settled, this track was the main access from Lyttelton and, for early settlers laden with baggage, must have been a daunting introduction to their new home. It's easy to see why the Lyttelton rail tunnel, opened in 1867, was such a priority. A monument commemorating the endurance of pioneer women can be found on the summit. Even today the Bridle Path is a challenging walk.

The track is now a 4WD road, and while well formed the trudge uphill from either side is a good workout. The views from the summit over both Christchurch and Lyttelton are superb, and you gain an appreciation of the pioneering spirit, even with modern clothing and a light backpack. An alternative to walking uphill is to take the gondola to the top and walk down to either the Heathcote Valley or Lyttelton, where the track ends near the southern entrance to the road tunnel. Even walking downhill you'll still need good footwear as the track has small loose stones that can be surprisingly slippery!

8 Harry Ell Walkway, Victoria Park

Bush and formal planting on the Cashmere Hills.

Grade: Medium. **Time:** Two hours return.

How to get there: The Sign of the Takahe, Dyers Pass Road, Cashmere.

First established in 1870, with formal planting under way in the 1880s, the park was named to celebrate Queen Victoria's 1897 Golden Jubilee. Now covering over 260 ha, the park is planted in a wide variety of native and exotic trees and is a maze of walking and mountain bike tracks.

A local MP, Harry Ell, envisioned a series of rest houses linked by walking tracks along the summit of the Port Hills. Originally the rest houses were to offer both accommodation and meals, but only the Sign of the Takahe was ever completed to the scale planned.

The Harry Ell Walkway begins at the Sign of the Takahe, and is an excellent well-graded track leading through regenerating bush, all the way to the Sign of the Kiwi at the top of Dyers Pass Road. The track parallels the road and unfortunately traffic noise can be a bit offputting. To avoid repeating the track on the way down, an alternative is to take the Thomson and Latters Spur tracks back to the start. These tracks can be confusing, but if you continue to walk downhill you won't go too far wrong. Be aware mountain bikers also use some of these tracks, though the Harry Ell Track is for walkers only.

9 Mount Sugar Loaf
Superb views over the Canterbury Plains.

- **Grade:** Medium. **Time:** 50 minutes return.
- **How to get there:** Starts opposite the Sign of the Kiwi at the top of Dyers Pass Road.

Easily recognised by the 120-m transmitter on top of Mt Sugar Loaf, this loop walk begins up the easy grade of the Cedric Track to a car park below the transmitter. It then follows the sealed road to the top, with amazing views over Banks Peninsula, Christchurch City, the Canterbury Plains and the Southern Alps.

From the top, walk down the eastern slope through the tussock to the stile, which is visible at the start. While there is no track, the tussock is short so you won't get lost. Immediately over the stile take the track to the right, which meanders through regenerating bush back to the car park.

10 Kennedy Bush/Sign of the Bellbird
A bush remnant on Banks Peninsula.

- **Grade:** Medium. **Time:** Up to one hour.
- **How to get there:** On the Summit Road 4.8 km from the Sign of the Kiwi at the top of Dyers Pass Road.

The signage for the walk is a bit confusing, but start the walk to the left of the rock shelter, which is the Sign of the Bellbird, and continue downhill through the bush. When you've had enough (remembering it's uphill all the way back) take one of the tracks to the right, which will lead back uphill to the shelter. It's a small reserve so you won't get lost. There is a superb view of Lyttelton Harbour across the road from the beginning of the walk.

Mainly consisting of mahoe with some totara and kowhai, this small bush remnant is a reminder the entire peninsula was once dense native forest.

11 Gibraltar Rock and Omahu Bush
Excellent views from a rocky outcrop.

Grade: Medium. **Time:** 40 minutes return.
How to get there: On the Summit Road, 9 km from the Sign of the Kiwi at the top of Dyers Pass Road.

The walk starts through a small patch of regenerating bush and continues over tussocky farmland to an outcrop of volcanic rock with great views over the city, plains and south to Lake Ellesmere. The walk is easy to the outcrop, but the less nimble might find the final scramble to the top a bit of a challenge.

Just 300 m from the Gibraltar Rock Track is the entrance to Omahu Bush. This small bush remnant on the Summit Road just below Coopers Knob harks back to a time of bitter conflict between Ngati Mamoe and Ngai Tahu. After a clash with Ngai Tahu, some of the defeated Ngati Mamoe escaped and hid in the dense bush below the peak, which took the name Omahu, a blended meaning of 'running silently' and 'a place of healing'.

While the large trees have gone, the bush is surprisingly dense, with open country revealing great views of Lake Ellesmere. Three interconnecting tracks loop down the hillside, so it is easy to choose a walk to suit. While the track is well formed, it is steep and muddy in parts.

12 Quail Island/Otamahua, Lyttelton Harbour
A fascinating volcanic island.

Grade: Easy/medium. **Time:** Complete circuit around 2 hours.
How to get there: Black Cat Cruises runs regular trips to the island through summer. Ph 03 328 9078 www.blackcat.co.nz

Quail Island is no single geological entity, but was built up by three distinct volcanic eruptions, with the oldest rocks on the island dating back to an eruption at the head of the harbour 14 million years ago. The youngest rocks are from lava flows during the Mt Herbert/Te Ahu Patiki eruption 6 million years ago. The island's volcanic origins are very clear from the distinctive cliffs of columnar basalt rock on the eastern side.

The European name for the island stems from the native quail, which appear to have been confined to the island and quickly became extinct once it was cleared for farming. For many years the island was used as a quarantine station and several buildings from this period still remain. Today the island is virtually devoid of native trees, but it is slowly being replanted by volunteers, although still at an early stage. The complete circuit of the island takes around 2 hours with a shorter walk taking around 50 minutes.

13 Montgomery Park Scenic Reserve
A gnarled old totara tree.

- Grade: Easy. Time: 20 minutes return.
- How to get there: From Hilltop on the Akaroa Road turn left into Summit Road – the reserve is on the left, 500 m from the intersection.

Montgomery Park Scenic Reserve is the location of an ancient totara tree believed to be at least 2000 years old. While not a particularly large specimen (it has a girth of 8 m), it is rather battered and certainly looks its age. This ancient tree is a poignant reminder that the peninsula, now largely grass and tussock, was once thickly forested and alive with birdsong.

14 Ellangowan Scenic Reserve
Spectacular views over the peninsula.

- Grade: Medium. Time: 45 minutes return.
- How to get there: On the road from Duvauchelle, 3 km north of Akaroa turn right into Long Bay Road. At the top of the hill, at the intersection of Summit and Long Bay roads, take the metalled road off to the left (Hickory Bay Road) – the reserve is marked 1 km on the left.

From this high rocky bluff in the Ellangowan Scenic Reserve there are spectacular views over the peninsula, while to the west lie the Southern Alps and Pegasus Bay far to the north. Not a hard climb, the track varies from rough to nonexistent and the top can be very exposed and windy.

It's easy to lose the track, but it's impossible to get lost in the open, waist-high vegetation. You will need long trousers as the stunted gorse and wild Spaniard can be nasty. Unless you know what it looks like, you'll feel the pain of wild Spaniard, *Aciphylla colensoi,* before you see it. A small grass-like plant, it has very sharp spikes on stiff narrow leaves all facing outwards from a central crown and is common above the tree line, growing among tussock and alpine shrubs in open, well-drained locations. The yellow flowers appear on long, tall stems.

15 Otepatotu Reserve
An ancient totara forest.

- **Grade:** Medium. **Time:** 45 minutes return.
- **How to get there:** On the summit road, 4 km from the Okains Bay/Summit Road junction.

Otepatotu Reserve is one of the best bush remnants on the peninsula, with ancient totara hung with moss and a groundcover of hardy ferns nurtured by the mist that often envelops this peak. The track to the peak is steady rather than steep, but slippery and uneven in parts and poorly signposted. Initially, the path winds through bush; at the junction not long after starting take the track to the left. The track quickly emerges into a flax field from where a short detour to the top of a rocky bluff gives great views over Akaroa Harbour. The track then enters dense bush dominated by fine old totara, before emerging into low scrub (mainly mountain five-finger) kept short by the fierce winds on the summit, known as Lavericks Peak. After admiring the views, take the track to the right along the fence line and at the next junction (unmarked) take the wide track to the right, which emerges not far from the car park.

16 Onawe Peninsula
An historical pa site with great views.

- **Grade:** Easy. **Time:** One hour return.
- **How to get there:** At Barry's Bay turn into Onawe Flat Road – the walk starts from the car park at the end.

Onawe Peninsula (100 m) juts into Upper Akaroa Harbour, linked to the mainland by a narrow strip of land. Virtually cut off at high tide, this was the ideal position for a fortified pa.

After the fall of Kaiapohia, Ngati Toa chief Te Rauparaha turned his attention to Onawe. He cut off the pa, dividing his forces to cover both sides of the narrow isthmus. The terrain allowed the attacking force to take a position on the hills above where they could observe pa defences; more importantly, with the isthmus sealed there was no escape.

The pa was difficult to capture. Seeing Te Rauparaha's frustration, the Ngai Tahu defenders decided to harry him. The attack failed and Ngai Tahu retreated. Ngati Toa warriors followed, using captives from Kaiapohia as a screen. Reluctant to fire for fear of hitting their relatives, the defenders left the gates open too long and Ngati Toa poured in. The well-defended pa became a trap and few escaped the terrible massacre, followed by a cannibal feast at Barry's Bay.

When peace was finally established in 1839, Ngai Tahu returned to the peninsula, but were a shadow of their former force, never recovering from the deadly raids.

The track starts to the right of the car park and skirts around the beach, though difficult right on high tide. From there it's an easy walk through open grassland to the top.

17 Stanley Park Loop Walk and the Garden of Tane

A bushy walk with an intriguing reserve.

Grade: Medium. **Time:** One hour 15 minutes return.
How to get there: Starts to the left of the fire station on Beach Road, Akaroa.

This walk is a bit rough and not well signposted, but very pleasant with views of the harbour. In the bushy areas keep an eye out for unusual jet-black fantails.

Soon after starting the walk you reach a grassed area. Take the track to the right over the stile and walk uphill through regenerating bush to another large open area, with views over Akaroa Harbour. From here follow the fence line to the right, taking the track downhill to Walnut Place and Rue Jolie. Walk up Rue Jolie to the Garden of Tane.

Originally the Akaroa Domain, this 4.5 ha reserve is both a bewildering maze of tracks and a dazzling collection of trees. Established in 1876, the more formal aspects of the garden have long since disappeared and the very large trees which survive were planted well before 1900. The current shape of the garden was largely determined by Arthur Erikson, who from 1964 until his death in 1991 tirelessly cleared away weeds and planted hundreds of native trees, renaming the domain after Tane, god of the forest.

18 Akaroa Historical Walk

Grade: Easy. **Time:** One hour.

How to get there: Northern end of Rue Lavaud (where the road from Christchurch enters the town). Of course you can start from any point along the walk, but as parking is at a premium in Akaroa especially during the summer, the northern end of the town has more parking particularly for campervans.

In 1838, Captain Langlois, a French sea captain who had earlier visited Akaroa, established the Nanto-Bordelaise Company, and in 1840 set sail for New Zealand with a small contingent of French and German families with the intention of establishing a French colony. By the time they arrived in August 1840 on the ship Comte de Paris, the Treaty of Waitangi had been signed, and the French found themselves in what was now a British colony. Not wishing to return, the French and German emigrants established themselves around Akaroa Harbour, and were later to be joined by British settlers.

The town has numerous historic buildings all within a short walking distance either on or near the two main streets Rue Lavaud and Rue Jolie. The following walk features the highlights of this historic town.

- 2 and 6 Rue Lavaud. Along with French settlers, there were many Germans and Number 2 Rue Lavaud was the home of Christian Waeckerle who became a prominent businessman and later mayor of Akaroa in 1878. At number 6 he built the Grand Hotel in 1860 which burnt down in 1882 to be replaced by the hotel still standing.
- 25 Rue Lavaud. Although two French priests arrived with the settlers in 1840, Akaroa's Catholic Church is named St Patricks after an Irish saint, and was built in 1865 to replace an older chapel.
- 40 Rue Lavaud. Italian settler Joseph Vangioni and his son Louis were notable merchants in Akaroa and built this store in the late nineteenth century to replace an older grocery store established in 1878.
- Detour here to the left up Rue Brittan for 50 m to the Orion Powerhouse, one of the oldest power stations in the South Island built in 1910. The

short walk up to the French Cemetery starts here.
- 46 and 50 Rue Lavaud. Hailing from the Portuguese island of Maderia, Antonia Rodrigues arrived in Akaroa in 1858. This building dating from 1860, was at first a butchery, then a bakery and after he extended the building, The Madeira Hotel. In 1907 he further extended the hotel and both buildings still survive.
- Several former civic buildings cluster around the town centre on the Rue Lavaud. No. 60, the Town Hall, No. 62 the Police Station, No 69 the Courthouse. At 73 Rue Lavaud is the BNZ (1875) and still a bank, while on the opposite corner is the old Post Office (1915).
- 71 Rue Lavaud. The Langlois-Eteveneaux Cottage is Akaroa's oldest building constructed immediately after the French settlers arrived in 1840 by Aimable Langlois. By 1858 the building became the home of Jean-Pierre Eteveneaux. The simple cottage was extensively renovated in 1900 by Jean-Baptiste Eteveneaux, Jean-Pierre's son, to give it a more 'French' style and today the cottage is the most conspicuous (other than street names) reminder of Akaroa's French past.
- Detour to the right at the intersection of Rue Lavaud and Rue Balguerie down to the wharf and the tiny Customs House built in 1858 to control the smuggling of alcohol.
- Continue south along Rue Lavaud where the street changes to Beach Road and walk directly ahead into Rue Jolie.
- 103 Rue Jolie. The Coronation Library began life as the Literary and Scientific Society in 1875 and after renovations in 1911 changed its name to mark the coronation of George V. It is still in use as a library today.
- 105 Rue Jolie. An Akaroa landmark, the Gaiety began life in 1879 as the Loyal Good Intent Lodge and later became a theatre, public hall and picture theatre.
- 109-117 and 110-116 Rue Jolie. On both sides of the street are a fine group of historic homes built between 1850 and 1905.
- Detour to the right into Church St to view number 6 which was originally the bakery built in 1884 and the Shipping Office across the street at number 3. The Shipping Office. Built in 1895 it is typical of many early New Zealand buildings, which although very small, were designed to look very grand.
- Rue Jolie Bridge. This brick and stone bridge was erected in 1878 to replace an older wooden structure.
- 160 Rue Jolie. Constructed to replace a lodge that burnt down, the aptly named Phoenix Lodge dates from 1881.

19
short walks in
South Canterbury, Mackenzie Country and North Otago

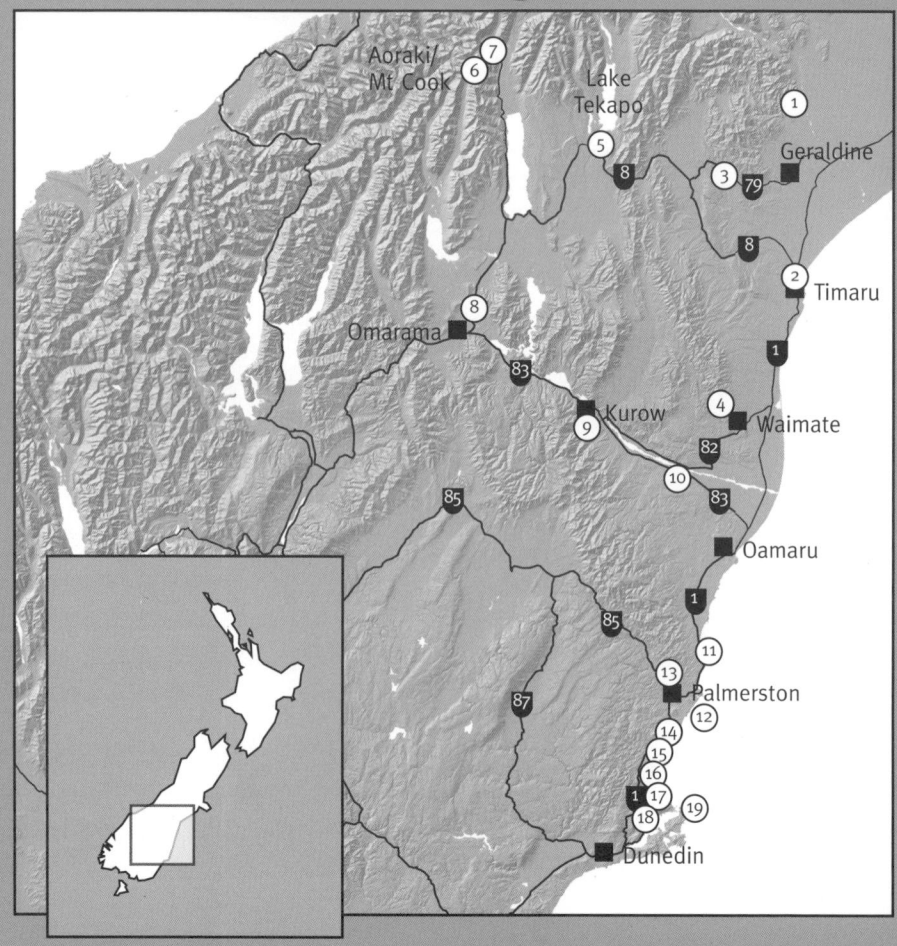

1 Peel Forest Park
Spectacular foothills of the Southern Alps.

Grade: Easy. **Time:** Dennistoun Bush loop walk – 45 minutes, Te Wanahu Flat car park short walk – 30 minutes; Acland Falls – one hour 20 minutes return.

How to get there: These three short walks are clearly signposted and all within 2 km of Peel Forest Village.

Covering over 700 ha on the southern bank of the Rangitata River in the foothills of the Southern Alps, Peel Forest Park is a remnant of a much larger forest burnt by early Maori and milled by Pakeha settlers. The climate at Mt Peel is distinct from both the plains and the high country further inland. With a much higher rainfall supporting a rich and diverse flora and fauna, this forest is home to a large number of native birds and trees, including giant totara, matai and kahikatea. The variety of ferns is surprising – one third of all native fern types are found here.

The Dennistoun Bush loop walk is an easy 45-minute stroll on the Blandswood road, 1.7 km from Peel Forest Village. Highlights include the enormous totara, matai and kahikatea, and a short detour to an old sawpit, testament to extensive milling in the late nineteenth and early twentieth centuries.

The Te Wanahu car park (toilets and a shelter), 2 km from Peel Forest Village, is the starting point for two walks. The shortest is an easy 30-minute return through dense bush to a massive totara, estimated to be at least 1000 years old and 31 m tall with a girth of 8.5 m.

The second, to the Acland Falls, takes one hour 20 minutes return and is a medium grade. From the car park take the Allans Track, which leads steadily uphill on a path that can be muddy in places. Just before the waterfall the track drops down and follows a creek to the waterfall – this last short section is in the creek bed and a bit rough and slippery. The 14-m waterfall is more like a waterslide, dropping gently down a mossy rockface into a shallow pool. On the return trip take the Acland Track, which leads straight downhill to the road, from where it is a quick 500-m walk back to the car park.

2 Dashing Rocks Walk
Ancient lava flows along a coastal bluff.

- **Grade:** Easy. **Time:** 30 minutes return.
- **How to get there:** The track begins at the corner of Pacific and Westcott streets, Timaru.

This loop walk just north of Caroline Bay follows a coastal bluff, once a whaling lookout, with wide views back to the city over Waimataitai Beach. Two small rock arches, once a feature of the walk, have now collapsed but equally attractive geometric patterns in the ancient lava flows from distant Mt Horrible underlie the clay.

The beginning of the track is just below the road and the sign is a bit hard to see. For those wanting a longer walk, there is a track from Caroline Bay along Waimataitai Beach to Dashing Rocks (the origin of their rather descriptive name becomes obvious when a heavy easterly swell is running).

3 Kakahu Escarpment
A smooth wall of rock rises above farmland.

- **Grade:** Easy. **Time:** 30 minutes return.
- **How to get there:** Hall Road, off the Winchester–Hanging Rock Road, 15 km from Geraldine via Hilton. The walk begins 200 m from the lime kiln by the bridge.

The Kakahu Escarpment is a magnificent wave of rock sculpted by the elements, rising dramatically above farmland. Huge weathered mushroom-shaped boulders lie at the base of the escarpment. The short walk is across farmland, which is muddy in places. Take time to visit the historic and well-preserved lime kiln built in 1876, and just 200 m down the road.

The area contains the largest colony of New Zealand long-tailed bats in the eastern South Island. One of just two surviving native bat species and closely related to other long-tailed bats in Australia, Papua New Guinea, New Caledonia and Norfolk Island, it is thought to have arrived here within the last two million years. Aerial feeders, the bats catch insects on the wing, and have a home range of around 100 sq km.

4 Kelcey's Bush Walk, Hunters Hills, Waimate
An elegant waterfall in a rare bush remnant.

Grade: Easy. **Time:** 30 minutes return.
How to get there: At the end of Mill Road, 8 km from Queen St, Waimate (the main street).

Kelcey's Bush is a remnant of extensive forests which covered the Hunters Hills. The hills are a long, low range of primarily greywacke rock, raised above sea level by tectonic uplift. Stretching from Tengawai River in the north to the Waitaki River in the south, the highest point is Mt Nimrod (1525 m). While the tops are subalpine with tussock, the foothills were once densely forested and still have small areas of totara, tree fuchsia, matai, kowhai, mahoe and (in the north) silver beech. This short easy walk leads through beautiful old tree fuchsias to the modest but pretty Sanders Falls. Tree fuchias are the world's largest fuchsia and one of only two deciduous native trees.

Now known as Hunters Hills, the name has a Maori origin. When surveyor Charles Torlesse visited in 1849, the local chief Te Huruhuru told him he often hunted in the hills. Back in Akaroa, Torlesse told mapmaker Captain John Stokes, who labelled the range the Hunter's Hills on his 1851 map.

A disastrous fire swept the hills in 1878, burning down 70 homes, a Maori settlement and destroying the forest, ruining the flourishing timber industry. The Hunters Hills are also home to Bennett's Wallaby, released in 1875 to foster a fur industry. Now considered a pest, they're sought after by hunters. For an up-close view there is a wallaby enclosure in town, in Victoria Park.

5 Mount John Summit
Superb views of the Mackenzie Country and Southern Alps.

Grade: Medium. **Time:** Two hours return.
How to get there: From SH8 at Tekapo turn down to the lake on Lakeside Drive and the camping ground. Go through the camping ground to the end of the road by Tekapo Spring, where the track begins to the right.

Mt John is famous for ultra-clear night skies, especially in winter, and the University of Canterbury operates an astronomical observatory on the summit (tours arranged through Earth and Sky: www.earthandsky.co.nz). At 1030 m, the climate is definitely alpine. While the heights are exposed and extremely windy, rainfall is low, sunshine hours are high and in summer it can be a very hot climb. This is officially our windiest spot, with a wind gust on 18 April 1970 hitting 250 kph.

Below is Lake Tekapo, largest of the three Mackenzie Basin lakes (87 sq km with a maximum depth of 120 m). Formed by ancient glaciers, the lake is fed primarily by the Godley River, with the Mistake, Cass and Macaulay rivers. The distinct turquoise colour is caused by finely ground rock suspended in melting ice water. Even on the hottest summer day swimming is only for the very hardy.

Walkers have two options. The first is up from the lake where the Summit Track begins (see above), a steady rather than steep walk to the top. Initially through larch, once clear of the tree line the terrain is open tussock. Just beyond here the Summit Track meets the Circuit Track – continue straight ahead, the easiest uphill grade to the top, where there is a café and the observatory buildings. On your return, drop down to the Circuit Track below the café and turn left, taking you to an excellent information board. Continue the circuit around the summit to the left until you rejoin the Summit Track for the return downhill.

The second option is the Circuit Track, meandering around the summit (easier to do anticlockwise) through deep tussock and including the excellent information board. There is a small fee to use the road to the summit.

Whichever option, the views are unrelenting, encompassing the whole Mackenzie Basin, Lake Tekapo, Lake Alexandrina, tiny Lake McGregor, the headwaters of the Godley River and the Southern Alps.

6 Kea Point Lookout, Aoraki Mount Cook
An excellent lookout point for Aoraki Mount Cook and the Mueller Glacier.

- **Grade:** Easy. **Time:** One hour return.
- **How to get there:** Just before Mt Cook village turn right into Hooker Valley Road and drive to the Whitehorse Hill campground car park, from where the track starts.

New Zealand's highest mountain (3754 m), also known as Aoraki 'the sky piercer', sits at the head of a dramatic glacial valley. The mountain is at the heart of the Aoraki Mount Cook National Park, an area of 70,000 ha containing all but one of New Zealand's peaks over 3000 m.

The first successful ascent was on Christmas Day 1894. Before a massive landslide in December 1991 the mountain was another 10 m higher – 12 million cu m of rock and ice raced over 7 km down the mountain at a speed of 200 kph.

In Maori legend Aoraki was one of the three sons of Rakinui (Ranginui), the Sky Father, who journeyed from the heavens to the earth in a waka. However, a terrible storm overturned it, forcing the brothers to clamber onto the upturned hull. A cold southerly sprang up, and within a short time they froze to death and turned to stone. Aoraki was the tallest and oldest brother, while his brothers and crew became the other mountains. What we know as the Southern Alps became Te Waka o Aoraki, the upturned canoe of Aoraki.

The DOC office has excellent displays on the natural and human history of the area and up-to-date information on weather and track conditions.

Meandering through matagouri and mountain totara, the walk skirts the Mueller Glacier's debris, to a spectacular lookout in an alpine basin. Below is the terminal of the Mueller Glacier, strewn with gravel, the terminal lake with huge blocks of ice slowly melting.

While Aoraki Mt Cook dominates at the end of the Hooker Valley, Mt Sefton looms above the Mueller Glacier with the Huddleston Glacier clinging to its slopes. The return trip offers great views back down the glacial carved Tasman Valley.

7 Tasman Glacier and Blue Lakes Walk
New Zealand's longest glacier.

- **Grade:** Medium. **Time:** 40 minutes return to the lookout – add 10 minutes for Blue Lakes and 30 minutes for Tasman Lake.
- **How to get there:** Just before Mt Cook Village turn right into Tasman Valley Road and continue 8 km to the car park – the road is gravel but in good condition.

With Aoraki dominating, it's easy to overlook the Tasman Glacier, which at 30 km is our longest, reaching far into the mountains. The main track from the car park is a steady uphill trek with steps and a short rocky scramble to the top at the end. The lookout point is on a hill of debris overlooking a vast landscape of rock and ice, torn apart by the glacier.

However, don't expect shimmering blue ice – the glacier has been steadily shrinking over the past 100 years, and a thick layer of rocks and gravel cover the ice. While the glacier might resemble a quarry, the ice is much deeper than it looks – over 100 m thick. From the lookout, Aoraki is visible to the left. The Blue Lakes – these days distinctly green – are visible from the track, and for a closer look there's a short side track leading down, but watch out for the prickly wild Spaniard! A side track leads to the terminal lake of the glacier with huge blocks of melting ice drifting ponderously in the icy green water.

8 Clay Cliffs
Dramatic 'badlands' landscape in the high country.

- **Grade:** Medium. **Time:** Allow 50 minutes return.
- **How to get there:** 4 km north of Omarama, turn left into Quailburn Road and after 4 km turn into Henburn Road – 4 km along this road is a gate, and the carpark is another 4 km on.

A 'badlands' landscape is created over many thousands of years by water eroding soft, gravelly soils to cut deep gullies, leaving tall pillar-like formations known as 'hoodoos'. These unusual natural structures are formed when rock protects the soil from rain and prevents the soft gravels beneath from eroding, creating high, fluted configurations.

While you can walk along the 4WD track along the bottom of the cliff, it's worth exploring the formations themselves, although these side tracks are pretty rough and involve pushing your way through briar and matagouri. The cliffs are on private land and there is a small entrance fee.

9 Kurow Hill Walk
Views over the Waitaki]Valley, Hunters Hills and the Hakataramea Valley.

- **Grade:** Hard. **Time:** One hour 15 minutes return.
- **How to get there:** From SH83 in Kurow go north past the shops in the town and then turn left in Grey Street – the track begins at the end of the street.

Forming the boundary between Otago and Canterbury, the 100 km-long Waitaki River is the main river draining the Mackenzie Basin and is fed by Lakes Pukaki, Tekapo and Ohau, as well as the Hakataramea and Ahuriri rivers. A classic braided river with a wide shallow bed and numerous channels, the Waitaki has been dammed at Benmore, Aviemore and Waitaki, but its lower reaches are free of development.

After crossing the irrigation channel at the end of Grey Street, the track zigzags up the face of Kurow Hill; while it's a solid uphill climb, the track is well graded and within reach of the moderately fit. As you climb, Kurow township gradually recedes into toy-town dimensions, while the grand view over the Waitaki Valley unfolds. The vegetation is sparse in the dry and exposed location, so the views are continuous as you climb. About two-thirds of the way up the hill the track forks at an unmarked junction. At this point continue to the left. Near the top the track reaches a ridge; again you need to continue to the left to reach the top of the hill.

From the summit the views are wonderful, not only over the lower Waitaki River, but also to the rolling hills of the Hakataramea Valley, and northeast to the Hunters Hills. While the views are great, the top of the hill can be very exposed in windy weather.

10 Duntroon, Waitaki Valley
Three walks into the distant past.

- **Grade:** Easy. **Time:** Two to three hours, depending on how much walking you want to do.
- **How to get there:** On SH83, 42 km northwest of Oamaru. Earthquakes Valley – turn off SH83 by the church, onto Earthquakes Road. The walk begins 6.5 km down this road on the left. Elephant Rocks is 6 km from Duntroon on Island Cliff Road, off Danseys Pass Road, while Anatini Whale Fossil is on the same road, just 1 km on.

The area around Duntroon has fascinating rock formations and fossils, all easily accessible from the road. The Vanished World Centre is an excellent starting point, with a collection of impressive fossils up to 30 million years old, including penguins, whales and dolphins and some species still unknown to science. There is a small entrance fee (www.vanishedworld.co.nz).

A short loop drive from Duntroon covers three easy walks. The first is in the Earthquakes Valley, where huge rocks have broken away from the cliffs in a massive landslide, exposing fossils on an ancient seabed. The highlight is a well-preserved whale fossil from the late Oligocene period, approximately 23–28 million years ago. From here the track wanders in and around huge weathered boulders, a rich source of fossils. Take care as rocks are prone to fall and sudden drops and crevasses are concealed in the long grass. It will take 10 minutes return to the whale fossil and 40 minutes return for the whole valley.

Elephant Rocks also date from the Oligocene period. These huge weathered limestone rocks take their name from their grey colouring and general elephantine shape, but what makes them particularly appealing is the way they stand clear and stark amid the short grass, creating an unusual landscape. This walk will take 30 minutes. In 2005 parts of the first Andrew Adamson-directed Chronicles of Narnia film, *The Lion, the Witch and the Wardrobe*, were shot here.

The third walk to the Anatini Whale Fossil, is 7 km from Duntroon on Island Cliff Road off the Danseys Pass Road (1 km from Elephant Rocks). Just 10 minutes return from the road is the fossil of a baleen whale. The fossil is very clear and protected by perspex from weather and prying fingers. An interpretive board explains which parts of the whale are visible. If you have the time, the 40-minute return stroll down to the valley lined by ancient limestone rock formations is worthwhile.

11 Historic Thames Street and Harbour Street, Oamaru
Stunning Victorian heritage buildings.

Grade: Easy. **Time:** Allow one hour return.
How to get there: Begin at the junction of Thames Street and SH1.

Sheltered from the worst of the southerlies by Cape Wanbrow, Oamaru attracted early Maori settlement and was home to sealers and whalers in the first half of the nineteenth century. Construction of the breakwater began in 1871 and Oamaru became an important port, especially after 1884, and the first refrigerated export meat shipments. The picturesque harbour now shelters a small fishing fleet. The rocks for the breakwater came from a quarry which is now a blue penguin colony.

Oamaru has New Zealand's finest collection of Victorian buildings – the grandest along a short section of Thames Street. Most were built between 1870 and 1885 when the town flourished – eventually improved rail links replaced the port and Oamaru became a quiet backwater. What also makes the town unique is that local stone was used almost exclusively, giving the town a uniformity unusual in New Zealand. Know to geologists as 'totara limestone', Oamaru stone is formed from fossilised fragments of the calciferous shells of marine animals and plants dating back 30–40 million years, when this area was under the sea, and contains tiny fragments of sharks' teeth and whale bone. Soft enough to be cut by huge chainsaws, it hardens when exposed to the air.

The historic buildings are mainly in two areas, within easy walking distance of each other. The grandest are on Thames Street (part of which is SH1) and include the Bank of New South Wales (1883 – now the Forrester Gallery), the National Bank (1871), St Luke's Anglican Church (1876), the first Post Office (1864 – now a restaurant), the Post Office (1883 – now the Waitaki Council offices), the Courthouse (1882), the Opera House (1907) and the Athenaeum (1882 – now housing the North Otago Museum).

At the southern end of Thames St turn left into Itchen St and walk straight ahead into Harbour Street.

The working area for the port, Harbour Street has an appealing, intimate feel. The buildings here were warehouses, port offices and grain stores, and today house galleries, craft shops and cafés. Significant buildings include Smith's Grain Store (1881), the Union Bank (1878), the Customs House (1882), NZ Loan and Mercantile Warehouse (1882) and the Harbour Board Office (1876). A good place to finish your walk is the Criterion Hotel in Tyne Street. Built in 1877, the pub was closed in 1906 when Oamaru went 'dry', reopening in 1998.

At the end of Harbour Street turn right into Tyne Street and back to Thames Street. At this point you might like to continue walking to the harbour and breakwater (another 40 minutes).

12 Katiki Point Walk

An ancient pa, an historic lighthouse, penguins and seals.

Grade: Easy. **Time:** 45 minutes return.
How to get there: Turn off SH1 at Moeraki, then right into Tenby Street which becomes Lighthouse Road. Drive 3 km to the end of this gravel road.

The walk begins at the elegant wooden Moeraki lighthouse (1878). It was originally intended for Hokitika, but numerous shipwrecks along this wild coast convinced authorities to build it at Moeraki. The views are amazing – north to Cape Wanbrow near Oamaru, south to Shag Point, and the Otago Peninsula can be glimpsed beyond.

Just below the historic wooden lighthouse is a small area of protected coastal vegetation above a small, sandy cove in the rocky coastline. Both blue and yellow-eyed penguins nest here, coming ashore late in the day to rest and feed their chicks. Fur seals are common among the rocks along the shore.

From the lighthouse the track wanders downhill over open grass to a narrow rocky point, and involves some rock hopping to reach the pa site. The pa, known as Te Raka a Hineatua, is superbly located on a narrow spur of land almost surrounded by sea.

Established in the eighteenth century as the principal base for the Ngai Tahu invasion of Ngati Mamoe territory, the pa resisted many attempts at capture, but once conquered fell into disuse.

13 Trotters Creek Walk, Trotters Gorge
Lush bush reserve with an appealing swimming hole.

- **Grade:** Easy. **Time:** 45 minutes return.
- **How to get there:** Turn off SH1 2 km south of Moeraki into Horse Range Road. The walk begins from the picnic area on the right, but is not well signposted and easy to drive past.

Established in 1864, Trotters Gorge is a 152 ha reserve on the southern end of Horse Range, a popular picnic spot and walking area. The deep gorge is surrounded by high rocky bluffs which look like limestone, but are in fact a greywacke/breccia conglomerate. The creek itself is home to 12 native species of fish including koura (freshwater crayfish). In the thick bush which thrives in the deep, moist soils of the gorge, there are a surprising number of native birds, with the lyrical song of bellbirds almost constant.

A broad path continues across the stream from the car park, with flat walking all the way through the bush to a lovely grassy picnic area overlooking a large, attractive swimming hole in Trotters Creek. A rustic shelter provides a refuge if the weather isn't good. With six streams crossing this track, keeping your feet dry is a challenge.

14 Puketapu Summit/John McKenzie Memorial
Magnificent views from a memorial.

    Grade: Hard. **Time:** One hour return.

    How to get there: From SH1 just north of the Palmerston shops, turn into Stour Street, cross the railway line and go 500 m – the track begins on the left.

A steep climb leads to an unusual monument on the summit (343 m), in memory of local politician Sir John McKenzie. Champion of the small farmer, he was instrumental in breaking up huge land holdings in the late nineteenth century. Built in 1931 of local bluestone (an earlier monument collapsed), the cairn is 13 m high with an internal staircase and a spectacular view.

Once covered in dense bush, Puketapu was a favoured haunt of the patupaiarehe and, according to Maori tradition, heavy mists shrouding the summit allow them to reclaim the hill and play their music undetected.

For the very fit a race to the top is held in October in memory of Albert Kelly, a local policeman, who during World War II hiked to the top every day to scour the coastline for signs of the enemy.

There are two tracks to the top, both involving a good climb. From the road, the track steadily works its way uphill across farmland. At the water tank, the most obvious track goes straight up the hill – a steep and slippery climb which will have you panting. If you go immediately to your right, a much longer but more gently sloping track also takes you to the top, adding another 20 minutes. If you are up for a steep climb, go up the first track, and come down the easier one.

15 Matanaka
New Zealand's oldest farm buildings.

    Grade: Easy. **Time:** 25 minutes return.

    How to get there: Matanaka is signposted from SH1 at Waikouaiti – the road is mainly sealed but becomes narrow and gravel surfaced on the uphill stretch.

Believed to be the oldest surviving farm buildings in New Zealand, they were built during the 1840s by Johnny Jones, a Sydney wheeler and dealer originally involved in whaling at nearby Waikouaiti, who bought land to the north of the bay. Still standing are the stables, complete with old horse harnesses, the granary, a schoolhouse and a barn, which today houses an old boat, an echo of Johnny's connection to the sea. The simple, stylish old buildings provide a strong contrast with the utilitarian but charmless modern farm sheds.

As an extra bonus, there are marvellous views over Waikouaiti Beach and the verdant country inland, with an easy walk through farmland to the buildings.

16 Waikouaiti Beach and Hawkesbury Reserve Lagoon Walk
A flat walk with rich bird life and white sands.

- **Grade:** Easy. **Time:** One hour.
- **How to get there:** Turn off SH1 at Beach Road – go to the very end and park at the beach. Walk back down the road to the railway line and turn right into Scotia Road – the walk begins at the end.

The Hawkesbury Lagoon at the mouth of Patonga Creek is the perfect habitat for a wide range of wetland and wading birds, including stilts, paradise shelducks, shags, Canada geese, black swans, mallards, herons and the occasional grey teal. The lagoon is adjacent to Waikouaiti Beach, a magnificent stretch of white sand running from Cornish Head at the northern end to the mouth and lagoon of the Waikouaiti River, just below Huriawa Peninsula. This peninsula is volcanic in origin and has several blowholes in the cliffs on the southern side. Hooker's sea lions and fur seals are common along the shore.

Starting across the causeway through the lagoon, at the end of the lagoon turn right (don't cross the footbridge). Continue along the second causeway and at the end take the track along the river and through the pine trees to the beach. What makes this walk particularly appealing is that the causeways cut through the middle of the lagoons, with the birds just metres away. Follow the beach back to the car park or spend however long you want on the beach.

17 Huriawa Pa Walk, Karitane Beach
A spectacularly sited pa with magnificent coastal views.

- **Grade:** Easy. **Time:** 45 minutes return.
- **How to get there:** From SH1 turn off towards Karitane and take the road to the beach. At the beach turn left along Sulisker Street and continue uphill 500 m to the entrance.

The perfect location for a fortified pa, the volcanic Huriawa Peninsula has steep cliffs and sea on three sides, with uninterrupted views along the coast and over marshes to the east. A Ngai Tahu stronghold, this was the scene of an epic siege in the eighteenth century.

The rangatira of Huriawa, Te Wera, feuded with his nephew Taoka, the cause long since forgotten. When Taoka attacked Te Wera had vastly improved the defences. Well-stocked with food, even under siege the defenders could fish from a cove on the north side. Unable to take Huriawa, in the dead of night two warriors entered through blowholes and stole a wooden carving of Kahukura, the god of war, guarded by the tohunga Hatu.

Discovering the theft, despair swept through Huriawa, while Taoka's men performed haka and waved Kahukura above their heads. Invoking the gods, Hatu stretched out his arms, crying: 'Return to us, o Kahukura.' The carving flew through the air to rest at his feet, clearly showing who the gods favoured. Thoroughly discouraged, Taoka's men gave up their six-month siege and turned their fury towards Mapoutahi, just a little to the south.

Entrance to the pa is through a beautifully carved gateway. The track meanders gently to the end of the peninsula, with great views along the coast in both directions. The convoluted nature of Huriawa pa is such that specific evidence of terraces and defences is not so easy to spot, but the great blowholes through which the thieves stole into the pa at night can be found on the south side.

18 Mapoutahi Pa and Doctors Point
A beach walk to an old pa site with great views.

Grade: Easy. **Time:** Beach route, one hour 15 minutes return. Osborne Road, 30 minutes return.

How to get there: At high tide turn off SH1 at Waitati and take the road to the Orokonui Ecosanctuary. Turn left into Purakanui Road, then left again into Osborne Road and drive to the car park at the end. At low tide turn off SH1 at Waitati and turn left into Doctors Point Road. Follow this road to the end and park by the beach.

Steep cliffs and very narrow access made Mapoutahi easy to protect, while the sea and wide lagoons provided an excellent food resource. In either direction the views are extensive – Orokonui Lagoon and the Otago Peninsula to the south and Purakaunui Inlet immediately to the north, with Huriawa in the distance.

At first Taoka could make no impression on the impregnable fortress, but his attack took place in the middle of winter and on a particularly cold night, the sentries set up dummies and retreated to warm fires in their huts. Alerted to the ruse, Taoka attacked, quickly seized the pa and massacred the inhabitants. The pa was never reoccupied.

While today the fortified ditches and terraces have largely disappeared, the site is nothing short of perfect. Blue penguins nest above white sandy beaches and aquatic birdlife is prolific.

There are two ways of getting to the pa – both easy. The most picturesque involves walking along the beach and around Doctors Point. From the car park, walk down the beach and head south (right) and around Doctors Point, passing through sea caves. This walk can only be undertaken at mid to low tide, and even then there is a short scramble over a rock slide which has tumbled down the cliffs.

If the tide isn't right, the northern access to the pa is via Osborne Road and a short walk through the sand dunes.

19 Orokonui Ecosanctuary
New Zealand's tallest tree among mature forest.

Grade: Medium. **Time:** From 30 minutes to two hours return.
How to get there: Located at 600 Blueskin Road, the sanctuary is well signposted from SH1 at Waitati, and from Port Chalmers. www.orokonui.org.nz. There is an entrance fee.

Established in 2007 this 'mainland island' is a 307 ha reserve of old and regenerating forest with mature podocarps as well as kaikawaka or New Zealand cedar. Orokonui is protected by an 8.7 km predator-resistant fence and rare native birds are gradually being introduced including kiwi, tieke (South Island saddleback) and South Island kaka, while birds such as pukeko and paradise shelduck have already established themselves here.

What makes Orokonui particularly appealing (though it doesn't make for easy walking) is that the reserve stretches from mist-cloaked high hills down to sea level, with the vegetation reflecting the altitude. There are three main tracks looping down the hill from the education centre and café. The shorter loop tracks close to the entrance are well formed and suitable for all age groups, while the longer track requires a higher degree of fitness.

At the bottom of the reserve is New Zealand's tallest tree – not a towering totara or kahikatea, which holds first place as New Zealand's tallest tree, but an Aussie import, *Eucalyptus regans*. Reaching almost 70 m tall, the tree is in a large grove of gum trees that were self-sown after a fire in 1900, with the ash from the fire providing a fertile base to give the trees a good start in life.

Before beginning any of the walks at Orokonui, it is worth spending some time brushing up on your knowledge in the extensive education centre, and when your ramble is complete the excellent café provides a good reward. Entrance fee, www.orokonui.nz

16
short walks in
Central Otago

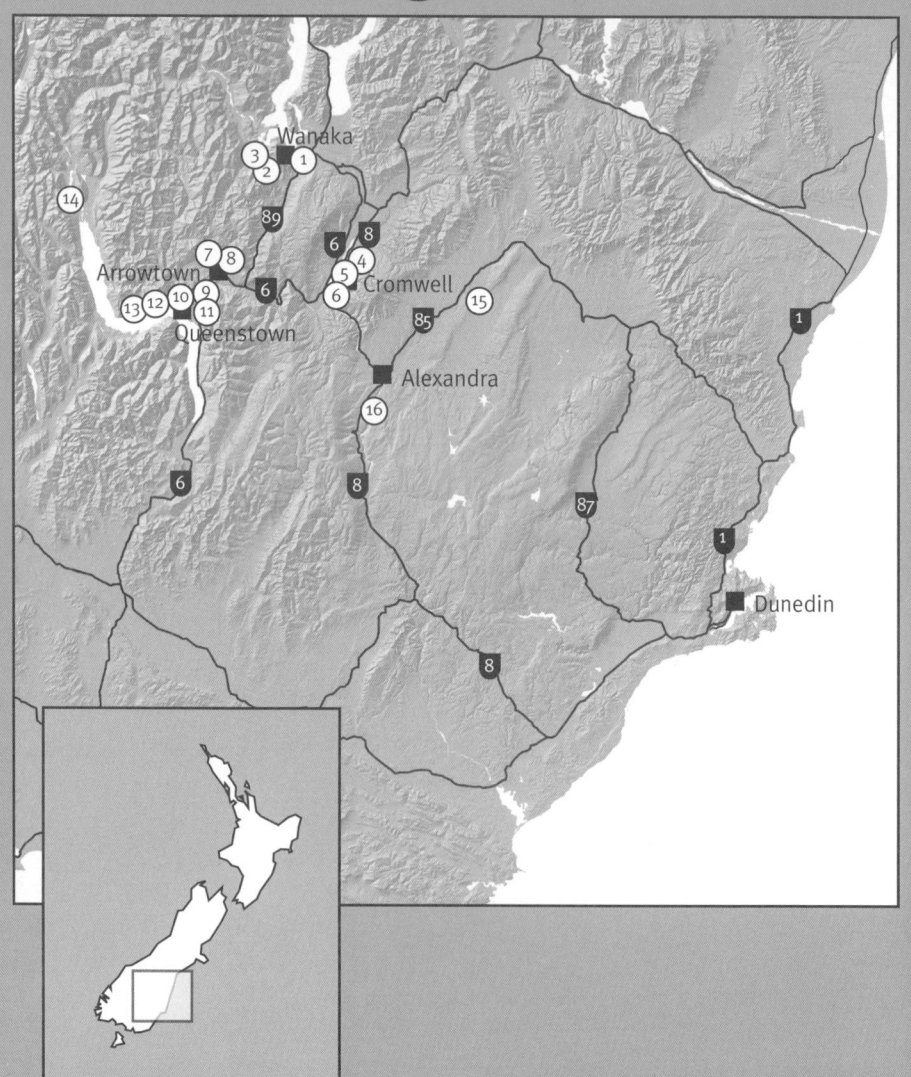

1 Mount Iron Walk

Fantastic views from a glacial mountain.

- **Grade:** Medium. **Time:** One hour 30 minutes.
- **How to get there:** 1 km east of Wanaka on SH6.

Mt Iron (548 m) lies to the east of Wanaka. Isolated from surrounding mountains, it offers fantastic views in every direction. The mountain bears the scars of an earlier time when this landscape was scoured by massive glaciers. Known as a roche moutonnée (or 'sheepback'), glaciers have ridden over its western side, leaving it relatively smooth, while the eastern side has been sharply scraped away forming steep cliffs and rocky bluffs.

There are two meanings of Wanaka. One version has Wanaka as a form of Oanaka, 'the place of Anaka' – an early chief; or it can be interpreted as 'a place of renewal'. Wanaka and Hawea were two of the lakes created by the legendary Rakaihautu when he journeyed the length of the island, digging out lakes and heaping up mountains with his magical ko or digging stick.

The walk to the top takes around 30 minutes and it's easier to walk the loop track clockwise, up the gentler western slope and down the steep eastern side. The open nature of the low vegetation ensures endless views. From the summit these extend south along Cardrona Valley, east to the broad terraces of the Clutha River, north over Lake Hawea and west across Lake Wanaka and beyond to the Southern Alps.

2 Waterfall Creek Walk

Views of the mountains and lake and a side trip to a vineyard.

- **Grade:** Easy. **Time:** One hour return from the western end of Wanaka Station Park on the lakefront park, two hours return from the town centre.
- **How to get there:** From Wanaka town centre follow the lake shore to the Wanaka Station Park at the western end of Roys Bay. The track begins right by the water.

This easy flat walk follows the Lake Wanaka shore, with pleasant views over the lake and mountains. At Waterfall Creek (there is a creek but no waterfall) the walk ends at a wide shingle beach. A popular detour is up through the Rippon Vineyard for a spot of wine tasting, with views over the vineyard to the lake and mountains that are simply stunning, and even more so in autumn when the vines turn golden.

You can start the walk from the town centre or from Wanaka Station Park, which is also an excellent place for a picnic. A word of warning – some mountain bikers barrel along this track, so be prepared for a quick dive into the bushes to avoid being knocked down.

3 Diamond Lake Lookout
Excellent views of Lake Wanaka and the Matukituki River.

Grade: Diamond Lake – easy, Lake Wanaka Lookout – medium, Lake Circuit – medium. **Time:** Diamond Lake – 25 minutes return, Lake Wanaka Lookout – one hour return, Lake Circuit – two hours return.

How to get there: 20 km from Wanaka on the Mt Aspiring Road and 6 km past the Glendhu Bay camping ground – the turnoff to the track is just before the bridge over the Motutapu River.

Rocky Mountain is a small peak (775 m) which once lay deep under grinding glacial ice, which in turn gave the mountain its distinctive rounded shape. Like Mt Iron, it is a roche moutonnée. Nestled in the southern lee of the mountain is Diamond Lake, a small raupo-fringed tarn which reflects the surrounding landscape in its still waters, with small patches of native bush clinging to the steep hillside above.

The track starts off gently uphill. From Diamond Lake the track climbs more steeply through bush to a dramatic bluff overlooking the lake far below. Just beyond this point the track goes off to the right to the Wanaka Lookout with views over the lake and the Matukituki River.

If you're feeling fit, continue on and complete the Lake Circuit, which will take a further hour. The track becomes rougher from the lookout, as it meanders up the scrubby hillside to the top, from where there are even more spectacular views.

As the track is on the southern side and totally shaded in winter, it can be very icy.

4 Bendigo Goldfields walk
Picturesque ruins of mining huts and an old hotel.

Grade: Easy. **Time:** One hour.
How to get there: From Cromwell take SH8 towards Tarras and after 14 km turn right into Bendigo Loop Road. Continue for 2 km then turn right at Bendigo township, to Welshtown.

Gold was discovered here in 1863, by Thomas Logan, and the area is a labyrinth of mine shafts, old townships and ruined batteries. The dry climate has preserved many of them and the high altitude provides a magnificent backdrop.

The loop walk from Welshtown takes 40 minutes and has some of the best-preserved miners' huts in Central Otago. The walk winds through tussock and scrub past mineshafts, old rock walks and ruined cottages to the Matilda Battery. Opened in 1878, the shaft went down 178 m and the steam-powered 16-stamper battery crushed ore hauled from the depths. In 1884 the mine closed and in 1908 ten of the stampers were relocated to the Come In Time battery, where they remain.

Magnificent vistas over the Tarras area and the mountains to the west and north are a bonus, though many shafts aren't covered – keep an eye on youngsters if you don't want to lose them down a deep, dark hole.

Back at the car park, walk in the opposite direction and follow the 4WD road across the dam to Pengelly's Hotel. While the ruins are visible from the car park, they're worth a closer look. Pengelly's is incredibly small, with rooms so tiny it's hard to imagine them holding more than three or four burly miners, let alone a bar! Continue up the creek and past the ruins of several miners' huts, then back to the car park. This will take just 20 minutes.

5 Cromwell Old Reservoir and Firewood Creek Walk
A wild rocky landscape and excellent views.

- **Grade:** Medium. **Time:** 50 minutes return.
- **How to get there:** Opposite the Cromwell Lookout on SH8, 1.5 km south of the bridge over Lake Dunstan.

Moderately steep, the track ascends through a sparse landscape of rock and wild thyme to an old reservoir. Now dry, this stone-lined reservoir once supplied Cromwell with water. The exit pipes and depth measuring posts are still here, and the supply pipe is visible along the track.

Above the reservoir, the landscape is a sea of rocky outcrops, tors and loose stones where even the hardiest plants struggle to survive the bone-dry slopes. Thyme growing in Central Otago is thought to be the only wild population outside its natural range in the Mediterranean and most likely introduced by miners. Thyme thrives in the harsh dry climate and its distinctive bouquet is now part of the local landscape. Growing to 30 cm tall, its mauvey pink or white flowers occur from September to December.

Superb views encompass Lake Dunstan, Cromwell and beyond to the Pisa Range. Lake Dunstan was created by the construction of the Clyde Dam, which flooded the old town and its famous gorge, and large areas of fertile river flats. Historic buildings were removed and reconstructed above the water level, but the old stone bridge over the gorge remains, 11 m below the surface. Local legend has it that a car is still parked on the bridge.

Having put the steepest part of the walk behind you, head uphill to a 4WD track, then downhill for a short section before joining another track to the right and back onto the road.

6 The Sluicings and Stewart Town
This barren and dramatic landscape will fascinate.

- **Grade:** Easy. **Time:** One and a half hours for the loop walk.
- **How to get there:** Well signposted in Felton Road, Bannockburn.

The Sluicings is an area of cliffs, gulches, pinnacles, tunnels and old ruins set amidst a barren landscape – all man-made. In the late nineteenth century gravelly soils were worked with high pressure sluicing hoses, resulting in a drastic revision of the landscape. Blasted by water, the flat terrain near Bannockburn has been altered beyond recognition and has a strange appeal all of its own. This is a great place to work up an appetite – or walk off your lunch at one of the excellent vineyards.

The walk begins gently, uphill through a deep gully cluttered with stacks of rock debris from the sluicing, and tunnels leading deep into the base of fluted cliffs. From here the climb leads to a flat terrace with grapevines, the original level of the land before the 1880s, when mining began. A short walk takes you to Stewart Town, with a handful of ruins. Almost intact, and only missing its roof, is the small cottage of David Stewart and John Menzies, both bachelors, who made their money by providing the vital water supply on which the miners depended. Surrounding the house old apple and pear trees still bear fruit.

Just east of the house a number of channels are clearly visible – these carried water from the dam to the workings. From Stewart Town the loop walk follows a parallel valley to the east, past the remains of a blacksmith's forge and miners' huts and back to the car park.

7 Tobins Track, Arrowtown
Wide views over Arrowtown from an old gold mining settlement.

Grade: Medium. Time: One hour 30 minutes return.
How to get there: Signposted from the car park by the river behind the Buckingham Street shops.

Gold was discovered in the Arrow River in 1862, by shearer Jack Tewa, and a shantytown was established, only to be washed away the following year. Rebuilt on higher ground, the town's population rose to 7000, with further settlements at Macetown, Skippers and Bullendale. Today over 60 buildings remain from this period, including a row of miners' cottages dwarfed by huge trees well over 100 years old. The cool Central Otago climate makes this one of the few places in New Zealand to experience spectacular autumn colour; the best time to visit is between the summer peak and the winter ski season.

From the car park follow the river downstream for 10 minutes then cross over the footbridge. From the bridge the track goes steadily uphill on a well-graded 4WD track. Initially through larch and sycamore, halfway up the trees begin to thin and extensive views unfold over the Arrowtown Basin and the mountains beyond. The land at the top is surprisingly flat and the site of Crown Terrace settlement, a substantial township in the 1860s and 70s, though nothing remains. Thomas Tobin, after whom the track is named, built the road to Crown Terrace in 1874, and lived just uphill from the river. The ford by the bridge was the location of the famous scene in the first *Lord of the Rings* film, when Arwen calls on the river to sweep away the Ringwraiths.

The views from the top are superb and include the Remarkables, Arrowtown, Lake Hayes and Lake Wakatipu.

8 The Chinese Settlement Walk, Arrowtown
A glimpse into the lives of Chinese miners.

- **Grade:** Easy. **Time:** 30 minutes return.
- **How to get there:** Bush Creek Reserve at the very end of Buckingham Street.

Chinese miners occupied the margins of society both socially and physically in the Central Otago goldfields, and although 1200 Chinese miners arrived to rework old claims in the Wakatipu Basin in 1869, today very little remains of their humble homes. At Arrowtown the small Chinese section of town has been preserved and in some places reconstructed, to provide the best overview of the life of the Chinese miner on a New Zealand goldfield. As well as simple stone cottages there is a tiny store, and excellent information panels along the track enhance this easy walk.

9 Lake Hayes Walkway
A gentle stroll beside placid waters.

- **Grade:** Easy. **Time:** Around the lake in two and a half hours.
- **How to get there:** Begin at either the recreation ground on SH85 from Queenstown to Cromwell, just before the turnoff to Arrowtown, or at the large picnic area at the northern end of the lake.

Lake Hayes is much favoured by photographers for stunning autumn colours and the reflection of the mountains in its still waters. These held the same appeal to early Maori, who named the lake Wai-whaka-ata, the water that reflects.

Following the shoreline, this walk meanders along the lake under the shade of old willows and poplars, with tranquil views over the lake and mountains. The reserve at the northern end is popular in summer; Lake Hayes is much shallower than the deep mountain lakes and the water not so cold for swimming. This is a great spot on a hot day and especially appealing in autumn, when the trees turn vivid yellow and gold.

Not marked at either end, this track isn't hard to find as it follows the shoreline. At the northern end, the track begins where the access road to the picnic ground meets the main road, while at the recreation ground it starts to the right of the car park by the boat ramp. If time is tight the walk from the recreation ground to the reserve picnic ground will take 30 minutes.

10 Oxenbridge Tunnel Walkway, Queenstown
A walk leads to dramatic views.

Grade: Easy.   **Time:** 30 minutes return.
How to get there: At the Shotover Bridge turn into Oxenbridge Road (a narrow gravel road) and continue until it drops down to the river and a large car park. There are no signs indicating the track, but follow the river upstream for a short distance and it becomes obvious.

This short walk along the Shotover River leads to a lookout point above the rugged gorge and the Oxenbridge Tunnel. The Oxenbridge brothers, whose intention was to divert the river and make a fortune from the gold on the riverbed, built the tunnel between 1906 and 1910. Unfortunately for them, the scheme only returned a small amount of gold. Today this is a good spot to watch jetboats on the river. Keep an eye out for the rusting steam engine strangely marooned on a rock in the middle of the river.

11 Time Walk, Queenstown Hill
Great views over Queenstown, Lake Wakatipu and the Remarkables.

Grade: Hard.   **Time:** One hour 40 minutes return plus 30 minutes if walking up from town.
How to get there: Kerry Drive, Queenstown.

The Time Walk is a loop track which officially starts at the beautiful wrought-iron gates and takes the walker from the past to the future, represented at the top by Caroline Robinson's simple sculpture 'Basket of Dreams'. Along the way the story of the Wakatipu Basin is told in a series of five illustrated panels, but to follow the panels you have to turn right at the junction where the track becomes a loop. This direction is also the gentler grade to the top. Most of the walk is through pine and Douglas fir, with the occasional lake view glimpsed through the branches. However, near the top the vegetation is open and a grand view of the lake, mountains and town is laid out before you. At the small tarn on top of the ridge veer left to the Basket of Dreams and the track downhill.

If you're feeling energetic after having come this far, the track to the right will take you to the summit of Queenstown Hill (907 m). This section of the walk is through open country to views of the lake and it will take just 15 minutes to get to the top.

12 Sunshine Bay Walk, Queenstown
A good walk with views over the lake.

Grade: Easy. **Time:** One hour 30 minutes return.
How to get there: From the centre of Queenstown follow the shoreline of the lake west from the town.

A pleasant walk from the centre of Queenstown, this track starts at Fernhill just out of Queenstown on the Glenorchy road, but is easily accessible from the centre of town by following the footpath along the edge of the lake. The footpath eventually becomes a track along the road then drops down below the road to wind along the lake, through a cool forest of mixed exotic and native trees. Once through the trees the track reaches Sunshine Bay, a small shingle beach with boat launching facilities.

On the opposite shore are the Remarkables, which run the length of the western side of the lake. The highest point is Double Cone at 2319 m, but what makes the mountains so appealing is that they rise in a sheer wall from the lake's edge. In winter when they're covered in snow they create a vista of lake and mountains that's hard to beat.

On the way back don't walk along the road, as it is narrow, there is no footpath and the traffic is fast.

13 Bob's Cove
A walk along the lake past historic lime kilns.

- **Grade:** Easy. **Time:** One hour 15 minutes.
- **How to get there:** 14 km from Queenstown on the Glenorchy Road.

Bob's Cove is named after a local boatman, Bob Fortune, and a feature of this lovely walk is several nineteenth-century lime kilns, one in particular very well preserved. Limestone was an essential ingredient of mortar used in local stonework, in an area where stone rather than wood was the preferred building material. The gum trees may have been planted to provide a supply of wood to fuel the kilns.

From the car park the track wanders downhill through a mixture of eucalypts and native trees to Bob's Cove, a small bay on the lake edged with white shingle. Just along the shore are the lime kilns and just past the kilns the track divides. At this point take the right-hand track as this is a more gradual climb to the top of the hill, with only a short steep section near the summit.

From here the views are marvellous in all directions, with the bush-fringed shore below and the Remarkables rising high on the far side of the lake. After taking in the view continue downhill. At the next junction take the track to the left and return to the car park.

14 Bridal Veil Falls Walk, Routeburn Valley
A taste of the famous Routeburn Track.

- **Grade:** Easy. **Time:** 40 minutes return.
- **How to get there:** From Glenorchy follow the road to the beginning of the Routeburn Track, easily recognised by the large car park and public shelter (the last section is gravel but the road is in good condition).

In contrast to the dry Central Otago landscape, this basin in the Mt Aspiring National Park is more typical of Fiordland, so if a trip there isn't possible, this is a taste of what Fiordland has to offer. The lower reaches of the Routeburn river occupy a wide montane valley, dense with old beech forest, mosses, ferns, swiftly flowing streams and tumbling waterfalls. This is the beginning (or end) of the famous Routeburn Track and an excellent short excursion is to Bridal Veil Falls, a short, flat, easy walk through magnificent beech forest. The track leaves from the main car park, beyond which is a very attractive picnic area. Keep an eye out for the friendly native robin, common along the tracks.

If you have time, just a short distance down the road is Lake Sylvan. This small glacial lake is surrounded by the stark peaks of the Forbes and Humboldt mountains and encircled by beech forest. The lake is a haven for ducks, including paradise shelduck and grey teal, and there is also a simple camping site among beech trees. The easy walk to the lake will take about an hour return.

15 Poolburn Gorge, Otago Central Rail Trail
The most dramatic section of the rail trail and two tunnels.

Grade: Easy. **Time:** One hour 45 minutes.
How to get there: From Alexandra head north to Omakau, and at Omakau turn right into Ida Valley Road. After 10 km turn left into Auripo Road and continue down this road for 12 km to Thurlow Road on the left. The trail is just a short distance down Thurlow Road. You can also start the walk from Lauder, which will add another 40 minutes.

Operating for over 80 years, the Clyde to Middlemarch railway line was closed in 1990 and acquired by DOC in 1993, reopening in 2000 as the Otago Central Rail Trail. The trail is in six sections, each between 19 and 32 km in length, passing through tunnels, over bridges and viaducts and through some of New Zealand's most dramatic landscapes. While biking is the most popular way to travel, this short walk is along the most scenic part of the trail.

From Thurlow Road the track follows the flat rail line to the Poolburn Viaduct. This is the highest viaduct on the trail, rising 37 m above the gorge. Built in 1904, the viaduct stands on massive beautifully crafted stone piers, quarried and shaped on location. Much of the old timber is in its original position, with the spikes holding the rails in place still visible. Some of the old railway iron is stacked on the northern side of the viaduct.

Both tunnels are short so you don't need a torch, but the first one curves slightly so you will need to stand for a little while and let your eyes adjust. Between the two tunnels the views of the rocky Poolburn Gorge below are dramatic and a short walk to the top of the longer tunnel gives great views over the surrounding countryside. If you're keen on a picnic, just beyond the exit to the first tunnel you can scramble down the hillside on a rough track to a pleasant shady spot down by the river. This is the home of the New Zealand falcon, and these can be seen from the trail, patrolling the gorge for prey.

16 Flat Top Hill and Butchers Dam
A short walk though dry tussock land.

- **Grade:** Easy. **Time:** Loop walk 30 minutes.
- **How to get there:** On SH8, 5 km south of Alexandra.

Flat Top Hill lies at the foot of the Old Man Range near Alexandra and is the driest place in New Zealand, with less than 300 mm of rain a year. The rocks here are ancient by New Zealand standards, dating back 100 million years, forming a stone known as schist. Derived from the Greek word 'to split', schist is old mud and sandstone with a high quartz content and easily split, making it an ideal building material.

Equally unique is the rare surviving example of dry short tussock grassland. At first glance the vegetation seems dull and uniform, but over 180 native plant species have been recorded here, most of which are rare and highly localised. It's surprising to learn 12 native ferns are found here, given the exceptionally dry conditions.

Gold was first discovered here in 1862 and originally the town was called Hill's Gully, then Londonderry and finally Butcher's Gully, a name which finally stuck, though nothing now remains of the town. The dam itself was constructed from 1934 to 1937, to irrigate local orchards.

A loop walk with excellent interpretive panels takes around 30 minutes, while a walk up the slope to the summit of Flat Top Hill is longer than it looks and will take up to 2 hours return. From the top there are great views over Alexandra and the Clutha River.

19
short walks in Dunedin, South Otago and the Catlins

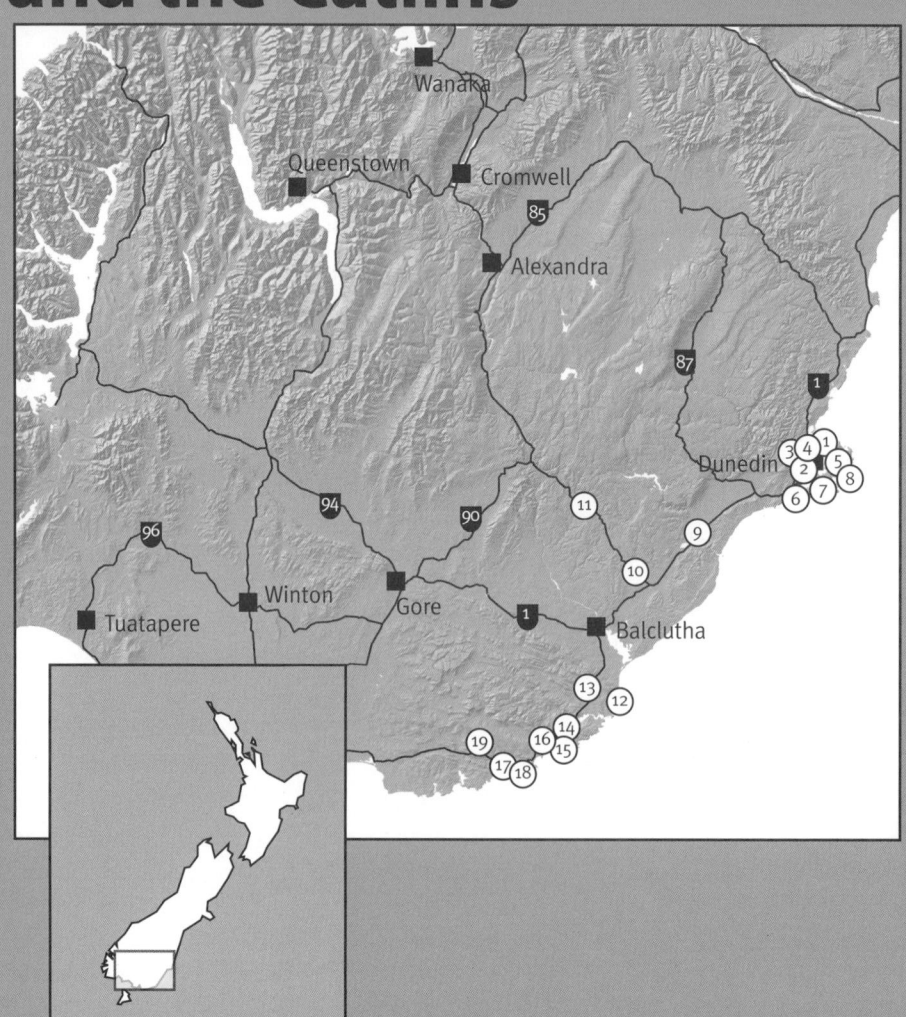

1 Mount Cargill and the Organ Pipes Walk
Magnificent views with volcanic rocks.

- **Grade:** Medium. **Time:** Organ Pipes – 40 minutes return; Mt Cargill – two hours return.
- **How to get there:** From North East Valley follow North Road. From the point where North Road morphs into Mt Cargill Road, the car park is 3 km on left, with very limited parking space.

Looming over the city, and just a short drive away, Mt Cargill (676 m) is exposed and often shrouded in cloud, creating a unique subalpine summit environment. Known to Maori as Kapuka-taumahaka, the mountain represents the body of either a warrior or a princess, with Buttars Peak the head.

While there is a road (very rough on the last section), the best way to experience Mt Cargill is on foot, via the Organ Pipes. All the hard climbing is in the first 15 minutes – the track goes solidly uphill with quite a few steps, before levelling off. From there it's an easy walk, well within the capabilities of anyone with reasonable fitness, with another short uphill stretch at the very top. The early part of the walk is through bush, ferns and mosses. What look like carefully shaped steps are in fact natural – broken rock from the Organ Pipes. The pipes are volcanic basalt rock, shaped in the cooling process into precise geometric forms. The formation isn't easy to see properly, but the jumble of broken rock below is interesting in itself.

From the Organ Pipes the track leads through subalpine vegetation to the top of Mt Cargill, where a cairn indicates key features. The 360-degree views over Dunedin and the coast are spectacular on a clear day. If the weather isn't good don't bother with this hike as you won't see a thing, but if the day dawns fine, make this your first priority.

2 Historic Dunedin
Some of our finest Victorian and early twentieth century buildings.

- **Grade:** Easy. **Time:** Allow one hour.
- **How to get there:** Begin this walk in the Octagon.

When gold was discovered in the 1860s, Dunedin became a boom town. While most miners came away empty-handed, merchants and bankers made their fortunes, their prosperity reflected in the grand buildings of Dunedin. This walk begins in the Octagon, heads south along Princes Street as far as Liverpool Street, then back along Princes Street to the Exchange. From the Exchange walk down High Street to the Railway Station and then back up Stuart St to the Octagon.

The city's central public space, the Octagon has remained people-friendly with a mix of historic buildings, cafés, picture theatres and the city art gallery. The magnificent Municipal Buildings (1880) were designed by prominent local architect Robert Lawson. Considerably altered in 1939 and 1963, the building is now restored, with its 40 m clocktower. In the heart of the Octagon is a statue of the Scottish poet Robert Burns, unveiled in 1886 to a crowd of over 8000, and the annual venue for poetry reading every 25 January – his birthday.

Princes Street, once the heart of the commercial district, has been left behind as the central retail area moved north along George Street. Major buildings here are: the ANZ Bank (1874); the Bank of New Zealand (1883); the National Bank (1912); the Old Post Office (1937); the Union Bank (1874) and Wains Hotel (1878).

Just off Princes Street, in Moray Place, is the First Church of Otago (1873), one of New Zealand's most elegant buildings. Built of Oamaru stone on a base of local volcanic rock, it was designed by Robert Lawson. The visitor centre at the back of the church has a display of his architectural drawings as well as photographs of the construction.

The Exchange was the hub of the financial area with the elaborate Cargill Memorial, honouring founding settler William Cargill, at its centre. Moved to the Exchange in 1872 and converted to a drinking fountain, the monument was first erected in 1863, in the Octagon.

Just uphill on the corner of Rattray and Smith streets is St Joseph's Catholic Cathedral (1866). Built in bluestone, it was designed by renowned church architect F.W. Petre in the Gothic revival style.

From the Exchange walk down Rattray Street to Queens Gardens and the Railway Station, past Dunedin Prison (1896), built of brick and only recently closed, then across the road to the distinctive art deco lines of the New Zealand Railways Road Service Building (1937), now part of the Otago Settlers Museum.

Built in 1906, Dunedin Railway Station was the largest and busiest in the country. The two-storey building is in the Flemish Renaissance style, constructed of dark volcanic stone and lighter Oamaru limestone, with stunning Royal Doulton tiles in the foyer. Mosaic flooring, magnificent stained glass windows and Edwardian ironwork along the platform are all original.

Lower Stuart Street, linking the railway station to the Octagon, houses the Law Courts (1899) built, like the railway station, in the Flemish Renaissance style.

3 Ross Creek Reservoir
A bush-fringed Victorian reservoir.

Grade: Easy. **Time:** 45 minutes return.
How to get there: The walk begins just over the bridge on Rockside Road near the intersection with Malvern Road, Dunedin.

As Dunedin grew, the city needed a reliable water supply and in 1867 the Ross Creek Reservoir was built to supply the rapidly growing settlement. Still in use today, the reservoir's distinctive Victorian valve tower and earth dam are the oldest in existence and fine old stone walls still line the dam. The reservoir is recognised as an outstanding engineering achievement by IPENZ (Institute of Professional Engineers New Zealand).

The gentle uphill walk to the reservoir is part of the much longer Leith Valley walkway and leads through a mix of introduced and native trees, including some very large native tree fuchsias. On reaching the dam, the walk becomes a flat loop around the reservoir.

4 Woodhaugh Gardens
An attractive mix of native trees and formal gardens.

Grade: Easy. **Time:** 30 minutes return.
How to get there: North end of George Street just before Pine Hill Road, Dunedin.

At first glance these gardens appear to be a rambling combination of bush, grassy picnic spots, ponds and playgrounds, but this is in fact a rare native forest remnant within walking distance of George Street. The flat paths and tracks meander through 12 ha alongside the Water of Leith and make this an ideal spot to let the kids run a little wild.

5 Aramoana Breakwater
A white sandy beach and a long breakwater.

Grade: Easy. **Time:** One hour return.
How to get there: From Port Chalmers continue east along Otago Harbour to the very end of the road.

Aramoana is essentially a large sandbar protecting the sheltered waters of Otago Harbour from the open sea. Facing the ocean is a wide sweep of white sand, interrupted by the Mole, a long breakwater constructed to stop the harbour channel from silting up. Directly opposite Taiaroa Head, Aramoana is a good spot to watch albatross in flight (binoculars will come in very handy), and fur seals and blue penguins are not uncommon on the beach.

Just inside the breakwater a track and boardwalk lead through the tidal saltmarshes, home to numerous wading birds, including godwits in the summer months, while to the north of the breakwater the wide sandy beach of Aramoana is ideal for a leisurely beach amble.

6 Tunnel Beach Walkway
A short tunnel down to a rocky cove.

Grade: Medium. **Time:** One hour return.
How to get there: End of Blackhead Road, St Clair, Dunedin.

In an area with a surfeit of coastal vistas, it's hard to go past Tunnel Beach. A short walk over farmland leads downhill to a large sea arch. From the top there are marvellous views south along the coast. In wild weather huge waves thunder against the rocks below and the rougher the weather the more impressive the wave action. From the top of the arch a low tunnel with shallow steps leads down to a small cove. The tunnel was built by John Cargill, son of the prominent settler William Cargill, so his daughters could go swimming away from the more public beach at St Clair. Sadly one of his daughters drowned, so needless to say this isn't a particularly safe place to swim.

7 Sandymount Loop Walk
Some of the best coastal scenery on the peninsula.

Grade: Easy. **Time:** Loop Walk one hour, Sandfly Bay one hour return.
How to get there: End of Sandymount Road off Highcliff Road – the main road running along the top ridge of the peninsula.

Sandymount consists of sand driven up from Sandfly Bay to cover the rocky summit (319 m), and is best known for dramatic cliffs over 200 m, at The Chasm and Lovers Leap.

The short loop walk begins through an avenue of macrocarpa, then crosses tussock farmland with views of Allans Beach, Hoopers and Papanui inlets and Mt Charles. The Chasm is a massive vertical drop to a rock base and foaming sea. From here it's a short walk to Lovers Leap, a sheer cliff dropping to a large sea arch. In windy weather it's very exposed, so come prepared. The track up to the summit is basic but not difficult, and then it drops back down through tussock to the carpark. A better track, although still rough, leads up from the car park. The views are panoramic – south to Nugget Point, north to Moeraki, and a glimpse of the city.

The track to Sandfly Bay leads down from Sandymount, crossing farmland before entering dunes driven inland by fierce southerly winds – the beach taking its name not from the pesky insect but wind-blown sand. The beautiful white sandy beach is flanked by cliffs, with small rock stacks offshore. Yellow-eyed penguins nest in the dunes and seals are common.

You can walk to Sandfly Bay from Sandymount, although it's quicker to drive back along Sandymount Road, take Ridge Road to the left and drive to the end (don't block the farm entrance and note the track is closed for lambing from 1 September to 1 November). Another access point is at the end of Seal Point Road, off Highcliff.

8 Okia Reserve/Victory Beach
A magnificent sweep of white sand beach.

- **Grade:** Easy. **Time:** One hour 30 minutes return.
- **How to get there:** Victory Beach is 24 km by road from Dunedin CBD, and accessed from Portobello (gravel road). At the end of the road a 2 km walkway leads past the Pyramids.

This large coastal reserve is an extensive area of dune, wetland and a pristine beach wide open to the Southern Ocean, and as wild as it gets on the Otago Peninsula. The dunes behind the beach are the nesting grounds for both yellow-eyed and blue penguins and a resting area for New Zealand sea lions. The Pyramids, two aptly named small hills, are volcanic in origin – which is made very obvious by the geometric basalt columns on the seaward side of the smaller pyramid (similar to the Organ Pipes on Mt Cargill).

The beach takes its name from the ship *Victory*, which came to grief on the shore while under the command of the proverbial drunken sailor, although very little of the wreck remains. The beach is undeveloped, open to the Southern Ocean and pristine.

Beginning through farmland, this walk passes between the Pyramids and continues through wetland and dune terrain to the beach. There is a short scramble to the top of the smaller pyramid for a view over the dune country.

Take care in the scrub-covered dunes behind the beach as New Zealand sea lions rest here, and are well camouflaged. Not called sea lions for nothing, they can be quite aggressive when disturbed. Penguins also nest in the dunes; give them plenty of latitude.

9 Sinclair Wetlands
The only remaining wetland on the Taieri Plains.

- **Grade:** Easy. **Time:** One hour return.
- **How to get there:** 854 Berwick – Clarendon Road, South Taieri. This road runs west of Lakes Waihola and Waipori and is off SH1 south of Mosgiel.

Covering 315 ha, and adjoining Lakes Waihola and Waipori, these wetlands are all that remain of the huge swamp covering most of the Taieri Plains, long since drained for farmland. The wetlands have only survived through the far-sighted actions of Horrie (Horace) Sinclair, who purchased land in 1960, and allowed it to revert to its original state, saving one of our most important wetlands. In addition to 40 bird species which breed here, another 45 bird species have been recorded.

By their very nature, wetlands are flat and damp, and it's often hard to see anything. The Sinclair Wetlands are fortunate in having a causeway through their heart, linking two small islands, both of which have excellent views over the entire reserve. There is camping on site (Ph 03 486 2654) and a koha/donation is requested to enter the wetland.

10 Manuka Gorge Tunnel Track
A beautiful rail tunnel complete with glow-worms.

Grade: Easy. **Time:** 30 minutes return.
How to get there: On SH8, 11.5 km from the SH1 turnoff, 3 km south of Milton.

In 1876 a railway was constructed from Milton to Alexandra, linking the coast with the goldfield towns further inland, which operated until 1968. The brick-lined Mt Stuart tunnel at Manuka Gorge is 442 m long and the walk to the tunnel is flat and easy. While the tunnel itself is now closed, the glow-worms can still be seen at the wetter eastern entrance

11 Gabriel's Gully
New Zealand's first gold rush.

Grade: Medium. **Time:** One hour.
How to get there: From the main street of Lawrence (SH8) turn into Gabriel's Gully Road and drive a further 4 km to the car park.

New Zealand's first major gold strike occurred in May 1861, when Gabriel Read struck gold here. Within months 6000 miners had poured into the area and nearby Lawrence quickly blossomed into a town of over 11,000 people. At the time Dunedin had a population of around 6000. Gold was also discovered in several locations nearby, but the easy gold was quickly won and the miners moved on to new discoveries on the West Coast.

Almost nothing tangible remains at Gabriel's Gully – what was not carted off to be used elsewhere has long since quietly rotted away in a climate much wetter than further inland. Today the site is overgrown with sycamore, broom, gorse and manuka, but excellent interpretive panels which include historical photos make the walk worthwhile. The loop walk begins with a steady uphill section with an overview of the valley, then drops into the gully and meanders among old workings, the most substantial of which is a tunnel. A little way on from the car park is a small pond and a picturesque picnic area among shady trees.

12 Nugget Point
Coastal views, an historic lighthouse and wildlife on the rocks.

Grade: Easy. Time: 30 minutes return.

How to get there: From Balclutha drive to Port Molyneux and then on to Kaka Point – follow the unsealed coast road for 8 km to Nugget Point.

Nugget Point takes its name from the group of jagged rocks just offshore and is the location of an historic lighthouse. This was built in 1870 when Port Molyneux, just to the north, was an important port and the rugged Catlins coast took a high toll on local shipping.

Wild and windswept, the track to the point has spectacular views north and south. Just before the lighthouse a steep track leads down to Roaring Bay (10 minutes one way), where there is a hide to watch both the blue and yellow-eyed penguins, which come ashore to nest late in the day. On the rocks below the point is a unique seal colony, the only place in New Zealand where elephant seals, fur seals and New Zealand sea lions share the same territory. The seals aren't easy to see as the track is 130 m above the rookery. As these animals blend in with the colour of the rocks, binoculars are very useful.

13 Tunnel Hill
A beautifully constructed railway tunnel.

Grade: Easy. Time: 20 minutes return.

How to get there: 3 km north of Owaka on SH92.

Catlins River Branch Railway was opened in 1895, to speed the extraction of timber, the mainstay of railway at the time. However, as the line opened, the timber began to run out, though the line was not finally closed until 1971. Constructed with pick and shovel, this 276 m long rail tunnel is lined with fine stonework on the lower half of the tunnel, with brickwork above. A torch is helpful.

14 Pounawea Scenic Reserve
A particularly fine stand of virgin lowland forest.

- **Grade:** Easy. **Time:** 40 minutes return.
- **How to get there:** Turn off SH92 and drive 5 km to the end of the road at Pounawea – the track is accessed through the camping ground.

The superb bush in this small reserve is a good example of what drew timber millers to this isolated region. This virgin forest has all the important lowland trees, including totara, southern rata, rimu, miro and kahikatea – all helpfully identified by good signage. The birdlife is prolific and the song of the bellbirds is a constant accompaniment.

The walk begins in the camping ground, straight ahead past the office at the main gate, and forms a loop through the bush back to the far side of the camping ground. A side track leads down to a lookout over the Owaka River estuary.

15 Jack's Blowhole Walk
A booming blowhole inland from the sea.

- **Grade:** Easy. **Time:** One hour return.
- **How to get there:** Turn off SH92 at Owaka and drive towards Pounawea. After 2 km turn right into Jacks Bay Road and drive the 8 km to the end of the road – the track begins at the southern end of the beach.

Jack's Blowhole, over 200 m from the sea, is a 55-m deep hole linked to the sea by an underground cave. You'll hear it long before you arrive – the booming of the blowhole at high tide is impressive.

An easy track across private farmland leads from the southern end of the beach at Jack's Bay, with excellent views of Jack's Beach, where small cribs snuggle along the shore, dominated by the cliffs of Catlins Heads. A track around the blowhole, known to Maori as Opito or 'the navel', has two excellent lookouts.

Jack's Bay and Jack's Blowhole are named after Tuhawaiki, or 'Bloody Jack' – nothing to do with bloodthirstiness, but rather his fondness for using the word 'bloody'. A great Ngai Tahu warrior who played a key role in the 1831 defeat of Te Rauparaha near Cape Campbell, in 1835 he helped push back Ngati Toa forces in the South Island, finally defeating Te Puoho in 1836, near Mataura.

In April 1840 he signed the Treaty of Waitangi on board the HMS *Herald* at Ruapuke Island in Foveaux Strait. Known for shrewdness, intelligence and vast knowledge, Tuhawaiki was also fond of being grand, with a liking for splendid military uniforms. When he signed the deed of sale for the Otago Block, he called himself the 'King of Bluff'.

Tuhawaiki drowned in 1844 when his ship hit rocks south of Timaru at what is now Tuhawaiki Point. Nearby Tuhawaiki Island is also named after him. When Te Rauparaha trapped Tuhawaiki on False Island, to the north of the Owaka river mouth, he escaped by swimming.

16 Purakaunui Falls
Picture-postcard perfect waterfall in lush beech forest.

Grade: Easy. **Time:** 20 minutes return.
How to get there: Well signposted off SH92 south of Owaka, the falls are 9 km off the main road just past the Catlins River Bridge.

Purakaunui Falls is the most popular stop in the Catlins, with water gently cascading down a stepped rock face. While the waterfalls in the Catlins area are not especially high or dramatic, they are particularly picturesque, surrounded by beautiful native bush.

The best view is from the lower lookout accessed by a short flight of steps, and the walk to the falls is through a particularly handsome forest of beech, ferns and mosses.

17 Traill Tractor and Cook's Sawmill Walk
An old sawmilling town and the fascinating Traill Tractor.

Grade: Easy. **Time:** 20 minutes return.
How to get there: The track begins on the southern side of the Fleming River bridge on SH92.

Timber underpinned the settlement of the Catlins region, and this walk focuses on the extensive timber milling industry rather than the area's natural beauty. The track leads through the site of the settlement supporting the mill, to the remains of Cook's sawmill and the restored Traill Tractor. This unusual vehicle is a Fordson tractor adapted to run on rails, either pushing or pulling log-laden carriages from the bush to the mill. At intervals along the track are signs indicating where buildings once stood, though nothing remains today.

18 Cathedral Caves
Dramatic sea caves accessible at low tide.

- Grade: Easy. Time: Allow one hour.
- How to get there: 2 km south of the Tautuku River on SH92.

Cathedral Caves are a group of spectacular sea caves, with the main cave over 30 m high, while others go deep into the cliff. It's a 20-minute walk to the first cave, but take some time to explore the other caves along the shore and be prepared to get your feet wet, even at low tide. The walk is very tide-dependent and the caves are only accessible for 1½ hours either side of low tide, depending on the sea and the sand base. While the tide times are helpfully posted on the gate avoid disappointment by checking the website www.cathedralcaves.co.nz or at the Owaka information centre There is a small entrance fee and the gate is closed if the tide is not right. The caves are closed over winter, usually from Anzac Day to Labour Weekend.

19 McLean Falls
The most impressive waterfall in the Catlins.

- Grade: Easy. Time: 40 minutes return.
- How to get there: 1 km south of Cathedral Caves, turn into Rewcastle Road – the beginning of the track is 3.3 km on the right.

One of the higher waterfalls in the Catlins, McLean Falls is not one but four interlinked cascades. The highest single fall is 20 m high, with water spreading across a rock face. The stream is then forced through a narrow gorge and over a further three falls. Equally attractive is the walk along the bush stream to the falls themselves, with trees and rocks covered with thick mosses, and bellbirds and tomtits flitting in the trees.

20 short walks in Southland, Stewart Island and Fiordland

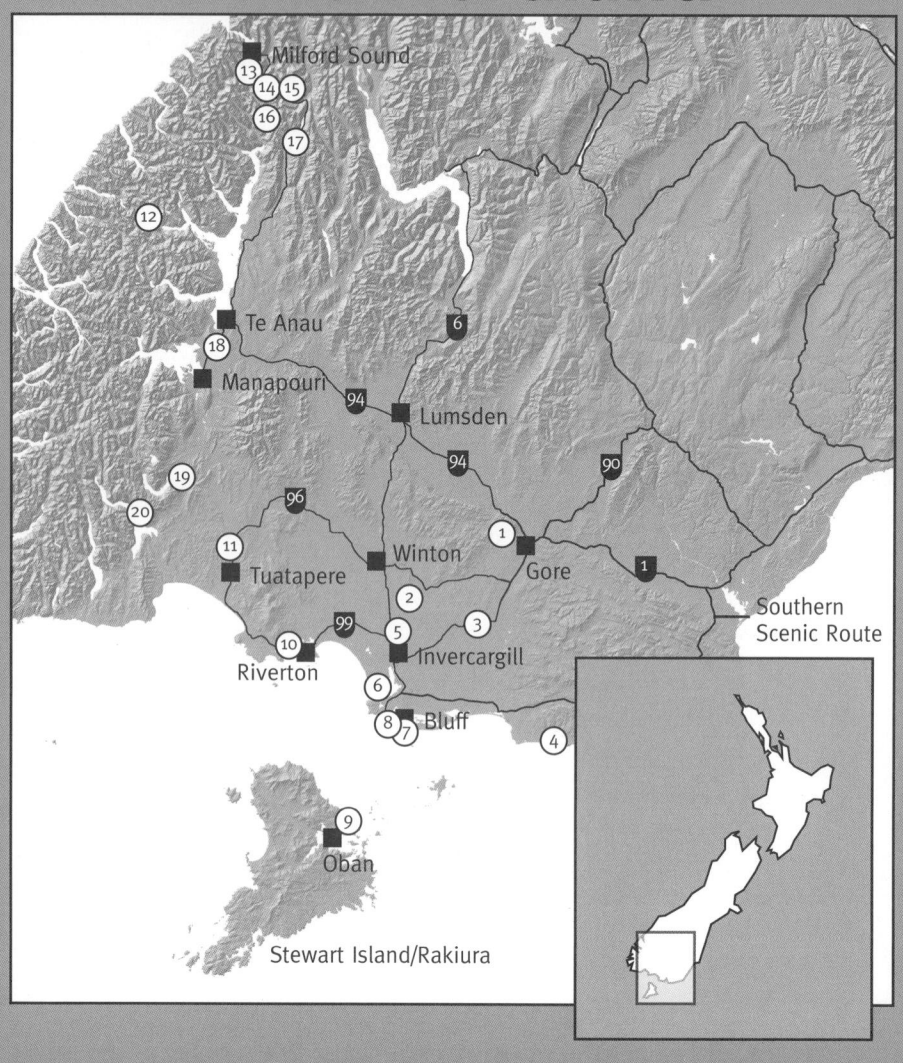

1 Dolamore Park and Croydon Bush Reserve
Untouched bush in the famous Hokonui Hills.

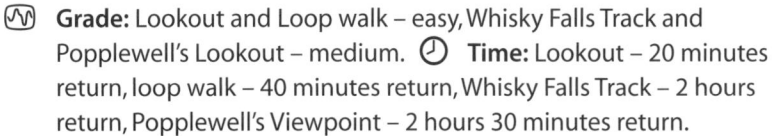

- **Grade:** Lookout and Loop walk – easy, Whisky Falls Track and Popplewell's Lookout – medium. **Time:** Lookout – 20 minutes return, loop walk – 40 minutes return, Whisky Falls Track – 2 hours return, Popplewell's Viewpoint – 2 hours 30 minutes return.
- **How to get there:** Take SH94 west of Gore for 5 km and turn left into Kingdon Road. Continue along this road which after 2 km changes into Reaby Road. After a further 5.5 km turn right into Dolamore Park Road; the entrance to the park is about 1 km on the right. Both short walks start opposite the main entrance on the far side of the large grassed area.

Covering nearly 1000 ha, Dolamore Park and Croydon Bush are two adjacent reserves in the Hokonui Hills, parts of which were set aside as a reserve as early as 1895. Most of the forest, which completely covered these hills and much of the plain beyond, was milled for timber in the late nineteenth century. The forest was so dense the Hokonui Hills were famous for illegal whisky production with stills set up in the deep forested valleys, and for 50 years these hills produced the best bush whisky in the country. The Dolamore Park area has been more formally developed, with an arboretum, rhododendron garden, picnic areas and children's playground, as well as very good camping facilities.

The walk to the lookout is on a well-graded uphill path to a 304 m point with views south over the plains to Bluff Hill. The loop walk is flat and wanders through huge mature trees with a lush undergrowth of ferns and moss. For those wanting to stretch their legs even further, try the loop walk on the Whisky Falls track, with Popplewell's Viewpoint at 460 m another 30 minutes on from there.

2 Forest Hill and Tussock Creek Reserves

Grade: Easy. **Time:** Lookout – 1 hour 30 minutes return; Derek Turnbull Track – 2 hours one way.

How to get there: From Invercargill take SH6 towards Winton, after 26 km turn right into Wilson's Crossing Road and after 7.5 km turn left into Pettigrew Road – the track starts from Tussock Creek picnic area, 2 km, at the end of this road.

The only native bush left in Central Southland, the two adjoining reserves of Forest Hill and Tussock Creek, just southwest of Winton, contain some outstanding examples of rata and tree fuchsia. Despite their isolation from any other bush, the reserves are home to a surprising number of native birds including bellbirds, tui, tomtits, kereru and brown creepers. In addition, among the limestone outcrops are a number of small caves, the perfect habitat for cave weta.

This track has the most fantastic gradient, with the steady uphill grade hardly noticeable. A 500-year-old rata has toppled on its side, but is still vigorous and growing strongly. From the lookout the views are over the rich Central Southland Plains, south to Stewart Island and Bluff, west to the Longwood Range and northwest to the Takitimu Mountains.

The Derek Turnbull Track traverses the entire length of both reserves, with the exit on Forest Hill Road, 7 km south of Winton.

3 Seaward Downs

Outstanding rimu, kahikatea, miro, totara and matai.

Grade: Easy. **Time:** 30 minutes.

How to get there: From Invercargill take SH1 toward Gore and 2 km beyond Dacre turn right to Morton Mains – 1 km past Morton Mains, turn left into Tramway Road; the reserve is 3 km down this road, on the right.

Throughout Southland numerous placenames have their origins in the vast forest once covering this plain – Heddon Bush, Ryal Bush, Gummies Bush, Centre Bush. The forest is long gone and this small bush reserve is a reminder of what has vanished. In particular, it has fine examples of major podocarps, rimu, totara, kahikatea, miro and matai. The short loop walk is flat all the way and, although not signposted, is easy to find and it is impossible to get lost. However, take note that it is very muddy in places.

4 Slope Point

The most southerly point on the South Island mainland.

Grade: Easy. **Time:** 25 minutes return.

How to get there: From Tokanui on SH92 turn off towards Haldane and follow the signs to Slope Point, 6 km south of Haldane.

While most tourists flock to Bluff, Slope Point is the most southerly point of the South Island and at 46.4 degrees south is almost equidistant from the South Pole and the Equator. While it is bleak and windswept, there are excellent coastal views across to Stewart Island, and the more northerly Bluff Hill is just visible in the distance. The track crosses farmland and leads to a simple sign marking the point's position. The track is closed for lambing from 1 September to 1 November.

5 Thomson's Bush, Invercargill

Easy walking through kahikatea, matai and beech trees.

Grade: Easy. **Time:** 40 minutes.

How to get there: Queen's Drive, Invercargill.

A surviving remnant of the great forest which once covered the coastal plain where Invercargill now stands, the bush had been milled prior to its protection as a reserve in 1912. Named after J. Turnbull Thomson, New Zealand's Surveyor General who planned the settlement of Invercargill in 1857. Despite earlier milling, the reserve still contains large kahikatea, matai and beech.

Numerous short tracks weave through the trees, but for a longer walk begin from the second car park (the first is right by the road), cross the small bridge over the stream known as the Waihopai Backwater and take the first track to the right. This track continues around the outer edge of the reserve, via a section along the stop bank of the Waihopai River and back through the bush to the car park.

6 Sandy Point, Invercargill

Viewpoints over the New River estuary, Invercargill and Bluff.

- **Grade:** Easy. **Time:** Noki Kaik Beach – 20 minutes return; Daffodil Bay – one hour 10 minutes return.
- **How to get there:** From Invercargill take Stead Street and drive towards Oreti Beach (Otatara). After 7 km turn left into Sandy Point Road and continue down this road for 6 km – just past the end of the tarseal is a parking area on the left.

Sandy Point is a large sand peninsula between the Oreti River and the open ocean at Oreti Beach. Much of the area is now highly modified, though patches of bush remain along the estuary. The drive to the walk is like a roll call of every outdoor club imaginable.

From the car park a short uphill walk leads to Hatch's Hill lookout with views over the wide tidal New River Estuary (essentially the estuary for the Oreti River), Invercargill city and beyond that to Bluff. This is particularly picturesque at sunset. The track leads downhill to the small, sandy Noki Kaik beach. This area was a rich source of food for early Maori. The main settlement here was Oue, though the pre-European population would never have been more than a few hundred people. In 1836 a whaling station was established here, though it only lasted a short time.

From the beach retrace your steps back to the Daffodil Bay track, which goes off to the right. This section of the walk leads through a surprisingly dense and dark, but not very tall forest of matai and totara to Daffodil Bay, another small beach with views over the estuary.

7 Bluff Hill Summit, Foveaux Walkway, Bluff

- **Grade:** Medium/hard. **Time:** Lookout – one hour 20 minutes return, Summit via Lookout – two hours return; Summit via Topuni Track – 50 minutes return.
- **How to get there:** Stirling Point, the end of SH1 – Bluff.

Rising to 265 m, Bluff Hill is an ancient volcanic cone dating back to the Permian, well over 200 million years ago when New Zealand was part of the Gondwanaland supercontinent. Mt Anglem on Stewart Island, the Longwood Range and the Takitimu Mountains all date from the same period.

It is known to Maori as Motupohue, 'motu' or island refering to the way the hill appears like an island; 'pohue' refers to native convolvulus growing there. The area around Bluff was used for seasonal hunting and gathering, with the main pa occupying Ruapuke Island, the home of Tuhawaiki, or 'Bloody Jack'. Bluff was also a source of argillite, a tough stone worked into adzes.

There are two ways of walking up to the summit. The first, Topuni Track, branches off to the right immediately after the beginning of the Foveaux Walkway and is a solid uphill walk.

The longer but more picturesque walk follows the flat, easy Foveaux Walkway to the lookout then turns uphill along the Millennium Track to the summit. This superb coastal walk on an excellent flat track winds around the rocky shore of Bluff Hill through salt-resistant flax and hebes to a lookout with views far to the west and to the offshore islands. Stewart Island looms across the wild waters of Foveaux Strait. Return down the Topuni Track and this becomes a loop.

8 The Glory Track, Foveaux Walkway, Bluff
A verdant, lush forestscape.

- **Grade:** Easy. **Time:** 50 minutes return.
- **How to get there:** Stirling Point – Bluff.

Despite proximity to constant salt-laden winds and spray, the even temperature and consistent rainfall has created a forestscape which is verdant and lush. There are many fine old trees including kamahi, kahikatea, rimu and rata; the close relationship between rata and pohutukawa is abundantly clear, with rata here growing twisted and spreading much like pohutukawa. Some of the rata are so gnarled and twisted they look as if they have been wrung out to dry.

This track takes its name from an English ship, the *Glory*, which was wrecked on the rocks below, ironically while taking on board the local pilot. Today, however, the name could equally refer to this glorious stretch of bush.

Begin the walk by following the Foveaux Walkway till you reach the entrance to the track, to the right. From the coast, the Glory Track is a steady uphill walk on a good graded path, looping back towards the car park. Not far from the exit the track drops steeply passing a substantial World War II gun emplacement. Just below is a low concrete lookout pit – both were built in 1942.

This track is very sheltered and a good option if the weather makes the longer Foveaux walk an unpleasant prospect.

9 Ulva Island, Stewart Island/Rakiura
An unspoiled island is now an important bird sanctuary.

- **Grade:** Easy. **Time:** Allow at least two hours.
- **How to get there:** The ferry company is Stewart Island Experience, Ph 03 212 7660, 0800 000 511 (www.stewartislandexperience.co.nz); they also operate a bus service from Invercargill to Bluff. Stewart Island Airway also has regular flights (www.stewartislandflights.co.nz) ph (03) 218 9129.

New Zealand's third-largest island is home to Rakiura National Park, covering 85 percent of the island. The island has an exceptional unspoiled landscape of untouched bush, hidden bays and rugged mountain ranges, with the highest point Mt Anglem (980 m).

Stewart Island was likely joined to the mainland during the Pliocene ice ages, when the sea level was lower. However, a number of important trees and plants including beech, one of New Zealand's most widespread and ancient, are absent. This may indicate the island has been isolated for much longer.

Known to Maori as both Rakiura, 'heavenly glow' (perhaps a reference to spectacular sunsets), and Te Punga-o-te-waka-a-Maui, or 'the anchor stone of Maui's waka', Maori history is sketchy; it's likely the island was a refuge for vanquished tribes.

With just 25 km of road, 250 km of track and only 400 residents, the island has a gentle, relaxed feel, with a range of accommodation, a great pub and some good places to eat. A day trip to Stewart Island will enable you to visit Ulva Island, take a boat trip and have a wander around Oban – anything more will require an overnight stay. While the ferry from Bluff is fast, taking an hour, Foveaux Strait has a well-deserved reputation as a wild stretch of water. The ferry is fairly small and frequently booked out in summer, so book ahead.

Ulva Island is in Paterson Inlet, just around the corner from Halfmoon Bay, and popular with day-trippers. The island has been cleared of pests and rare native birds have been reintroduced. Keep an eye out for kaka, kakariki, saddlebacks and Stewart Island robins. Inquisitive weka are common, especially on the beaches, where they'll peck at your backpack looking for something to steal. Waters around the island are now protected by a 1000 ha marine reserve. Ulva Island is a short water-taxi ride from Golden Bay, in turn a 20-minute walk from the wharf at Oban, although there is transport. The Ulva Island Experience also runs boat trips from the main wharf at Oban. The island is small and relatively flat, with a network of well-marked, excellent tracks, linking very attractive beaches. Sydney Cove is the pick and just a short 20-minute return walk from the wharf, though South West Beach (1½ hours return) is also well worth it. The old post office, over 100 years old, still stands near the wharf.

Around Oban a number of short walks can be included on the walk to and from Golden Bay. Raroa and Fuchsia Walks are short side tracks through the bush, an alternative to walking on the road. Observation Rock, just 10 minutes from the road, is a wonderful lookout point over Paterson Inlet and Ulva Island.

10 Mores Lookout, Riverton
Excellent views over coastal Southland and the offshore islands.

Grade: Easy. **Time:** 45 minutes return.
How to get there: Head west from Riverton and turn left towards Riverton Rocks immediately after crossing the bridge over the Jacobs River – after 800 m turn right in Richard Street and take the gravel road up to the car park.

The Maori name for Riverton is Aparima, named after a high-born Waitaha woman, and today the river retains this name. Original estimates put the Maori population around 300, centred around an area later known as the Kaike. Riverton began life as a whaling station established by Captain John Howell in 1836 and is one of New Zealand's oldest European settlements. Now a picturesque seaside and fishing township on the estuary of the Jacobs River (the confluence of the Aparima and Pourakino rivers), it once promoted itself as the 'Riviera of the South'.

Mores Reserve centres on two small rocky outcrops once used to spot whales passing through the strait, when Riverton was a whaling station. From the top, the islands of Foveaux Strait are clearly visible including Stewart, Codfish, Centre and Pig islands. Below is the estuary, to the west the view follows along the coast to Colac Bay and, in the distance, the mountains of Fiordland. To the north lie the Takitimu Mountains, Eyre Mountains and the Hokonui Hills, while to the east is the white sweep of

Oreti Beach and beyond that Bluff Hill.

The walk to the Hilltop Lookout will take 15 minutes return, while the longer walk to Mores Lookout takes 45 minutes return but is a more appealing stroll through lush regenerating bush, alive with bellbirds.

11 Tuatapere Domain Walk
A 1000-year-old totara is the centrepiece of this short walk.

- **Grade:** Easy. **Time:** 25 minutes.
- **How to get there:** From Tuatapere head west on SH99 and immediately after crossing the Waiau River bridge turn right into the domain – the track begins on the left just before the sports ground.

Part of the Tuatapere Domain is a small patch of ancient trees which include totara, matai, kahikatea and beech; the highlight is a massive 1000-year-old totara. The walk is flat and easy. Equally impressive is a huge felled tree, which was lifted back onto its stump in 1984 by the power of floodwaters. The white railing around the oval sports ground harks back to the days when the domain was a horse-racing track.

12 Fiordland National Park
Our largest national park.

- **Grade:** Varies. **Time:** Varies.
- **How to get there:** The Milford and Hollyford roads.

Established in 1952 and with an area over 1,252,000 ha, Fiordland is our largest national park and was recognised in 1984 as a World Heritage Area. Much of the park is rugged and mountainous with a hard and very wet climate, but this untouched part of New Zealand is spectacular and home to some of the rarest plants and birds in the world.

For most visitors the park is accessible only at the fringes and tourists tend to travel directly to Milford Sound, take the boat trip and return. However, some short excursions along the way are worthwhile. The road is sealed and in excellent condition, though subject to road closures during winter, mainly due to snow and icy conditions around the Homer Tunnel. Make sure you have a full tank of fuel before leaving Te Anau, you'll need to carry chains in winter (available for hire in Te Anau). Cell phone coverage is limited to Te Anau and Milford Sound (if that), and facilities and accommodation at Milford itself are very limited.

The road is very busy in the morning with buses to catch the midday boat trips, which tend to stop at selected viewpoints on the way to the Sound. Up to 100 coaches per day use the road in the peak of the season but fortunately most of the traffic is travelling in the same direction and most coach tourists do the boat trip as a lunchtime excursion. If you want to avoid the worst of the crowds leave before 8 am, travel straight to Milford Sound, do the boat trip, and stop for the walks on a leisurely drive back. The following walks are on the basis of travelling from Milford Sound back to Te Anau.

13 The Chasm

Grade: Easy. **Time:** 20 minutes return.
How to get there: On the Milford road, about 12 km from Milford Sound village.

The Cleddau River is forced through a narrow gorge creating an impressive torrent of water. Over thousands of years this has worn the rock into smooth sculpted formations. Given the high rainfall in the area, the Chasm is always dramatic viewing.

14 Homer Tunnel Nature Walk

Grade: Easy. **Time:** 30 minutes return.
How to get there: The walk is to the left of the entrance to the Homer Tunnel coming from Te Anau.

The area around the tunnel is 945 m above sea level and the highest point on the road. Prior to the tunnel, the only access to Milford Sound was either on foot via the Milford Track, or by sea, with considerable pressure on the government to build a tunnel through the Homer Saddle to open up the area to tourism. Government work schemes during the Depression provided a ready source of labour and in 1929 work began on the road, and in 1935 on the tunnel. Progress in the harsh environment was slow and dangerous, and although the breakthough was achieved, work on the tunnel was halted during World War II. Work resumed after the war and in 1953 the tunnel was finally completed. The road on the western side of the tunnel is dramatic, with sheer cliffs and hairpin bends dropping steeply to

Milford Sound. The single-lane tunnel is 1.2 km long, slopes steeply down towards the Milford end with a gradient of 1 in 10, and is controlled by traffic lights (though the wait isn't usually long).

A short walk on the eastern side of the tunnel leads through alpine vegetation and kea are common in the area.

15 Humboldt Falls, Hollyford Valley
An attractive side trip down an unsealed road.

- **Grade:** Easy. **Time:** 30 minutes return.
- **How to get there:** Turn off the Milford Road (SH94) at Marian Corner, about 87 km from Te Anau. The track starts at the end of the unsealed road.

If there is time, the Hollyford Valley is an attractive side trip. While the road is unsealed, it is flat and in good condition. The total height of these falls is 275 m, though they fall in three stages of which the tallest single drop is 134 m. Naturally more impressive after heavy rain, the falls are reached by walking through beech forest, though the view of them is quite distant, from a lookout across the Humboldt Creek.

16 The Key Summit

- **Grade:** Medium. **Time:** Three hours return.
- **How to get there:** The track begins at the Divide, 10 km from Lake Gunn.

The track to the top of Key Summit (919 m) is one of the most accessible points to high alpine scenery along the Milford road and ideal if one of the longer walks is not an option. From The Divide (515 m), the walk to the top follows the Routeburn Track for most of the way, branching off for the climb to the summit. Along the way the vegetation changes from beech through to subalpine tussock and shrubs. From the top the views of the Darran and Humboldt mountains are superb.

17 Cascades Creek/Lake Gunn Nature Walk

Grade: Easy. **Time:** 40 minutes return.
How to get there: On the Milford Road, 75 km from Te Anau.

A flat loop walk through red beech forest thickly smothered in moss leads to a view of high snow-capped mountains looming over the bush-lined shores of Lake Gunn. The track then follows the shoreline to the lake outlet stream and back to the car park. An added plus is good signage to help with plant identification.

18 Dock Bay Walk, Lake Te Anau
Pristine beech forest lines the shores of Lake Te Anau.

Grade: Easy. **Time:** Brod Bay – two hours return, Dock Bay – one hour return.
How to get there: From Te Anau, head south towards Manapouri and turn right into Golf Course Road, then right again at the sign 'Kepler Track'; drive to the car park by the control gates at the end. From the car park, walk down the sealed road to the control gates and cross over to the other side.

This walk, which follows the lakeside, is the beginning of the Kepler Track. Covering an area of 344 square km and 65 km long, Te Anau is the largest lake in the South Island and the second largest in the country after Lake Taupo. The eastern and western sides could not contrast more. To the west the rugged Kepler, Murchison and Stuart mountain ranges rise to over 1500 m and are snow-clad in winter and bush-clad at the shoreline. Three arms of the lake, unimaginatively named South, Middle and North Fiords, reach deep into the mountains, while to the east the landscape is flat, open and much drier.

Following the shore of Lake Te Anau, the track meanders along the lake edge, through virgin beech forest with a lush understorey of moss, crown ferns and beech saplings. Dock Bay is a very pretty beach of white sand, overhung with beech and kowhai trees. While sheltered from the westerly wind, the lake is cold, even in summer. Brod Bay is very similar and just another 30 minutes further on.

19 Lake Monowai Walk
A stroll through beech forest to a mountain lookout.

- **Grade:** Easy. **Time:** 30 minutes return.
- **How to get there:** From SH99, 34 km south of Manapouri, turn into Lake Monowai Road and travel 14 km to the lake at the end of the road – about half this road is gravel.

If for no other reason, this lake should be visited as an example of the disastrous and lasting effect on the environment of careless development. The Monowai power station was built in 1925 and the lake raised, yet over 80 years later the result is still evident with stumps and logs of the drowned forest still visible along the shore. Created by a long-vanished glacier, the lake is long and narrow and surrounded by high mountains, shrouded in mist and cloaked in virgin beech forest. Like Hauroko, Monowai is undeveloped (the power outlet is unobtrusive) and it doesn't attract many visitors, retaining a timeless, primordial feel.

This flat walk is through mature beech forest, the ground thickly carpeted in mosses, and leads to a lookout point with long views down the two arms of the lake and far into the Fiordland mountains.

20 Lake Hauroko Lookout
Superb views over one of the world's deepest lakes.

- **Grade:** Lake Hauroko Lookout – medium/hard, Lake Hauroko track – easy.
- **Time:** Lake Hauroko Lookout – 3 hours return, Lake Hauroko Track – 30 minutes.
- **How to get there:** From Tuatapere, drive 13 km north to Clifden on SH99 and then turn into the Lake Hauroko Road. Lake Hauroko is 32 km down this road, of which more than half is gravel.

One of the few accessible points in the southern area of the park, Lake Hauroko at 462 m is the deepest lake in New Zealand and one of the 10 deepest lakes in the world. Deep within the mountains, wild and undeveloped, the location at the end of a long gravel road deters most visitors, creating a place of quiet beauty.

In April 1967, local George Evans pulled his boat onto Mary Island in Lake Hauroko and decided to poke around the clefts in a rock face. To his great surprise, he found a skeleton held upright and covered in a cloak.

George had found the body of a woman of high rank dating back to the seventeenth century, who was later identified as Te Maiairea Te Riri Wairua Puru of Ngati Mamoe. What makes the burial particularly curious is that the lake and the island were remote from major Maori settlements, and those who buried this woman took exceptional care to protect the location of the burial site. Now known as the 'Maori Princess', her burial site is protected by a metal grille and is highly tapu. The best view of the lake is from the Lake Hauroko Lookout. This track for the most part follows the lakeshore until the steep climb to the lookout, where you'll be rewarded with spectacular views as far as Foveaux Strait. However, the track is a bit rough and steep towards the end. For something less demanding, there is a flat easy loop walk through forest and swamp from the car park.

This edition published by New Holland Publishers in 2020
First published in 2013 by New Holland Publishers
Auckland • Sydney

Level 1, Fox Valley Road, Wahroonga, NSW 2076 Australia
5/39 Woodside Avenue, Northcote, Auckland 0627, New Zealand

newhollandpublishers.com

Copyright © 2021 in text: Peter Janssen
Copyright © 2021 in photographs: Peter Janssen
Copyright © 2021 New Holland Publishers
Peter Janssen has asserted his right to be identified as the author of this work.

Group Managing Director: Fiona Schultz
Production Manager: Arlene Gippert
Managing Director: David Cowie
Editor: Duncan Perkinson
Designer: Yolanda La Gorcé
Maps: Adapted from originals by Bruce McLennon/Island Bridge

Front cover image: Waitakere Dam
Back cover images from top to bottom: Te Werahi Beach, Oamaru, Wairere Falls
Title page: New Zealand's oldest farm buildings at Matanaka,
near Waikouaiti, Otago.

A record of this book is held at the National Library of New Zealand

Janssen, Peter (Peter Leon)
A walk a day: 365 short walks in New Zealand / Peter Janssen.

ISBN: 9781869665326

1. Day hiking—New Zealand—Guidebooks. 2. Trails—
New Zealand—Guidebooks. 3. New ZealandvGuidebooks.
l. Title.
796.510993—dc 23

10 9 8 7 6 5 4 3

All rights reserved. No part of this publication may be reproduced, stored in a retrieval system, or transmitted in any form or by any means, electronic, mechanical, photocopying, recording or otherwise, without the prior permission of the publishers and copyright holders.

While the author and publishers have made every effort to ensure that the information contained in this book was correct at the time of going to press, they accept no responsibility for any loss, injury or inconvenience sustained by any person using this book.

New Holland Publishers places great value on the environment and is actively involved in efforts to preserve it. The paper used in the production of this book was supplied by mills that source their raw materials from sustainably managed forests.

Keep up with New Holland Publishers:

NewHollandPublishers

@newhollandpublishers